JONATHAN FREJUSTE

THE BRIDGE TO CHANGE

MENTORING TOOLS FOR PARENTS, TEACHERS, COACHES, AND COUNSELORS

Copyright © 2020 Jonathan Frejuste All rights reserved.

Scripture quotations marked MSG are taken from THE MESSAGE, copyright © 1993, 1994, 1995, 1996, 2000, 2001, 2002 by Eugene H. Peterson. Used by permission of NavPress. All rights reserved. Represented by Tyndale House Publishers, Inc.

Scripture quotations marked NLT are taken from the Holy Bible, New Living Translation, copyright ©1996, 2004, 2007, 2013, 2015 by Tyndale House Foundation. Used by permission of Tyndale House Publishers, Inc., Carol Stream, Illinois 60188. All rights reserved.

Scripture quotations marked NIV are taken from THE HOLY BIBLE, NEW INTERNATIONAL VERSION®, NIV® Copyright © 1973, 1978, 1984, 2011 by Biblica, Inc.™ Used by permission. All rights reserved worldwide.

Scripture quotations marked KJV from The Authorized (King James) Version. Rights in the Authorized Version in the United Kingdom are vested in the Crown. Reproduced by permission of the Crown's patentee, Cambridge University Press

Scripture quotations marked GW are taken from GOD'S WORD®, © 1995 God's Word to the Nations. Used by permission of God's Word Mission Society.

Scripture quotations marked NCV are taken from the New Century Version®. Copyright © 2005 by Thomas Nelson. Used by permission. All rights reserved.

Scriptures taken from the Holy Bible, New International Version®, NIV®. Copyright © 1973, 1978, 1984, 2011 by Biblica, Inc.™ Used by permission of Zondervan. All rights reserved worldwide. www.zondervan.com The "NIV" and "New International Version" are trademarks registered in the United States Patent and Trademark Office by Biblica, Inc.™

Scripture quotations marked ERV are taken from the Holy Bible: Easy-to-Read Version (ERV), International Edition © 2013, 2016 by Bible League International and used by permission.

Scripture quotations marked GNT are taken from the Good News Translation in Today's English Version- Second Edition Copyright © 1992 by American Bible Society. Used by Permission.

Scripture quotations marked (TLB) are taken from The Living Bible copyright © 1971. Used by permission of Tyndale House Publishers, a Division of Tyndale House Ministries, Carol Stream, Illinois 60188. All rights reserved.

Scripture quotations marked (NIrV) are taken from the Holy Bible, New International Reader's Version®, NIrV® Copyright © 1995, 1996, 1998, 2014 by Biblica, Inc.™ Used by permission of Zondervan. All rights reserved worldwide. www.zondervan.comThe "NIrV" and "New International Reader's Version" are trademarks registered in the United States Patent and Trademark Office by Biblica, Inc.™

This book is designed to provide information and motivation to our readers. It is sold with the understanding that the author and the publisher is not engaged to render any type of psychological, legal, or any other kind of professional advice. The content of each article is the sole expression and opinion of its author. No warranties or guarantees are expressed or implied by the publisher's choice to include any of the content in this volume. Neither the publisher nor the individual author(s) shall be liable for any physical, psychological, emotional, financial, or commercial damages, including, but not limited to, special, incidental, consequential or other damages. Our views and rights are the same: You are responsible for your own choices, actions, and results.

Dedication and Acknowledgment

I AM THE SON OF Haitian immigrants. As a first-generation Haitian American who was raised alongside black people who were descendants of slaves in America, I empathize with their pain.

As a child of Haitian immigrants, I had a different cultural value system than my black American friends, but I never saw myself as superior to black Americans. I have always seen black people as one. Sadly, black immigrants often misunderstood the intergenerational pain of black Americans.

I was born and raised in Newark, New Jersey. I witnessed my community torn apart over several decades by the forces of hopelessness and despair as close friends and neighbors went to prison. As a teenager, I could not see the through-line of black American history that lent itself to the feelings of helplessness and anger. I can see a bit more clearly today.

Haiti became the first independent slave nation on January 1, 1804. The national flag says, "L'Union Fait La Force" meaning "Unity Makes Strength." One of the reasons why they achieved their liberation is because of unity.

That same spirit needs to be cultivated today in America, to ensure that this country becomes a place where black people can heal from the legacy of pain and trauma experienced during hundreds of years of white supremacy. We will need unity.

I want to acknowledge and dedicate this guide to the men and women who are putting in the work by setting positive examples, breaking cycles, and leading in their own ways to turn our communities around.

I initially wanted to name the people who served as a force for good in the life of healing black people in America, but I realized there would be too many to name, and I don't need any more drama in my life by inadvertently missing anyone.

As black people in America, it's important to note that we never signed up for this experience. We never received a comprehensive tutorial on what it meant to be black. We cannot conceal or run away from being black, though some of us try to.

We didn't have a say in whether being black could subject us to slavery and segregation, or the now-constant suspicion we live under, or our forced silence about the economic, judicial, emotional, and psychological hurdles we experience. Though much progress has been made and a cultural beauty has emerged from our journey, we still have more work to do to heal from the legacy of white supremacy.

To all the men and women who continue to fight to build a life in America, despite all the challenges you face: Never quit. Though you stumble, get tired at times, and feel helpless and hopeless, you keep going.

I acknowledge you and dedicate this to you.

Table of Contents

Mentor's Guide to a Bridge the Gaps Workshop · · · · · · · · · · · 1
Maturity Assessment: Are You in Condition to Lead? · · · · · · · · 5
Bridge the Gaps Maturity Assessment Scores and Interpretation
Guide · 13
Bridge the Gaps – Tool Descriptions · · · · · · · · · · · · · · · · 17
What a Safe Mentor Looks Like · · · · · · · · · · · · · · · · · · · 25
Introduction · 31
The King I Never Learned About · · · · · · · · · · · · · · · · · · 39

Part 1: Sense of Self · **51**
1: Knowledge of Self Toolkit · 53
   Identity and Esteem: How Do I See and Feel about Myself? · · · · · *55*
   Words: Speak Life, Not Death · · · · · · · · · · · · · · · · · · · *61*
   Sankofa: Know Your History · *64*
2: Values Toolkit · 71
   Go Beneath the Iceberg: · *74*
   Values and Integrity Reflection: · · · · · · · · · · · · · · · · · *77*
   Virtues roadwork: · *81*
3: Confidence Toolkit · 85
   Emancipate and Guard Your Mind: · · · · · · · · · · · · · · · · · *87*
   Stand: Remember Whose Shoulders You Stand Upon · · · · · · · · *103*
   It's Your Life: Take Responsibility · · · · · · · · · · · · · · · · *115*
4: Community Healing Toolkit · · · · · · · · · · · · · · · · · · · 119
   Never Stop Asking Questions · · · · · · · · · · · · · · · · · · · *121*
   Is Willie Lynch Real? · *125*
   Talented Tenth: Beat the Odds to Change the Odds · · · · · · · · · *139*

Part 2: Productivity ··············· **151**
5: Purpose Toolkit ··················· 155
   Find Your Lane: There's Less Traffic ············ *157*
   Code of Conduct: Bring Order into Your Life ········ *164*
6: Process Toolkit ··················· 175
   Define Your Success: What Do You Look Forward to Achieving? 177
   Dreams to Reality: What Will You Do to Get There? ····· *188*
   Expertise: Greatness Takes Time ·············· *196*
7: Permission to Be Courageous Toolkit ··········· 205
   Fear of Reality: Denial and Procrastination ········· *209*
   Fear of "Breaking the Rules": Conformity and Dependency ··· *218*
   Fear of Raising Expectations: Self-Sabotage and Mediocrity ··· *230*

Part 3: Emotional Health ············· **251**
8: Well-being Toolkit ················· 255
   Grieve Your Losses: Fix the Hole in Your Bucket ······· *257*
   No More Shame: Write Your Own Story ·········· *263*
   Present: Limit/Eliminate Social Media and Phone Use ····· *271*
9: Healthy Relationships Toolkit ············· 277
   Supplement: Work on Your Love ·············· *278*
   Do the Work: Understand Your Family Background ······ *281*
   Emotionally Safe Communities ··············· *295*

Part 4: Community issues ············· **305**
10: Collateral Consequences of a Felony ·········· 309
11: Children of Incarcerated Parents ············ 325
12: Innocence ····················· 331
13: Healing: No Longer Used to Dysfunction ········ 337

Recommended Resources / Reading List ·········· 345
Endnotes ······················· 347

Tools to be Reflective,
Productive, and Attentive

Mentor's Guide to a Bridge the Gaps Workshop

ONE OF THE BIGGEST CHALLENGES in our communities today is the breakdown of the family. Ideally, we all are raised in homes with loving parents who prepare us for every aspect of the journey we will face in life. They learn who we are. They help us identify our talents and provide opportunities for us to exercise them. They help us grow and develop as people, teach us how to take care of every aspect of our personhood, and facilitate the healing of the wounds we suffer.

Many of people I've worked with had a common denominator: They were raised in broken homes. They came from homes where there was mistreatment, abuse, and intentional or unintentional neglect. Their parents might have done the best they could, but they left areas of their children's development unattended. Parenting is a skill that's learned on the job. Unfortunately, raising children doesn't come with a manual or a complete toolbox. When parents are not fully equipped, the children they raise suffer from gaps in their well-being and development, often because of the gaps in the parents' well-being and development.

None of our parents are perfect. As a result, many people enter adulthood with a sense of incompleteness, a sense that they have gaps or deficits in their understanding and resources for life. Those gaps carry over into adulthood, and affect nearly every dimension of life: their relationships, finances, employment, and involvement in the community.

Children raised this way might grow up to be adults who make career missteps or poor life and relationship choices. Their lives might be marked by wasted time and continued emotional and mental pain—all of which could have been prevented if the necessary tools had been available.

Many of us have learned these life lessons the hard way. If, somehow, we never learned them at all, we might be living lost, confused, and disillusioned with life. If this is you, please have compassion for yourself. Remember, it's unloving and unkind to expect yourself to do something that you were never taught to do. Many of us have never been taught how to live. We might have been taught how to survive, or how to get along without causing any trouble, or how to protect ourselves. But we've never been taught how to live wholeheartedly and abundantly. Fortunately, there is hope. Healing is possible, and it's never too late to grow and reposition yourself to live your life wholeheartedly.

We are, at all times, both leaders and followers. We lead, but we also are called to follow or submit to a system to achieve progress in a given area of life. The best leaders are the best followers.

We must ask the question, "What could I have done better?" along the way to learn from our mistakes and help others avoid mistakes. We often don't want to deal with the pain of confronting flaws in our character. I know I don't! But I've witnessed the best leaders re-examine their choices. This kind of reflection shows humility and a commitment to growth.

Our society conditions us to always be right. "Never make mistakes" and "never show weakness" are the mantras we often hear. Despite subcultures that promote emotional health, the dominant cultures don't allow us to be that vulnerable.

History has revealed that a lack of integrity will reflect in your leadership and eventually hurt you and those you are called to lead. To be frank, the price of leadership is often loneliness, responsibility, criticism, and discomfort—because you will not change what you learn to tolerate.

The reward for leadership is the breaking of generational cycles in your own life and the lives of others. The following assessment is based on the book *Bridge the Gaps – Lessons on Self-Awareness, Self-Development, and Self-Care*. If you haven't read this book, you can visit the website www.thebridge330.com or visit www.amazon.com to pick up a copy. You also can download this assessment at www.thebridge330.com under "Start a Book Club."

Maturity Assessment: Are You in Condition to Lead?

You can't turn out better than your teacher; when you're fully taught, you will resemble your teacher.
Luke 6:40, The Voice

Use the following scoring scale:
True – 5
Often True – 4
Occasionally True – 3
Rarely True – 2
Not True – 1

Self-Awareness

_____ 1. I have a conscious awareness of the problems that I am called to solve in this world. I know what I am passionate about and use that passion to serve others. (Ch.1)

_____ 2. I refuse to compromise my true self when I am under pressure. I don't measure my worth by my performance, possessions, or popularity. (Ch.2)

_____ 3. I know my values and am intentional about incorporating them in my life. (Ch.3)

_____ 4. I know my gifts and talents and consistently work to develop them into strengths. (Ch.4)

_____ 5. I pursue feedback from peers, subordinates and managers on my strengths, areas of improvement, style of conflict resolution, and perceived purpose in life. (Ch.5)

_____ 6. I know my ideal work style and strategize to create a work life that honors how I'm wired. (Ch.6)

_____ 7. I am able to determine my goals, values, and beliefs despite the pressure around me. (Ch.7)

_____ 8. I have dreams and visions for my future that I am patient, committed, and persistent in pursuing. (Ch.8)

_____ 9. I have role models and mentors who inspire me, teach me lessons, and help me stay committed on my journey to living out my calling. (Ch.9)I am committed trusting the process of finding and fulfilling my calling using the tools mentioned above. (Ch.10)

Total _____

Self-Development

_____ 1. I am able to define and set my own goals based on personally motivating factors. (Ch.11)

_____ 2. I hold in balance all the dimensions of life when I set my goals. (Ch.12)

_____ 3. I consistently work to develop confidence and self-respect through developing my talents and accepting my areas of improvement while living in healthy community. (Ch.13)

_____ 4. I set financial goals, live below my means, and avoid reckless and unnecessary spending. (Ch.14)

_____ 5. I know how to set GOALS that are specific, measurable, written, personal, and time bound. (Ch.15)

_____ 6. I have created a personal development plan and timeline through reading/listening to books and attending educational workshops/conferences. (Ch.16)

_____ 7. I know what my main focus should be in this season of my life – physical health, professional growth, financial health, or emotional recovery post-life transition/trauma, etc. (Ch.17)

_____ 8. I use my time wisely by focusing on important and urgent activities. (Ch.18)

_____ 9. I develop a clear focus by measuring the number of hours invested in my activities. (Ch.19)

_____ 10. I have the ability to be self-disciplined in the pursuit of my goals and cultivating my talents. (Ch.20)

_____ 11. I take time to assess the areas of my character that need improvement and find help when I get stuck or need guidance. (Ch.21)

_____ 12. I have a safe environment that supports me in my growth and healing including resources such as coaching and counseling when I get overwhelmed. (Ch.22)

_____ 13. I make quality decisions using a framework that includes a process of information gathering, rational analysis, and internal reflection. (Ch.23)

_____ 14. I focus on the mastery of a craft by incorporating deliberate practice for 10,000 hours. (Ch.24)

_____ 15. I examine the regular tendencies and practices that I've become acclimated to and am proactive about cultivating habits aligned with one's calling. (Ch.25)

_____ 16. I address challenges head on and incorporate quality problem solving strategies when facing difficulties. (Ch.26)

_____ 17. I use the obstacles to grow one's character and increase my focus on one's calling. (Ch.27

_____ 18. I have a redemptive perspective of failure and use it to fuel my next endeavor and stay aware of the mental traps that may keep me from taking risks. (Ch.28)

_____ 19. I understand the fear of success and how it can keep me from relentlessly pursuing my calling. I understand what the possible criticisms will be and how to compensate for the fears through restructuring one's mental framework. (Ch.29)

_____ 20. I anticipate changes in life and take initiative to engage the mental, emotional, and practical aspects of change and transition. (Ch.30)

Total _____

Self-Care

_____ 1. I give myself emotional permission to process grief and loss as often as necessary to live emotionally free and healed. (Ch.31)

_____ 2. I don't allow my bitterness towards those who have hurt me to overrule my compassion. I work to let go of the pain of my mistakes and someone's offense towards me. (Ch.32)

_____ 3. I protect and steward my time, talents, treasures, and thoughts and refuse to compromise my mental judgment or emotional safety for any relationship. (Ch.33)

_____ 4. I am aware of how my past mistakes and wounds are affecting my ability to live freely. I can see the worst in others and still believe the best for them. I can love myself and others despite failures or shortcomings. (Ch.34)

_____ 5. I am able to stand up for myself and am proactive against unhealthy relationship practices such as people pleasing, mind reading, and setting invalid expectations. (Ch.35)

_____ 6. I work to break the stigmas associated with issues that affect community relationships and make people feel safe to discuss tough issues. (Ch.36

_____ 7. I avoid stigmatizing mental illness and work to stay safe for people who are affected by mental illness. (Ch.37)

_____ 8. I am aware of the legacy of white racism and work to grow in my understanding of how it affects the world around me. (Ch.38)

_____ 9. I work to break the stigma of sexual abuse, understand the emotional experience of survivors in order to break the cycle of fear, shame, and isolation, and raise awareness about resources to help others find healing. (Ch.39)

_____ 10. I work to understand fatherlessness, its causes, and effects. I work to get equipped to provide people with tools to heal and deal with fatherlessness. I am also aware of ways to provide fathers with an on-ramp to engaging and/or re-engaging with their children. (Ch.40)

_____ 11. I work to understand mass incarceration in the US and to end the stigma of incarceration for returning citizens. I raise awareness about the common issues returning citizens face and resources available. (Ch.41)

_____ 12. I work to become a mature listener who can understand people despite having differences of beliefs and opinions. (Ch.42)

_____ 13. I work to spread hope and love by sustaining my motivation and consistency along the journey to building a life of impact and significance by maintaining priorities, taking actions, reflecting on regrets, and being more thoughtful going forward. (Ch.43)

Total _____

Bridge the Gaps Maturity Assessment Scores and Interpretation Guide

Bridge the Gaps Maturity Assessment - Your Scores			
	Self-Awareness	Self-Development	Self-Care
Community Leader	41-50	81-100	53-65
Mentor	31-40	61-80	40-52
Adult	21-30	41-60	27-39
Adolescent	11-20	21-40	14-26
Childhood	10	20	13
Your Scores	____/50	____/100	____/65

Interpretation Guide: Levels of Maturity

Self-Awareness

Community Leader – I help train leaders to serve those they work with to find and live out their calling.

Mentor – I have taken ownership of my calling and help others find their calling when asked.

Adult – I am aware of my calling and know what steps I have to take to unlock that calling.

Adolescent – I have a sense of what I am called to do but need to get clear with what that calling is.

Childhood – I need to work to get aware of my calling.

Self-Development
Community Leader – I help train leaders to serve those they work with to set goals and reach them.

Mentor - I set and reach my goals consistently and help others learn the tools needed to set and reach their goals.

Adult – I know what my goals are and have the tools needed to reach my goals.

Adolescent – I know my goals but am not sure where to start to pursue those goals.

Childhood – I'm not sure what goals I should set and will get started.

Self-Care
Community Leader – I help train leaders to love themselves and others well.

Mentor – I know what tools I need to love myself and others and share those tools with others when asked.

Adult – I know what tools I need to love myself and others.

Adolescent – I know a few of the tools needed to love myself and others but use them inconsistently.

Childhood – I am not aware of tools I needed to love myself and others.

Bridge the Gaps – Tool Descriptions

Skill/Tool	Purpose
Chapter 1 - Your Calling Is Your Compass	To increase awareness of and live in alignment with one's calling through reflection exercises that focus on one's passion, personality, and risk tolerance.
Chapter 2 – False Self	To get aware of the mask that is worn in order to fit in out of fear of judgment, ridicule, and/or shame and implement strategies to fortify one's true and unique self out of which one's calling is pursued.
Chapter 3 - Values	To determine one's core values and develop strategies to be intentional about staying grounded in those values.
Chapter 4 – Gifts, Talents, Skills, and Strengths	To reflect on and take ownership of your talents in order to develop them into strengths.
Chapter 5 – What Do People See in You?	To obtain feedback from one's closest family, friends, and/or coworkers about your talents, growth opportunities, and areas of greatest impact.

Chapter 6 – Work Styles	To determine one's ideal work style in order to organize one's life in a way that is most fulfilling and meaningful.
Chapter 7 – Be Differentiated	To determine one's own life goals, beliefs, desires, vision, mission, and values apart from outside pressure.
Chapter 8 – Visions and Dreams	To provide principles and a framework to cultivate the tenacity and fortitude to pursue and sustain one's dreams and vision.
Chapter 9 - Models and Mentors	To describe the role and importance of mentors and role models and how they can be used to provide courage and/or structure on the path building one's life.
Chapter 10 – Relax and Trust the Process	To ground one in the understanding that cultivating self-awareness is a journey that requires courage, effort, consistency, and patience.
Chapter 11 – Why You Should Set Goals	To define what a goal is, discuss the benefits of setting goals and provide examples of personally motivating factors to pursue one's goals that can serve as a canvas for discovering one's own set of personally motivating factors.
Chapter 12 – Define Your Success	To provide a paradigm of goal setting that holds in balance all the dimensions of life.

Chapter 13 – Self-Regard	To develop a strong sense of self by acknowledging and cultivating gifts and talents and an acceptance of one's areas of development using a healthy community and principles for wholeness.
Chapter 14 – Money	To determine one's finance goals, develop a budget, & develop countercultural consciousness about financial habits.
Chapter 15 – SMART Goals	To provide a framework to set goals that are specific, measurable, written, authentic, and time-stamped.
Chapter 16 – Personal Development	To provide motivation to develop a plan for growth and perspective on the benefit of becoming a lifelong learner through reading and listening to educational and inspirational materials.
Chapter 17 – One Major Focus	To help identify what is most essential and important based on one's season of life.
Chapter 18 – Time	To demonstrate how to prioritize one's activities to have the maximum effectiveness and efficiency.
Chapter 19 – Focus	To provide one with suggestions on cultivating an intense focus to accomplish any goal one sets out for.

Chapter 20 – Self-Discipline	To provide one with the perspective to cultivate an incomparable level of self-discipline and be comfortable with delayed gratification.
Chapter 21 – Character	To provide an opportunity to reflect on one's integrity within a value system and a make necessary adjustment to live a life above reproach.
Chapter 22 – Environment	To highlight the importance of having an environment that supports and bolsters one's true and best self and is proactive about its values.
Chapter 23 – Decisions	To provide a framework to make quality decisions through a process of information gathering, rational analysis, and internal reflection.
Chapter 24 – 10,000 Hours	To introduce the concept of mastery of a craft by incorporating deliberate practice for 10,000 hours.
Chapter 25 – Habits and Systems	To examine the regular tendencies and practices that one has acclimated to and be proactive about cultivating habits aligned with one's calling.
Chapter 26 – Problem Solving	To provide a framework for addressing challenges that occur over the course of life and tips to consider when facing difficulties.

Chapter 27 – Obstacles	To provide a framework to properly view inevitable obstacles, use the obstacles to grow one's character, and maintain focus on one's calling.
Chapter 28 – Failure	To provide a redemptive perspective on failure through a blueprint to use failure and its accompanying emotions to fuel one's next endeavor and the mental traps that may keep one from taking risks.
Chapter 29 – Fear of Success	To discuss the fear of success and the common objections to one's wholehearted pursuit of calling, the types of people in the arena of life that exist on the journey to calling, and ways to compensate for the fears through restructuring one's mental framework.
Chapter 30 – Change and Transition	To highlight the importance of anticipating change in life and taking initiative to engage the mental, emotional, and practical aspects of transition.
Chapter 31 – Grieving	To provide the emotional permission and framework to process grief and loss as often as necessary to live emotionally free and healed.

Chapter 32 – Forgiveness	To provide a healthy understanding of forgiveness and what forgiveness is not and provide steps to forgiveness.
Chapter 33 – Boundaries and Safe People	To provide a framework to take personal responsibility for the direction of one's life and a set of characteristics to use as an evaluation and standard for one's close relationships.
Chapter 34 – Survivor or Victim	To provide an assessment of one's habit patterns when facing challenges to eliminate unhelpful thinking, discuss the dynamics of shame, provide ways to combat toxic and shame-filled cultures and grow in greater emotional awareness.
Chapter 35 – Assertiveness	To explain the importance of standing up for oneself, describe the likely scenarios to prepare for, provide tools to avoid people pleasing and to be proactive against unhealthy relationship practices such as people pleasing, mind reading, and setting invalid expectations.
Chapter 36 – Community Care	To provide steps that one can take to break the stigmas associated with issues that affect community relationships.

Chapter 37 – Mental Illness	To provide a high level understanding of mental illness, a common perspective of mental illness that exists in the African American community, ways to address mental illness, and a framework to choose a counselor.
Chapter 38 – Colorism	To understand the nuance of white racism and its subsequent creation of racial hierarchy, specifically relating to skin tone.
Chapter 39 – Sexual Abuse	To provide an understanding of sexual abuse, the emotional experience of survivors in order to break the cycle of fear, shame, and isolation, and resources that one can use to find healing.
Chapter 40 – Fatherlessness	To understand fatherlessness and its effects, provide ways to heal and deal with fatherlessness, and provide fathers with on-ramp to engaging and/or re-engaging in a relationship with their children.
Chapter 41 – Mass Incarceration and Reentry	To highlight the rapid increase in the US prison population along with its racial disparities, end the stigma of incarceration for returning citizens, and provide a list of common issues and resources.
Chapter 42 – Listening	To provide an understanding of the importance of listening and an awareness of the maturity of one's listening skills.

Chapter 43 – Living a Life That Matters	To seal the lessons from the guide with a message of hope and love to sustain one's motivation and consistency along the journey to building a life of impact and significance.

What a Safe Mentor Looks Like

When a leader doesn't listen, he will, at some point, be surrounded by followers who have nothing to say.

It's been said that the only way to keep a secret between three friends is to kill two of them. Whenever I say this, people look at other people in an accusatory way. But we all need to evaluate ourselves, first and foremost.

We live in a day and age where people don't feel very safe to talk about the deep things in their heart. Change is the essence of life, but one of the missing ingredients in the process of change is safety. I think this is an area that mentors need to address more than most.

The doctor can't make the right diagnosis without knowing the symptoms. There is no change without the truth, but truth without grace is brutality, and grace without truth is enabling. Truth *with* grace is safety.

A sense of safety is a basic human need. Many of the relational issues in our culture today persist because people experience and create emotional violence. Social media and chronic texting has kept people connected, yet they are still isolated, relationally shallow, and feeling alone.

People need to feel safe more than ever before, because they are often going through secret storms. I believe that even holding onto painful secrets is a form of trauma.

I've had the privilege of working with people from all walks of life. I am no longer surprised at the level of secrets that people carry and are willing to unload once they feel a sufficient level of safety. I am privileged—but frankly, also burdened—with the pain that people carry and share with no one. As I hear deeply personal stories, my question is always, "Who have you told?" The response is often, "Only you" or "You and one other person."

Many people tell me their deepest secrets because they don't trust in those closest to them. People who are deeply wounded will often look to you for evidence of trustworthiness and safety. As such, we need to be safer for one another and confront the ways that we are unsafe for people, so that we can help facilitate healing.

As the saying goes, *hurt people hurt people*—but healed people heal people. Fortunately, pain always brings with it a gift. That gift will never be uncovered if people remain stuck in their pain due to fear of betrayal, judgment, or condemnation. More than ever, we need courageous, competent, and emotionally mature leaders who can help others find safety, healing, and an on-ramp to their destiny.

Emerging leaders—also known as *mentees*—need mentors who have depth of knowledge, critical thinking, and moral and emotional maturity to live in a wise way. Mentees are at the mercy of their mentors to provide this emotional safety.

This framework is designed to help you become more aware of your level of safety. To bolster the integrity of your work, you will want to do a thorough self-assessment, to ensure that you have the support necessary to serve in the best way possible.

One caring person can change someone's entire destiny by being a safe, non-anxious counselor who has an overall positive presence in the mentee's life.

Here are the ways in which you can be a safe leader.

1. Be mindful of your words.
a. "The one who has knowledge uses words with restraint, and whoever has understanding is even-tempered." Proverbs 17:27, NIV

b. "Observe the people who always talk before they think—even simpletons are better off than they are." Proverbs 29:20, MSG

A pre-condition for the progress of any group of people is that they have a sense of inner peace, a sense of stability, and the confidence instilled by the mentors.

2. Be a great listener and control your anger.
a. "Remember this, my dear brothers and sisters: Everyone should be quick to listen, slow to speak, and should not get angry easily." James 1:19, GW

b. "Fools vent their anger, but the wise quietly hold it back." Proverbs 29:11, NLT - Total honesty is for God, your support group, and your therapist.

c. Read Chapter 42 of Bridge the Gaps.

3. Keep secrets.
a. A gossip betrays a confidence; so avoid anyone who talks too much. Proverbs 20:19, NIV

4. Don't judge. Practice what you preach.
"Don't pick on people, jump on their failures, criticize their faults—unless, of course, you want the same treatment. That critical spirit has a way of boomeranging. It's easy to see a smudge on your neighbor's face and be oblivious to the ugly sneer on your own. Do you have the nerve to say, 'Let me wash your face for you,' when your own face is distorted by contempt? It's this whole traveling road-show mentality all over again, playing a holier-than-thou part instead of just living your part. Wipe that ugly sneer off your own face, and you might be fit to offer a washcloth to your neighbor." Matthew 7:1-5, MSG

5. Restore people who make mistakes with gentleness.
"If someone falls into sin, forgivingly restore him, saving your critical comments for yourself. You might be needing forgiveness before the day's out. Stoop down and reach out to those who are oppressed. Share their burdens, and so complete Christ's law. If you think you are too good for that, you are badly deceived." Galatians 6:1-3, MSG

6: Be discerning and don't believe everything you hear.
"Only a simpleton believes everything he's told! A prudent man understands the need for proof." Proverbs 14:15, TLB

7: Say what you mean and mean what you say.
"You need not swear an oath—any impulse to do so is of evil. Simply let your "yes" be "yes," and let your "no" be "no." Matthew 5:37, VOICE

8: Don't brag about your help. Do your work quietly. Attention is only required to highlight the work.
a. "When you do something for someone else, don't call attention to yourself. You've seen them in action, I'm sure—'play actors' I call them—treating prayer meeting and street corner alike as a stage, acting compassionate as long as someone is watching, playing to the crowds. They get applause, true, but that's all they get. When you help someone out, don't think about how it looks. Just do it—quietly and unobtrusively. That is the way your God, who conceived you in love, working behind the scenes, helps you out." Matthew 6:2-4, MSG

b. You can adjust your brother's collar without telling the world that it's crooked.

9. Don't be swayed by anyone's opinion.
"Teacher, we know that You are true. We know that You are teaching the truth about God. We know You are not afraid of what men think or say about You." Matthew 22:16, NLV

10. Commit before you correct.
a. "When they kept on questioning him, he straightened up and said to them, "Let any one of you who is without sin be the first to throw a stone at her." Again he stooped down and wrote on the ground. At this, those who heard began to go away one at a time, the older ones first, until only Jesus was left, with the woman still standing there. Jesus straightened up and asked her, "Woman, where are they? Has no one condemned you?" "No one, sir," she said. "Then neither do I condemn you," Jesus declared. "Go now and leave your life of sin." John 8: 7:11, NIV

b. As a mentor, you are an advocate. You are in a young person's life to point them in the right direction and to get to the root of and curb destructive behavior.

Introduction

IN MY SENIOR YEAR OF college, I attended the lecture of Dr. James Cone, a liberation theologian who has worked for more than fifty years as an advocate for black people in America. Black liberation theology is a faith perspective that interprets the work and life of Jesus in light of the social condition of black people in America and rejects the white American church that preaches a gospel of success based on white supremacy.

Dr. Cone taught that if America is going to live, then white supremacy and its accompanying atrocities have to die. His concern was not limited to a race or class or tribe or nation. However, his work was about recognizing and declaring a commitment to healing the legacy of the trauma that black people have experienced in America.

The black church, itself, was born out of rejection based on white supremacy. In the late 1700s, a black man named Richard Allen was praying in a whites-only section of the church. The people become angry and kicked him out of the church. That man went on to start the AME (African Methodist Episcopal) church. Over the last ten years, right-wing extremists—including white supremacists/nationalists—committed 70 percent of the 427 extremist-related killings. This includes the murders of nine African American members of Emanuel AME Church in Charleston, SC by white supremacist Dylan Roof.

Dr. Cone's perspective is particularly relevant today. His words offer a genuine response to oppression and marginalization in our world by affirming Jesus's social ethic in the work to end injustice and oppression, as well as our responsibility in the work. This is the Scripture he referred to that day in his talk:

> *"The Spirit of the Lord is on me, because he has anointed me to proclaim good news to the poor. He has sent me to proclaim freedom for the prisoners and recovery of sight for the blind, to set the oppressed free."* Luke 4:18, NIV

> *"For I was hungry and you gave me nothing to eat, I was thirsty and you gave me nothing to drink, I was a stranger and you did not invite me in, I needed clothes and you did not clothe me, I was sick and in prison and you did not look after me.' "They also will answer, 'Lord, when did we see you hungry or thirsty or a stranger or needing clothes or sick or in prison, and did not help you?' "He will reply, 'Truly I tell you, whatever you did not do for one of the least of these, you did not do for me.'* Matthew 25:42-45, NIV

> *"Speak up for those who cannot speak for themselves, for the rights of all who are destitute. Speak up and judge fairly; defend the rights of the poor and needy."* Proverbs 31:8-9, NIV

As a black man in America, I've wrestled with the intersection of my faith and the injustice and trauma that black people in America suffer. These words provide much comfort and perspective that the two could be reconciled.

I was given the honor of hosting Dr. Cone around campus and having lunch with him. He shared some encouraging pieces of advice. He gave me the courage to take steps to be unapologetic about working on behalf of black people in America. He said that black people had been taught to love everyone but themselves.

To help heal the frustration, oppression, and self-hatred that are the legacy of racial hatred and hierarchy in America, he encouraged studying the life and philosophies of Martin Luther King, Jr. and Malcolm X. He discussed some parts of his book *Martin & Malcolm & America*. The underlying tone was that the church should not only be focused on working to save souls to get to Heaven, but also working to save bodies right here on Earth. It was a piercing and life-shaping talk to me.

Later that day, my professor sent me the following e-mail. This was in 2008, twelve years ago:

Dear Jon,

I hope that you won't take this message as being too intrusive…. I just wanted to write to say that when I was listening to Dr. James Cone's final comments in which he said that he was confident that there were "Martins" and "Malcolm's" among the students in the President's Lounge this afternoon, I immediately thought of you. I know that you will make great contributions that will help others in whatever paths you pursue.

After receiving this message, I recall being lost and confused about what I wanted to do with my life and what I "should" do, based on family and societal expectations. I just wanted to make it to graduation. I had no idea that Dr. Cone's work and words would inform the course of the rest of my life and demonstrate the continuity of my calling from my childhood.

I didn't understand how to make the connection at the time, but I knew my destiny would be intertwined with helping people heal from the pain of the past. Hearing Dr. Cone planted a seed in me that did not begin to flourish until several years after I had started my career.

Over the last few years of my life, I've served as a coach, speaker, and workshop facilitator in schools, group homes, nonprofits, churches, and a substance abuse treatment center. It wasn't until I started facilitating life-coaching classes at a local adult prison and spending time in the juvenile detention center that I noticed the racial disparity.

My audiences were mostly, if not all, black males. According to the Bureau of Justice, one in three black males will go to jail or prison in their lifetime. There are 2.3 million people in prison. Black men make up about 6 percent of the American population but roughly 40 percent of the prison population.

New Jersey, the state where I was born and raised, leads the nation in racial disparity in prison. For every one white person incarcerated, there are twelve black people incarcerated. For every one white minor incarcerated, there are thirty black minors incarcerated. I knew that this was the issue I needed to focus on from the standpoints of healing, prevention, and justice.

The question I often ask myself is, how did white racists hold a notion of intrinsic goodness and nobility while engaging in acts of barbarism against black people? The answer is, they made up a lie that black people were inferior, which justified their behavior. As I see it, the sinister genius of racial dehumanization made many white people relabel and redefine black people in a degrading way, so they could justify acting egregiously towards them.

But it also made many black people believe negative things about themselves, which led them to inferior living. Unfortunately, those lies and programmed perspectives persist until this day. When the general society deliberately makes a person's skin color a stigma and teaches that they are less than human and incapable of taking care of themselves, the stigmatized group will reflect those beliefs in their practices and often take on the beliefs themselves.

Your life becomes a reflection of what you believe about yourself and about what's possible for your life. Your life is defined by how you love yourself and others.

I want to see change, not only in the men in the prisons but also in the leaders of the young people in the communities across this nation. I believe that when the leaders reflect the messages that they teach, the culture will change, and the outcomes of our young people will change as well.

True change is a protracted process that requires a deep shift in thought and behavior. Understanding how we got to the place where we are today will give us the ability to acknowledge the damage and then make a commitment to *be the change we seek*.

Historically, social change has been created in various ways: technological advances, physical force and violence, and people making small, personal, life-affirming choices rooted in a deep consciousness of the world in which they live.

If the goal is to have sustained social change in our communities, physical force has proven to bring about short-lived change. Science and technology can serve to reduce the barriers to participate in the change, but what tips the scale is when individuals who choose to make life-affirming choices from a deeply centered place reach critical mass.

For this to happen, we need mentors. A mentor is a generational messenger of vision, values, and history. A mentor is a facilitator of destiny and someone who helps the mentee develop a philosophy of life that sustains him from the cradle to the grave.

I would not have been able to take the necessary steps to pursue my calling without mentors—experienced and trusted guides who spoke life and destiny over my life, even when they were not sure when or how it would manifest. As the Word says, Paul "planted the seed, Apollos watered it, but it was God has been making it grow (1 Corinthians 3:6-8, NIV)." I am doing what I do today, in part because of the power of mentors.

This guide is written to those mentors, specifically parents, teachers, coaches, and counselors. Change in the world won't happen until it happens with the leaders. The truth is that you teach who you are. You cannot give what you don't have, and you can't take people to places that you've never been to. You can point folks in the right direction and even explain what you've studied, but to have full integrity, your life must reflect what you preach—and that is a journey.

Change is a journey. If we are going to have sustainable change in America, we need a paradigm shift. Facing the reality of the past's effect on the present is a prerequisite for engaging these issues with seriousness and commitment.

To be sure, there are different levels and forms of oppression against different groups of people, ranging from the genocide and displacement of the indigenous people of the Americas in the 1500s to the Chinese Exclusion Act in 1882 to the Internment of Japanese Americans in the 1940s to the Jewish Holocaust during World War II.

By no means do I want to reduce or minimize what other groups have endured. But I am responding to distinct, racially based needs and experiences of black people in America who are routinely underserved and whose issues are grossly misrepresented and much deeper than the general society chooses to acknowledge.

Some folks would say the main issues are economical and judicial, but I think the issues also go deeper to the emotional and psychological effects of living in a society that has not fully addressed the legacy of racial dehumanization and how that past affects black people and black families today.

To address black issues from a common point of reference and to break the issues apart, parts of this guide will address points made in the Department of Labor's controversial 1965 report *The Negro Family: The Case for National Action* written by American politician and sociologist Daniel Patrick Moynihan. Although significant social progress has occurred for many black Americans since 1965, many of the problems Moynihan identified in the report are still struggles for black people in America.

This guide is for anyone who works with black people in America and wants to understand the nature and impact of multigenerational beliefs and behaviors passed on and practiced within black culture. These beliefs and behaviors combined with the different treatment and access to opportunities afforded to others in a society that deliberately made his color a stigma.

It would be ridiculous to say that all the social ills that black people in America face can be attributed to the legacy of the trauma of slavery, but it's prudent to identify how the problem directly relates to the enslaved experience, Jim Crow, and lynching of black people until the mid-20th century.

Three of the major impacts of this treatment are black people having no sense of worth and value, learned helplessness, and a deep feeling of unresolved anger and frustration.

So much of what we learn is segmented, but life simply doesn't operate in segments. As such, this guide will combine the paradigms of personal development, emotional health, racial healing, and social justice.

Many people want to live in a post-racial world and collaborate on the level of ideas. But multiculturalism, while a noble idea, cannot work until the individual and institutional effects of the racial dehumanization of black people are acknowledged and addressed.

Can a non-black person read this work and benefit? Yes. Here's an important observation: The fact that I have to make a disclaimer for non-black readers speaks to the necessity of this book and books like it.

Personal development books written from a European standpoint rarely, if ever, make room for the black experience. Their books don't take into account the particularities of the experience of black people as a whole. For non-black readers, the tools listed here can give you a picture of what black people have to consider throughout their journey in America.

As Dr. Martin Luther King, Jr. discussed, what's more frustrating than total misunderstanding of the people of ill will is the shallow understanding from those of goodwill. Many of the tools here can transcend black culture, but they are geared toward the experience of black people in America who live and work in non-culturally receptive or even culturally violent environments.

Some of the tools are meant to help you grow as a person, which will help your mentorship, regardless of your race. Several of the tools will focus on the racial identity development and healing of black people in America in ways that are practical and socially applicable.

The tools in this guide are used to provide a general approach that you can tailor to your specific situation. When you're black in America, the paradigms given to you to be successful are often incomplete, so you have to learn as you go. I have no doubt that this guide will be incomplete, but it serves the purpose of being a bridge to getting/keeping the conversations going—and those conversations are the first step in creating sustainable change in one's individual life and the greater community.

As a mentor, even if you can't change the world, you can cast the stone across the waters that create the ripple.

The King I Never Learned About

If we don't face the past, it becomes the present.

As children, we are impressionable and vulnerable to the stories we hear. Unfortunately, there are certain stories that I never heard. My middle school and high school history classes never walked me through the full story of black people in America after slavery. I never learned how historical policies and events led to present-day social problems and structural inequalities that continue to impact black Americans negatively.

As it relates to black people in America, here are key historical accounts that get discussed in the mainstream.

- In 1863, slavery ended per the Emancipation Proclamation achieved through the Civil War.

- In 1963, Dr. King gave the *I Have a Dream* Speech where 250,000 people came out to hear the soaring rhetoric about a beautiful, multiracial nation where everyone comes together and everyone enjoys the same freedoms.

- In 1964 and 1965, segregation ended through the Civil Rights Act and black people got the right to vote through the Voting Rights Act.

The mainstream American narrative that I was taught tells us that great strides were made through these pieces of legislation, and that America now provides equal opportunities for black people to participate in the social, political, and economic order without interruption.

The problem is that, when you take time to review America's complicated and imperfect history—specifically the history of black life—you will quickly notice how the dominant culture's perspective either subtly acknowledges or very conveniently passes over the ugly truths of America's racist past, including the injustices of:

- Jim Crow, convict leasing, and more than 4,000 lynchings of black Americans between 1877 and 1950. See the report *Lynching in America: Confronting the Legacy of Racial Terror* by Bryan Stevenson, Director of the Equal Justice Initiative
  Website: https://lynchinginamerica.eji.org/report/

- Predatory housing practices against black Americans when they were kept out of the legitimate home-mortgage market between the 1930s and 1960s. See *The Case for Reparations* by Ta-Nehisi Coates
  Website: https://www.theatlantic.com/projects/reparations/

- Blatant refusal to desegregate schools, despite legislation. Fourteen Mississippi school districts refused for fifteen years to desegregate schools, even after the *1954 Brown v. Board of Education* decision. Look up *Alexander v. Holmes County Board of Education* in October 1969)

  Website: https://www.oyez.org/cases/1969/632
  (You can read and listen to the case at this site.)

This is a history that black people did not choose, but it's not a history that is obscure or unavailable. These facts are often deliberately left out of the general discourse, because the victors often have an *a la carte* relationship with the past. The victors, not the victims, write history, often in their own favor and with an exponential reflection on what favors them or disfavors those oppressed, without acknowledging root causes.

The news we choose to tell is just as important as how we tell the story. The dehumanization of black people continues with a refusal to acknowledge/fix the miseducation in American schools and a refusal to address the violence against black citizens in our criminal justice system.

As the victims rise to positions of power, the narrative that was once told is re-evaluated. Because of the evolving landscape of America's racial make-up, the once-vague understandings of racial injustice become clear and subsequently indict a nation that purports to represent liberty and justice for all. As Frederick Douglas alluded, the story of the master doesn't need more narrators. The story of the slave does.

What creates the clarity of the need for black healing is an acute understanding of black pain and the black experience. Unfortunately, many black people are conditioned to believe that speaking the unadulterated truth to white people about what they see and feel is a kamikaze mission. Black people's reticence to speak freely and honestly in front of white people is a result of the memory of violence against black people. This is where we need healing as a people.

Very few people more clearly explained this memory and the link between America's inception and the condition of black people than Dr. Martin Luther King, Jr. As you listen to Dr. King's speeches from the year before he passed, he unapologetically presented a well-defined picture explaining the contemporary social, political, and economic realities of black life rooted in America's racist past. Sadly, his words are still relevant.

In 1967, Dr. King gave an interview at Ebenezer Baptist Church in Atlanta, GA. I was surprised by some of the things he mentioned that I had never heard discussed in the mainstream. He admitted that the dream he had in 1963 had become a nightmare. He confessed that only a small minority of white Americans were committed to true racial equality for the Negro.

By 1967, he was beginning to fully grasp the alienation between whites and blacks. Integration for black people would be like moving into a burning house. The idea behind integration was equal access to opportunity. But as it turned out, that idea was untrue. Integration only let black people enter the belly of the beast.

Dr. King said that civil rights legislation, including the voting rights bill, didn't do too much to improve the fate of millions of Negroes in crowded ghettos in the Northern part of America. He also acknowledged the way racial dehumanization affects black people's sense of self and ability to progress in America.

That same year, Dr. King gave a speech called *"The Other America"* that described the existence of two Americas. One America provides nutrition and material provisions for the bodies, education and culture for their intellects, and human dignity and freedom for their souls. In this America, the promises of the Declaration of Independence are honored.

But, Dr. King said, there is the other America that turns hope into despair. Unemployment persists on a daily basis. The conditions of the communities are degraded. Poverty persists. Children grow up stripped of their dignity and develop a feeling of inferiority every day. Men are stripped of the hope of finding a job opportunity and fall victim to hopelessness and a psychology of self-defeat.

There were those who would ask Dr. King why black people can't "pick themselves up by the bootstraps" and do for themselves. These critics would use their lives as examples of how one can rise from poverty. But from Dr. King's perspective, it didn't help black people when insensitive and unfeeling people said that other groups (Italian, Irish and other European immigrants) had made more progress than black Americans.

Dr. King reminded the white immigrant that:

1. Black people arrived here involuntarily, in chains, while others came of their own volition.

2. No other immigrant group has been a slave on American soil except black people.

3. Racial terrorism persisted. Doors of economic opportunity and social engagement in the broader community were closed to black people, just because they were black. Their race remained a stigma after slavery, and it manifested itself in segregation, lynchings, housing discrimination until the 1960s, and police brutality.

As Dr. King said, many people were not willing to go all the way to ensure equality for all. That was in 1967. The following year, he was killed in Memphis while participating in a sanitation workers' strike.

Philosopher and historian Noam Chomsky said that, as long as Dr. King was focused on racist Alabama sheriffs, he was celebrated. But once he started addressing class issues, particularly reparations, he became widely criticized. From Chomsky's perspective, it is not ironic that Dr. King began to transition from a focus on civil rights to economic equality and that many people hated him for it.

In one of Dr. King's speeches, his argument for reparations was based on the logic of an innocent person who had been incarcerated for several decades. Upon discovery of the man's innocence, the man is released from prison with no bus fare, no money to get something to eat or to buy any clothes. He equated this to what happened to black people in America in 1863, when they were granted their freedom after 244 years.

The freedom was meaningless because there was no economic floor to start with, based on a broken promise by the government (See article titled "The Truth Behind '40 Acres and a Mule'

— https://www.pbs.org/wnet/african-americans-many-rivers-to-cross/history/the-truth-behind-40-acres-and-a-mule/).

In contrast, Congress provided white European immigrants millions of acres land in the west and Midwest. These white immigrants could receive farming education through land grant colleges and the help of county agents who would advise on farming and help them get low-interest loans to mechanize the farms.

Ironically, these people and their descendants now tell black people to pick themselves up by their bootstraps. White Europeans (Italians, Irish, etc.) didn't need bootstraps, because they were given an economic base on which to build.

This message of Dr. King rarely, if ever, gets discussed in the mainstream. Here's the latest reality of American leadership that can help us possibly understand how the "Other America" that Dr. King addressed came to be.

Where is America today?

- More than 75 percent of the US Congress is white.

- More than 90 percent of US Governors are white.

- More than 90 percent of music executives are white.

- 100 percent of highest ranked military advisors are white.

- More than 90 percent of studio executives are white.

- More than 80 percent of America's teachers are white.

- More than 70 percent of Fortune 500 senior executives are white.

- More than 80 percent of full-time college professors are white.

- More than 80 percent of book publishing executives are white.

- More than 90 percent of elected prosecutors are white.

- More than 60 percent of the federal prison staff is white.

If these figures showing racial disparities are surprising, it's because of ignorance of the racial legacy of America. Before any change can happen, there must be awareness. If you're white, you can afford to live in a bubble. You can afford to be "colorblind." The American social order caters to your understanding of the world.

If you're white, you're generally a result of a history your forefathers chose. But if you're black, you're generally a result of a history that your forefathers did not choose. History is not "accidental." It cannot be undone accidentally. You cannot undo something that was purposely done organically. In order to escape the legacy of racial dehumanization, we have to understand this concept.

I've been in enough failed, destructive conversations on race to know that the first mistake made in the dialogue is the failure to define terms. If you don't read anything else in this book, be sure to understand these three popular terms and their definitions: Racism, racial prejudice, and white privilege.

1. **Racism**: The use of structures of power to perpetuate unjust or unequal treatment or disadvantage against certain races or ethnicities.

    Note: Given the statistics above, can black people be racist? Simple answer: No. This is usually where people get stuck and degenerate into unhealthy, destructive conversations. It's better to debate the definitions than to move forward with different definitions.

2. **Racial prejudice**: The feeling of dominance, condescension, or superiority based on race or ethnicity.

3. **White Privilege**: The state of being free from the burden of being a racial minority and being part of the majority culture; not having to think about your ethnic identity constantly.

   Note: One of the mistakes made in dialogues about race is equating socioeconomics with race. For example, there are white communities that do not have socioeconomic privilege. White coal miners in Appalachia and whites in the Rust belt in Ohio and Michigan have not experienced socioeconomic privilege. Conversely, there are black people who *do* have a high socioeconomic status and enjoy the accompanying privileges and opportunities. Equating race and socioeconomics is misleading and insulting to black people who have overcome the barriers to achieve material success. White privilege just means the weight on your shoulders is generally lighter than it is for black people.

How does our disproportionate representation among decision-makers affect black people in this country? Black people are often forced to exist in environments that are culturally violent or remain on the margins of dominant culture. When power and discretion fall into the hands of one demographic, their ways of seeing the world are often superimposed on others.

America was built on the privileged treatment of white people. That legacy cannot change unless white people choose to step out of their comfort zones to create culturally safe and honest environments.

In America, we are being culturally formed into a *white* way of seeing life—a way that is generally unfamiliar with being on the wrong side of dehumanization, callous exploitation, internal division, abuse, and its accompanying legacy of pathology.

Legislation, policies, and interpretations of the world in mass media are determined mainly by people who were raised in a culture that showed their dominant experience and did not reflect those who have experienced the discrimination I've mentioned. Cultural norms have been established and reinforced by people who have a limited ability to understand the hopes, fears, joys, sadness, healing, and trauma of black people.

Black American singer, actor, activist, and close friend of Dr. Martin Luther King, Jr., Harry Belafonte, was asked in a 2018 interview what he believes it will take to make Dr. King's dream of a beloved community a reality. Belafonte said that, from his perspective, until white America regains or identifies a moral course of history and changes their course of conduct, nothing will happen. America will implode.

Belafonte said he'd never seen America more racially divisive, and that includes the time of segregation and the KKK terrorist attacks.

It's important to understand the nuances of white supremacy perpetuated by white society. I've observed three categories: blatant racism, insensitivity towards anti-black racism, and a lack of awareness of the legacy of anti-black racism. Without a nuanced understanding, a uniform approach will likely be misapplied, and further racial tensions and factions will form.

Sadly, in the year 2020, the sentiments and statements of another amazing thinker, James Baldwin, still hold true. In a conversation with Yale philosophy professor Paul Weiss on the Dick Cavett show on June 13, 1968, Baldwin contrasted the supposed well-meaning sentiments of white people and unequal outcomes for black people.

It can be hard to reconcile the supposed goodness of white people with the state of the institutions they govern. His conclusions about white people's feeling about him came from the conditions of their institutions. Here's the updated version of Baldwin's monologue.

I don't know if most white people hate me, but black people are five times more likely to be incarcerated for drug possession than white people and are twelve times more likely to be wrongfully convicted of drug crimes, though whites and blacks use drugs at similar rates, according to the National Registry of Exonerations.

I don't know if most white people hate me, but black youth are treated worse in the school system than white children who engage in the same disruptive behavior, according to the Department of Education.

I don't know if white people hate me, but black mothers die at three to four times the rate of white mothers, according the Center for Disease Control (CDC).

I don't know if white people hate me, but a young black man is twenty-one times more likely to be killed by police than a young white man, according to the Equal Justice Initiative.

I don't know if white people hate me, but in NJ, the average net worth of a black family is roughly $6,000 while the average net worth of a white family is roughly $300,000, rooted in a history of unequal access to mortgages. Though Congress granted every soldier the same benefits, many institutions were run with segregationist principles that resulted in racial injustice. (See article titled: "How the GI Bill's Promise Was Denied to a Million Black WWII Veterans"—Website: https://www.history.com/news/gi-bill-black-wwii-veterans-benefits.)

I don't know if white people hate me, but black youth are more likely to be prosecuted harshly, resulting in one in three black boys going to jail or prison, versus one in seventeen white boys. New Jersey, the state where I was born and raised, leads the nation in racial disparity in prison. For every one white person incarcerated, there are twelve black people incarcerated, partly due to "race-neutral" policies and practices that disproportionately impact black people.

I don't know if white people hate me, but white police officers use gun force twice as often when called on emergency operations and are five times more likely to use gun force in predominantly black neighborhoods, according to Mark Hoekstra, economics Professor, and CarlyWill Sloan, doctoral candidate from Texas A&M University.

Regardless of any singular person's experience, the numbers tell a story. Random, individual examples of equitable treatment, while great to see, cannot be used to exonerate a system that historically and contemporarily treats black people inequitably, as shown above. Jim Crow might be dead, but he had children that are alive and well.

Most Americans might have a general sense that these disparities exist, but they often don't sense a strong, cultural push to comprehensively address these issues. Why? Because in a society where white supremacy is not overtly addressed, integration leads to disregard, constant suspicion, subjugation, and unfair, severe treatment of black people.

The goal is not to demonize all white people, but to uplift black people by refusing to deny and invalidate our grievances. Such denial is the legacy of white supremacy. Until these issues are addressed, America will not be "post-racial."

These figures actually make perfect sense, given the length of time that this nation had racial dehumanization on the books. America is 243 years old. American chattel slavery and Jim Crow segregation existed for 189 years. Anti-black racial dehumanization has been on the books for about 80 percent of America's life.

Racial dehumanization won't come to a screeching halt because some laws were changed. The legislative leaps made it possible for significant strides to be made, and there are now many black Americans doing amazing things in academia, athletics, entertainment, and in business. But there's still a gap. The forces and effects of black dehumanization still need to be healed.

In addition, policies, laws, systems, and attitudes that promote black dehumanization need to be acknowledged, reviewed, and dismantled.

We have a long way to go to achieve equality from soup to nuts on the socioeconomic and justice fronts.

As a mentor, the great tragedy is that many black people in America allowed themselves to feel ashamed of their color. White supremacy is an evil ideology for some. For others, it's a psychological condition and sickness, and the first step to healing is truth. It's important to note that white supremacy is not solely possessed by loud racists, Nazis, and those with swastikas tattooed on their bodies. It's possessed by all of us raised in a culture that reflects white supremacy while denying its existence.

As American politician and sociologist Daniel Patrick Moynihan discussed in his 1965 report *The Negro Family: The Case for National Action*—specifically in the second section, called *The Negro American Family*—it's hard for white people to recognize the effects of 300 years of exploitation on the fabric of black America because the consequences of historic injustice are hidden from view and silent.

In 1965, Moynihan predicted that equal opportunities would not produce equal results, unless a novel and special effort was created. Sadly, his prediction was correct. He made this prediction for two reasons: the racist disease in white America leading to severe personal prejudice, and the unhealed trauma that black people in America suffered for three centuries.

My work as a coach is to give voice to these consequences, as part of this effort, and help us do exactly what Dr. King alluded to in his talk: the development of self-respect, dignity, personhood, and a sense of pride in our color. That is something that only we can do, and we must do. What happened to black people in America is not our fault, but much of our healing is our responsibility. Let's start.

Part I: Sense of Self

Being comes before doing.

IN 2007, THE HOUSE OF Representatives issued H. Res (Resolution of the House of Representatives) 194—an apology for slavery, segregation, and racial dehumanization. The apology included an acknowledgment of the lingering vestiges of racial dehumanization today.

The black race has been stripped of self-respect and self-will, divided internally, ruthlessly exploited, and rendered disposable. The apology also acknowledged the damage done, both tangibly and intangibly: loss of human dignity, obstruction of professional lives and careers, and a long-term loss of revenue and opportunity to acquire wealth.

Today, black people in America—who represent 12 percent of the American population—are the most artistically praised, culturally significant, and a prominent force in American life. As American politician and sociologist Daniel Patrick Moynihan discussed in his 1965 report - *The Negro Family – The Case for National Action*, specifically in the 4th section called *The Tangle of Pathology*, the fact the black people have endured is amazing. A weaker people would have died out. And not only did they endure, but black people entered national affairs as a constructive force, in part due to their inventive strength. Black people in America survived a great deal—but not without injury.

Since the first enslaved Africans came to America in 1619, the blueprint that white racists gave African people was rooted in black inferiority and lies about their inherent worth and value.

Unfortunately, there are forces in the world that have a vested interest in black people remaining ignorant, fearful, hopeless, and defeated.

When people have been told so many lies about themselves, they often begin to believe them. We have to undo the lies. Time alone will not undo it. It takes intentionality, critical analysis, the courage to question one's conditioning, and a resolve to develop a new blueprint for life.

To a great extent, your life will be a product of the source of your identity, values, inner belief, and community. Building your life is like building a skyscraper. Before you can build something tall and straight, you must dig deep to lay the foundation.

One of your goals as a mentor is to reveal your mentee's greatness to themselves. Your desire to get them to be and do more will begin with your ability to help them see this greatness. And that starts by you becoming the best version of you.

As a mentor, you cannot change a world that you are just like. You cannot erase flaws from the world that you still possess. You must be deliberate, because bad things grow naturally while good things have to be planted, particularly in a society that has been designed to destroy your sense of self and belief in yourself. Our view of the world is not dependent on the condition of the world, but on the condition of our heart and mind.

When you recognize that change is not an event, but a process, grace and patience will become your most useful tools to work with imperfect people. They are the same tools that you need to work with yourself.

Dr. Martin Luther King, Jr. and Malcolm X were both imperfect men who were willing to grow, change, and rethink some conclusions. If these men of tremendous virtue can change, why can't we?

Begin by being confident that you are right where you need to be and have everything you need to take the first steps toward personal and community change. We must begin by cultivating a sense of being self-rooted in our inherent value and dignity.

This guide will give you several tools to get you started.

1: Knowledge of Self Toolkit

To raise a people, help them raise themselves—and that starts with how they see themselves.

In 1967, at Ebenezer Baptist Church, the year before he was killed, Dr. Martin Luther King, Jr. was asked by a reporter what the Negro in America wants. Two words sum up his answer: humanity and equality.

He went on to say that black people have been scarred by a system of racial dehumanization, and that they experience a constant drain and a feeling of *nobodiness*. Black people who have endured a process of dehumanization, disenfranchisement, and disempowerment have to constantly fight the feelings of inferiority that would be the natural result.

American chattel slavery had a tremendous impact on the culture and soul of black people. Parts of that culture need to be acknowledged, redeemed, and celebrated. The dysfunctional parts need to be healed. The reality is that the culture of black people as it is today possesses certain behavior patterns that were cultivated in hostile environments and are neither healthy nor rooted in the African heritage.

As American politician and sociologist Daniel Patrick Moynihan discussed in his 1965 report — *The Negro Family – The Case for National Action*, specifically in the 2nd section called *The Negro American Family*— the ramifications of historic oppression are hidden from view and muted.

The role of the mentor is to identify the toxic parts of the culture that diminish the worth and dignity of black people and exercise sufficient integrity to lead in a way that empowers and restores humanity. That works starts with the mentor. The hardest work I've ever had to do was work on myself.

To undo some of the damage done by a non-culturally responsive environment, we must understand the damage done and learn how to heal. These three tools are designed to help begin the process of understanding the nature of the injury to your knowledge of yourself.

These tools will help you to think more critically and be immediately empowered to change what you know and believe about yourself.

Tools
1. *Identity and Esteem: How Do I See and Feel About Myself*
2. *Words: Speak Life, Not Death*
3. *Sankofa: Know Your History*

Identity and Esteem: How Do I See and Feel about Myself?

You can't break someone's leg and get mad if they limp.

As AMERICAN POLITICIAN AND SOCIOLOGIST Daniel Patrick Moynihan discussed in his 1965 report - *The Negro Family – The Case for National Action*, specifically in the 3rd section called *The Roots of the Problem*—American chattel slavery differed from other types of servitude in world history. He compared American and Brazilian slavery.

In the Catholic society of Brazil's religious and legal tradition, slaves were given a place as human beings. It was a miserable place, but still a place. The slave could marry, earn money to buy his freedom, and enjoy days of rest. The slave's family could not be broken up to be sold, and the freedom of infants could be bought for a small price.

The Brazilian slave understood himself to be a man. But the enslaved Africans had no similar protection in American society. Their marriages were not acknowledged. Their children could be sold. It was illegal for a slave to learn to write or read. Enslaved women could be violated and enslaved men could be tortured by the slave master.

It becomes pretty clear that, not only were African people stolen, but our sense of humanity and culture was stolen as well. Being cut off from your past can also make you hopeless about the future. American chattel slavery psychologically destroyed black people's connection to Africa. As a result, many black people feel an identity crisis and a psychological homelessness. Many black people feel like exiles in America due to this disconnection.

Because of the way they were treated, black people are vulnerable to perceptions of excellence and greatness outside of their community. As the Negro spiritual says, the black community is like a motherless child.

White supremacy created an atmosphere for black people that normalized cultural isolation and social invisibility (unless it's Black History month). As one civil rights leader said, black people in America are a nation within a nation, searching for a nationality.

The theft of their homeland affected one of the most crucial aspects of building a solid sense of self: identity and self-concept. Chattel slavery in America was the worst kind of slavery, not only because of the manner in which someone became a slave, the treatment of the slave, or the length of the servitude, but also because of the perception of the slave in their own eyes and the eyes of the oppressor population.

Four hundred years of perpetual abuse and victimization has conditioned many black people to believe they are inferior. Some black people did retain an intrinsic feeling of nobility and worth, in spite of the societal messages, but the effects of abuse on others was catastrophic.

What many black people struggle with is not low or high self-esteem, which requires a performance threshold. They struggle with a condition of having *empty* esteem. This type of esteem isn't about getting straight A's or hitting the game-winning shot. Empty esteem is about having a low sense of your own value. Empty esteem comes from consistent exposure to demeaning and degrading messages from society, community, and family rooted in white supremacy.

Empty esteem suggests that the fundamental sense of being seen, valued, and acknowledged has been greatly compromised. Unfortunately, people with empty esteem can be easily institutionalized, impressed upon, and intimidated.

Personally, I was raised to believe that I was a child of God and loved unconditionally, while simultaneously being taught that the lighter my skin, the straighter my hair, the thinner my facial features, the more valuable and handsome I was. These lessons weren't the result of the pastor's sermon. They came from racist socialization (teaching you what's okay and not okay) by those in my environment.

It's important to note that you come to understand yourself from those in your environment and you arrive at a sense of identity and self-concept from the appraisals and perspectives of those who play a role in your upbringing.

Racial Minority Identity Development

As American novelist and professor Toni Morrison says, every black person comes to the point when they realize they are not white. Race is a meaningful difference in our society. At some point, black people recognize that, in American society, they are the "other."

CNN broadcast a segment called, *The First Time I Realized I Was Black*. You can find the title on Google. You'll see videos of black figures who detail the painful moments when they first realized they were "the other."

Below is a set of stages that black people go through as they begin to realize that they have been forced to acquiesce to white cultural standards.

1. **Compliance**: At this stage, we give preference and considerable importance to the values of the dominant culture (European). We devalue our own racial/ethnic group. The best example of this is Samuel L. Jackson's character Stephen in the movie *Django*. Stephen loved and honored his white master while belittling and abusing those of his own race.

2. **Conflict**: Here, we begin to receive conflicting messages and challenges to the stereotypes of one's racial/cultural group. We feel a growing sense of our own heritage and move away from the perspective that the dominant culture's values are all good.

3. **Protest and Absorption**: At this stage, we feel pride in our heritage and a general distrust of and anger toward the dominant culture. Often, we recognize that a black person must leave the particularity of their experience at the door to make white people feel comfortable. We realize we've been wearing

a mask to get along in a world governed by white standards. As we learn the history of oppression (lynchings, false imprisonments until this day, police brutality), it might make us sad, enraged, or intensely focused on eliminating oppression. I can recall breaking down in tears. As Maya Angelou said, if you're not angry, it's because you're sick. Be angry, but not bitter. Bitterness feeds on the host. Warning: You can't stay there in anger; if you do, you will implode or explode. Extremism is not mentally, emotionally, or spiritually healthy. You should be angry at injustice, but do not let yourself be damaged by it.

4. **Self-Examination:** Here, we recognize the cost of intense feelings toward the dominant cultural group. We begin to focus on self-discovery and recognize that no culture is all good or bad. We might even feel disloyal as our perspective broadens. We might acknowledge a tension between feelings of allegiance to our own cultural group and feelings of autonomy.

5. **Multiethnic appreciation:** At this stage, we come to understand our intrinsic connection as human beings while maintaining the commitment to heal the legacy of anti-black racial dehumanization.

Reflection Question for Black People:

These stages involve a level of emotional labor that comes from feeling one way on the inside and displaying a different emotion on the outside. This is often referred to as "double consciousness." This term, coined by W.E.B. DuBois in his book *The Souls of Black Folk,* refers to the possession of a dual identity leading to an internal conflict in a society where one's culture is subordinated.

Black people have been conditioned to live next to people who don't mind dishonoring them. We are accustomed to placing other groups on a higher pedestal. How can black people be genuine and authentic when they are always trying to manage someone's perception of them? This type of practice is a burden and does injury to black people.

Unfortunately, the injuries that are most respected are the injuries that are most visible. Part of the conditioning is the fear of bringing up our own reality. It leads to an internalized racism which occurs when a black person is forced to conduct themselves in a way that reinforces or upholds white supremacy.

As a black person, at what point did you realize you were not white?

_____

_____

_____

How did it affect you, positively or negatively?

_____

_____

_____

If all people, including black people, have the right to not be invisible, to be respected and to develop their own identities, what can we do to ensure that black people can develop a racial identity in America without injury?

How do we heal?

The norm for black people needs to become the norm in the mainstream culture. Otherwise, black life will be seen as something to be discarded, dismissed, and/or disposed of.

As discussed in the first part of this chapter, one of the legacies of slavery is the robbery of our sense of self as black people, resulting in a condition of empty esteem. African Americans are living in a nation that has conditioned them to believe that they are not valuable. Even worse, black people have conditioned themselves to not feel valuable by acquiescing to the status quo.

As one black educator said, we have to make ourselves blank to wash away the guilt of white people. Things are certainly changing, but more work needs to be done. It takes time to get free from the lies that we've been told about ourselves. Here are several tools that we'll use to do that:

1. **Speak life.** Tool: *Speak Life, Not Death*.
2. **Learn your history.** Take the time to learn where you came from and develop an appreciation for the contributions of Africans to the human family. The next tool—*Sankofa: Know Your History*—will discuss that.
3. **Rebuild confidence.** Adopt a code of conduct. Guard your heart. Remember whose shoulders you stand on. See Chapter 3, *Confidence*.
4. **Help your community heal.** See Part 4, the Community Healing Toolkit.

Words: Speak Life, Not Death

WE RECEIVE A SENSE OF who we are from the appraisals of those around us. Our personal sense of worth and value is significantly influenced by what our mentors say and how they make us feel. As a life coach serving in prisons, most of the men I've counseled have heard negative words spoken from the time they were very young. They received little validation from their parents, and often were described in demeaning and degrading language. The stories I heard made a certain style of parenting very obvious. To be sure, not all black parents treat their children the same way, but some patterns of behavior are worth acknowledging and understanding. Here's an example of a black parent's response when receiving a compliment about her child's performance in class.

> **Teacher**: *Your son is doing really well in my class. We are so thankful that he is here. He really helps create a great learning environment.*
>
> **Black parent**: *Is he? Child, please! Don't let him fool you. That boy is a whole mess at home. Always fighting with his brother. You should see his room. He can barely keep it clean. Maybe you can come straighten him out at home, since he's doing so well here. Thank you anyway. You let me know if he gets out of line. Have a nice day!*

When I asked several black parents if they have either witnessed or even demonstrated this kind of behavior, 100 percent of them said yes. As an explanation, many black parents say they don't want their children to become arrogant, full of themselves, or too comfortable, which is why they barely praise their children. They might even try to instill a sense of fear.

I can understand the rationale, and in many ways, I agree. However, we must understand that this behavior oftentimes can affect a child for life.

What is the origin of black parents who talk about their children like this in public?

There's a secret that many black people know: the parent *is* proud of their child. Based on cultural studies and anecdotal evidence, the practice of degrading the child goes back to the days of American chattel slavery. When a slave master approached an enslaved mother with an eye toward selling one of her sons on the auction block or breeding her daughter, the mother would begin to speak negatively about the child in order to make the child seem less appealing. This might keep him/her from being sold or used for breeding.

> **Slave master:** *Is that your boy? He sure is coming along.*
>
> **Slave mother:** *No, Massa! He's no good, lazy, stupid…You don't want to sell him.*

According to the theory of social learning, we observe and imitate the behavior of those in our environment, and those individuals do what they learned in their environment. Hundreds of years after slavery, this style of parenting has become a kind of pathology (unhealthy behavior) that has been normalized in the black culture.

Unfortunately, a child often internalizes the messages spoken over his/her life. When you speak negative words over a child, the interior world of the child is reconfigured to fit the names spoken. Proof positive are the brothers I meet in prison. The tongue truly has the power of life and death. (Proverbs 18:21, NIV)

In light of this information, we have a responsibility to end negative cycles by speaking life-affirming messages to our mentees and interrupting the negative cycles in our respective communities. One educator says that it takes eleven positive words to overcome every one negative word spoken over the life of a child.

As a mentor, your words can aid or derail your mentee's future. Young people are vulnerable to your words. In your language and actions, you must work to affirm the mentee and let them know they are valued by the community and valuable to the community.

You must remember that those you work with cannot discern your intention as easily as they can see your action and hear your words, your work must be intentional and deliberate. You might mean well, but you must also do right.

We earn the right to speak into someone's life by the care that we take to speak words to uplift and not tear down. You can free people or put them in prison based on what you say, because someone's life is often a reflection of the words spoken over them. This becomes especially important for those who are building confidence. Sometimes you have to trust in someone else's faith in you before yours kicks in. Speak life.

The Mentor's Creed:

Whatever happens, you belong here. There's something the world needs to have done that only you can do. You have been fearfully and wonderfully made. You were loved and approved of before you were born. Know that you have worth and that your life has ultimate significance because you are made in the image of God. Don't allow anyone to make you feel that you are nobody. The image of God presents the life and dignity of the human person, which means you have worth and value regardless of popularity, titles, skills, association, and possessions. None of that makes you worthy of being loved, respected, and honored. Artificial, social, and human constructs don't determine who you are or what you can be. God does. In the mind of God, you are born with dignity, worth, and value. You are black and beautiful.

Sankofa: Know Your History
When lions can tell their own stories, the hunters will no longer be heroes.

ACCORDING TO AMERICAN POLITICIAN AND sociologist Daniel Patrick Moynihan in his 1965 report *The Negro Family – The Case for National Action*—specifically in the third section, called *The Roots of the Problem*—American chattel slavery differed from the types of servitude in ancient or modern history.

One of the main ways the enslaved African was injured was through being completely cut of and totally ignorant of his/her history. It was not in the interest of slave masters to keep track of the cultural heritage of his "property."

Under sanitized European history, black stories have been made invisible. Subsequent to that, there was no hope for the future. In order to justify the economic engine of the slave trade, black people had to be devalued. Any facts of black contribution to civilization that didn't go along with racial theories associated with white supremacy were ignored.

White supremacists not only colonized parts of the world, they also colonized the information shared. Even after slavery, the American government made no effort to help the enslaved Africans heal from the trauma of the slavery experience. It's foolish to expect the people who kidnapped you to tell you the truth about your history.

Today, black people are forced to piece together the broken fragments of the past. If the purpose of an education is to facilitate the development of a mature mind and a sense of self, then studying one's ethnic history should be a part of that process. If your worldview doesn't include an honest account of your history, you will build your identity on a foundation of lies.

It's been said that a child's worldview is formed by their early to mid-teen years. When I was sixteen, I visited the National Great Blacks in Wax Museum in Baltimore, Maryland. This wax museum features prominent historical black American figures. I didn't understand it at the time, but my visit instilled a sense of pride in me that would pay dividends until this day.

My cultural esteem began to increase as I learned about the amazing things that people like me had accomplished. My belief that I could contribute something significant in the world grew exponentially.

When I realized this, I realized that one of the worst things you can do to a people is to rob them of the memory of themselves. If you don't know your cultural history, you're like a tree without roots—and trees without roots cannot stand. To sever people from their cultural roots is equivalent to killing their sense of self.

My formal education, which reflected the perspective of the dominant culture, failed to give me knowledge of historical facts and events that would allow me to have a sense of pride in who I was and where I came from.

Our sense of self-worth and self-concept doesn't only come from our family heritage, but also from our racial and cultural history. When our race and culture are assaulted from birth, we will have to heal the damage to get a people back on track to achieving their destiny.

As Carter G. Woodson, author of *The Miseducation of the Negro* discussed, some of the damage began in school. The schools attempted to produce in white society a hatred of black people, and in black society, a hatred for themselves. The educational system has justified slavery, peonage, lynching, and segregation.

For many black people, this "historical amnesia" has led to an identity crisis. Identity comes from self-concept, out of which comes your sense of meaning and purpose. In order to heal this injury, black people have to engage in the process of *Sankofa*.

Sankofa is a word in the Twi language of Ghana, which means "go back and get it." There's also an associated proverb which says that there's nothing wrong with going back to get what you've forgotten. Research has shown that knowledge of cultural roots, values, and beliefs is central to the effectiveness of programs for education, reentry, and health.

The legendary actor Denzel Washington, in a 1992 interview with Barbara Walters, discussed his experience playing Malcolm X in the movie of the same name. He discussed what happens when you've been taught that your people have done nothing in the world.

Washington said his public school experience didn't teach him about the accomplishments of black people. His role in *Glory* taught him that 180,000 black men and women fought in the Civil War. His entire academic experience had excluded this information.

It's not that the history is not there or that the history is obscure; it has been *deliberately* left out. History taught to oppressed people has been sanitized to make it acceptable to live in the conditions of the world without challenging them.

Similar to the Prodigal son in the Word who "came to himself" (Luke 15:17, KJV) when he realized who he was and where he belonged, black people will come to themselves when they understand their history and what has happened to them.

The key difference between the prodigal son and black people is that the prodigal was responsible for his own misfortune. Black people are not responsible for their miseducation and dehumanization. White racism is responsible. But once we become aware, we become responsible to undo the damage by first learning our history.

If you don't know who you are, you can't figure out where you're going. To move forward, sometimes you have to first go backwards. The measure of a person's dignity depends on his estimation of himself.

Study black history—not to prove a point, but to gain back the pride we were stripped of. Higher standards have been set by those who have come before us. As Carter G. Woodson said, the lynching of black people begins in the school room. It's important for black people to know the revolutionary stories and accomplishments of their black ancestors, so they know that they are important by heritage.

Facts about Black History That I Never Learned in School
Don't ever forget. That's how you get lost.

1. The first man to die in the American Revolution was a black man, Crispus Attucks in 1770.

2. Benjamin Banneker, a black man, played a major role in the architecture of Washington D.C and may have even finished the designs in 1791. He also invented the first clock in 1753.

3. Nat Turner was an enslaved African who led a slave rebellion in 1831 in Southampton County, Virginia killing between fifty-five and sixty-five people. He gathered more than seventy enslaved and free blacks, some of whom were on horseback. The rebellion was put down in a few days, but in the after-math, one of the most interesting legislation changes occurred. Anti-literacy laws were enacted, because an educated mind cannot be enslaved.

4. Denmark Vesey was an enslaved African in Charleston, South Carolina who purchased his freedom at the age of thirty-two in 1799. After becoming free, he stayed close to the other slaves, many of whom were inspired by the success of the Haitian Revolution. Unfortunately, due to slave informants, their insurrection was stopped as those involved were arrested.

5. The Tuskegee Airmen were the first black military aviators in the US armed forces. During WWII, despite being subject to Jim Crow laws, these men served the US faithfully. By 1945, it was reported by the Chicago Defender that the 332nd Fighter group, which escorted bombers and defended from enemy

planes, had suffered no losses of bombers after completing 200 missions.

6. Mansa Musa, a black man, was once the richest man in the world. He was a 14th century West African ruler of the Mali Empire.

7. Jan Ernst Matzeliger, a black man, invented the automatic shoe lasting machine in 1883.

8. Charles Brooks, a black man, invented the street sweeper in 1896.

9. Frederick McKinley Jones, a black man, invented the first automatic refrig-eration system for trucks in 1935.

10. Garret Morgan, a black man, invented the traffic signal in 1923 and the military gas mask in 1914.

11. Henrietta Bradberry, a black woman, invented the underwater cannon, which made it possible to launch torpedoes from submarines in 1943.

12. Madam CJ Walker, a black woman, invented cosmetic products for women of darker complexion. She was the first woman of any nationality in the US to become a millionaire through her own efforts in the early 1900s.

13. Charles Richard Drew, a black man, contributed to blood banking and an understanding of blood plasma in 1940.

14. Daniel Hale Williams, a black man, completed the first successful open-heart surgery in the world in 1913.

15. Lewis Latimer, a black man, was the right-hand man of Thomas Edison. He came up with the light bulb filament in 1881.

16. Gabriel Prosser was an enslaved blacksmith who organized a slave rebellion in Richmond, VA in the summer of 1800.

When you study black history, you should come to several conclusions:

- When we understand the full history of the enslavement, you'll see how massive this crime was against black people. Slavery has been aptly referred to as the molestation of a nation. Reading about history should also make you proud of how far you have come. You have nothing to be ashamed of. Black people in America are some of the most resilient people to ever walk the face of the Earth.

- We have to keep digging to build a knowledge base of black history. The truth is, you have to work really hard to know the truth. It will not just be given to you. One of the greatest tricks of white supremacy is to convince black people not to study their own history. Michael Eric Dyson, the pre-eminent scholar from Georgetown University who holds a PhD from Princeton University, said that in his late fifties, he was still learning new things about black people. He didn't know about the black women (Katherine Johnson, Mary Jackson, and Dorothy Vaughan) who were mathematicians working for NASA, as portrayed in the movie Hidden Figures. He didn't know what black people had done in wars, in foreign countries, or in language. If this well-read, nationally acclaimed scholar admits he wasn't taught about black history, we all can learn humility from him and get on a path to uncovering who we are. Doing so will help us remember our greatness and our nobility—or discover it for the very first time.

- Memory is a powerful force in the way a society evolves. We must regularly engage in the moral and intellectual exercise of evaluating whether history is properly reflected in our culture. It's amazing how learning history forces you to see your reality differently. It goes a step further when current tragedies force a nation to see how the ugly, untold history still lingers today. In 2015, white supremacist Dylan Roof killed nine members of the African Methodist Church in Charleston, South Carolina. In that year, then-governor Nikki Haley made a decision to remove the Confederate flag from the South Carolina statehouse. Despite the Confederate flag having a history of representing racist causes, many Southerners see the flag as a symbol of Southern pride. This is just another example of the lack of truth and reconciliation that plagues America and allows people to live with their own versions of historical events. As history is unfolded, the legacy of white supremacy and racial hatred should be undone swiftly, to ensure that America truly represents a land that grants humanity and dignity to all people.

2 : Values Toolkit

I've always been a weirdo. It just makes sense now. Pharrell

IN A TRULY FREE WORLD, no one has the right to tell another what they ought to live and die for. This section bears witness to that truth. To be no one but yourself in a world that's always trying to change you is the hardest task.

The more in tune you are with your personal values, the more unique you'll be and the more you'll ultimately be able to contribute to your community. Each person has personal autonomy and the right to pursue goals and values apart from the pressures around them.

As a mentor, you need to know who you are and what your values are. Otherwise, you run the risk of becoming enmeshed in the views of others. Values are concepts, ideas, and beliefs that play a part in defining us. Values drive our behavior and govern our decisions. Our values are reflected in how we use our resources: time, treasures, and talents.

Setting goals without clarifying values is like building a house without a foundation. Not organizing your life around your values would be like climbing a ladder only to realize that it's leaning against the wrong wall.

Another way to look at it is, if you were building a home but forget to tell the contractor what kind of home you want, you couldn't be surprised if the house was built with the wrong number of bedrooms, the wrong lighting, and the wrong size kitchen. It's probably not going to fit what you want, because you never took the time to articulate what you want.

The things that matter most to us personally don't always make the most noise. Not everything that's good for us will be commercialized. It's up to us to ensure we give our values a place in our lives.

Most people derive a sense of self and purpose through the journey of life – the ups and downs, the joys and disappointments, the fulfilling and disillusioning experiences. That's a part of the process of discovering your God-given nature, and knowing your nature is the secret to finding the fulfillment.

Fulfillment comes from knowing what you value. We will generally fail at trying to be who we are "supposed" to be. The search for success starts by discovering who we actually are.

Being black in a Eurocentric society is not the only pressure humans must endure, but because race is meaningful in our society, it makes a difference. As a result of living in a way that doesn't attract unnecessary attention, many black people trade their genuineness for security. They disguise their true values for fear that they might disrupt their position in white society.

In other words, they wear a mask. When you wear a mask for too long, you become a stranger to yourself. One researcher says that when you exchange genuineness for security, you may experience a host of issues such as blame, eating disorders, addictions, anxiety, grief, and anger.

Often, it's not until you get around people who are safe—who don't pressure you to be anyone else—that you feel just how much pressure you've been under.

Walking an authentic path will always require a level of self-reflection. Great mentors give their mentees the space to discover their values. See the tools below to walk your mentee through this and give your mentee permission to live and walk authentically.

Tools

1. *Go Beneath the Iceberg: Teach them to journal and discuss their ideas, their deep-felt desires, and their personal history.*
2. *Values and Reflection Integrity: Help mentees translate their values into a set of consistent actions.*
3. *Virtues Roadwork: Develop the building blocks of character needed to protect the values you establish.*

Exercise: What is Your Mask?

Look up the poem *We Wear the Mask* by Paul Laurence Dunbar. (See the link below.) This poem, written in 1896, reflects what black Americans faced after the Civil War. Black people were forced to wear a metaphorical "mask" of contentment in front of white people to avoid racist attacks. The mask was integral to black people's survival in America. It hid the existence of the deep suffering and pain that blacks felt at that time, and for many in this time. In order to make life more tolerable, black people would sing and narrate poems that gave voice to their plight.

Website Link: https://www.poetryfoundation.org/poems/44203/we-wear-the-mask

After reflecting on the poem, in what ways have you ever worn a mask to hide your true feelings, compromise your uniqueness, and conform to the expectations of others? (Well-executed snaps or talking points, false expressions, carefully curated pictures on social media, etc.)?

_____

_____

_____

Go Beneath the Iceberg:
Teach them to journal and discuss their ideas, deep-felt desires, and personal history.

AS A CHILD, I LEARNED to silence who I was to make everyone else happy. Like the average boy growing up, I wanted people to be pleased with me. I silenced any deep-felt desires that might have contradicted with my family's worldviews and opinions. In the process, I deceived and betrayed myself in order to receive a sense of love, validation, and approval.

In my experience, many parents lack the tools to get a good sense of who their children authentically are on a deep level and to nurture that authenticity. They know about their children, but they don't know who they are: their insecurities, wounds, hopes, joys, how they are wired, and what motivates them.

These things are important to know, for two reasons. First, it's very hard to love someone well when you don't understand them. Second, it's hard to guide them in the right direction when you have little knowledge as to what drives them.

As a mentor, you want to spend time allowing your young people to talk and share what's in their hearts. There is greatness in all people. Unfortunately, some people need a little time (or sometimes a lot more time) and a feeling of safety to begin to tap into that greatness.

Behind your deepest and most consistent feelings are your values. You also want to pay attention to how you feel physically. Your body is a major prophet, not a minor prophet. Have you experienced muscle tension, a headache, or knots in your stomach at different moments in your life? Sometimes, what's going on in your body will tell you what your values are and if they are being violated.

This is a key part of the value assessment process. On a daily basis, take the time to ask yourself how your day went and which moments brought you tremendous joy and which moments made you feel uncomfortable or uneasy. Journal your answers, and use them to reflect. Your answers over time will give you an indication of what you find important and which frustrations you need to think about addressing more intentionally.

Your deep-felt passions and desires are not always discovered, but *recovered*. That's why journaling is important. Life is lived in forward motion, but it's understood with past reflection. You want to engage in the reflection process regularly, to spot trends.

Here's a list of questions that you can use to get started:

What makes you mad?
What makes you sad?
What makes you excited?
What makes you afraid?
What makes you feel generous?
What do you talk about without being asked?
What makes you feel complete?

Ask your mentee to keep a daily journal. Every thirty, sixty, or ninety days, help them review the journal for a theme of what their days have been like and what the *consistent* themes indicate. The word to think about is consistency. Your feelings can betray you, but when you journal, you get a sense of continuity in your emotions.

It can be dangerous to just follow your feelings. This piece is important, because one of the goals of life should be to identify, cultivate, and maximize your God-given talents in way that is consistent with your deep-felt desires or values and the needs of the world.

If you do this consistently and pay close attention, you will begin to spot trends in how you feel about different things and it will speak to the direction that your life should take in each season of your life. Whatever holds your attention will control the direction of your life.

When we reflect on the past, we give ourselves a chance to make the future more valuable. The goal is not to gather information but to watch for trends and figure out the point. This will be an ongoing process, because what stirs you emotionally at eighteen might not at thirty.

As a mentor, you might not be able to light the fire of purpose and destiny in the mentee's life, but you can create the conditions for the fire to burn brighter.

For additional exercises and tools, see Chapter 4 – Gifts, Talents, Skills, and Strengths – *Bridge the Gaps - Lessons on Self-Awareness, Self-Development and Self-Care – Tools for Building a Life that Matters.* Visit www.amazon.com or www.thebridg330.com to pick up a copy.

Values and Integrity Reflection:
Help mentees translate their values into a set of consistent actions.

The greatest gift you can give someone is the space to be authentic, without you walking away.

AFTER DOING THE LAST EXERCISE on going beneath the surface, let's identify the value that connects to the deepest emotions. In each season of life, there are certain values that are more important than others.

In our culture, we don't do a lot of work around values. Yet to increase personal power, we need to know our highest values. No one else has the authority or the right to pick what should and should not be important to you.

Unfortunately, many environments—from school to church to families—work to eliminate the distinctiveness of the individuality of people. This is problematic because it inadvertently teaches people to deny or undermine their own sense of self and values.

From the list below, choose three values that are among your top priorities—or choose your own. Then write a clarifying statement that makes your intent to manifest crystal clear. When you clarify your values, you can see your highest priorities clearly and can live your life with clear intention.

Make it a practice to regularly review your values and operationalize your values with clarifying statements of how they will manifest. Boil your values down to behaviors. Real values are reflected in the things you *do*, not the thing you say. This is a great exercise to guide you in deciding what you should make a priority to live a life that is personally meaningful.

Accomplishment o Achievement o Accountability o Accuracy o Adventure o Positive Attitude o Beauty o Calm o Challenge o Change o Collaboration o Commitment o Communication o Community o Comfort o Compassion o Competence o Competition o Connection o Cooperation o Coordination o Creativity o Decisiveness o Delight of being, joy o Democracy o Discipline o Discovery o Diversity o Effectiveness o Efficiency o Empowerment o Excellence o Fairness o Faith o Faithfulness o Family o Flair o Flexibility o Focus o Freedom o Friendship o Fun o Global view o Good health o Gratitude o Greatness o Growth o Happiness o Hard work o Harmony o Honesty o Improvement o Independence o Individuality o Inner peace o Innovation o Integrity o Intuitiveness o Justice o Knowledge o Leadership o Learning o Love o Loyalty o Management Maximum utilization (of time, resources) o Meaning o Modeling o Money o Openness o Orderliness o Passion o Peace - inner o Perfection o Personal Choice o Pleasure o Power o Practicality o Preservation o Privacy o Progress o Prosperity o Punctuality o Purpose o Recognition o Regularity o Relationships o Reliability o Resourcefulness o Respect for others o Responsibility o Results-oriented o Safety o Satisfaction o Security o Self-care o Self-reliance o Self-thinking Service (to others, society) o Simplicity o Skill o Solving Problems o Speed o Spontaneity o Standardization o Status o Structure o Succeed; A will to o Success o Achievement o Teamwork o Techniques o Timeliness o Tolerance o Tradition o Transformation o Tranquility o Trust o Truth o Unity o Variety o Wealth o Wisdom

Example:
Value: Personal development
Value-supporting behavior: I will attend two professional development conferences every year.

Value:
Value-Supporting Behavior:

Value:
Value-Supporting Behavior:

Value:
Value-Supporting Behavior:
Integrity Reflection: What We Value Will Reflect In Our Lives

> *Beliefs turn into thoughts.*
> *Thoughts turn into words.*
> *Words turn into actions.*
> *Actions turn into habits.*
> *Habits turn into values.*
> *Values turn into destiny.*

Wisdom is vindicated by her children. (Luke 7:35). In other words, *results speak for themselves.* When you do things that are not consistent with your values, you are out of integrity. Your goal should be to build and reinforce a foundation of behaviors that reflect your deepest values.

We have a hierarchy of values to consider in every season of life. When you get the chance to reflect, you can easily discern what's most important, what's not, and what's been misplaced or misprioritized.

Writing down values is easy. Living them is much more challenging. Our values systems do not immediately transform our lives or free us—but our core values *do* produce a predictable behavior pattern.

It's been said that 50 percent of your life should be used to reflect on the other 50 percent. Take a moment to reflect on your values and your behavior.

Reflection Questions:

- What values have you been communicating to your mentees by your actions?

- Is there any inconsistency between your values and actions? How might that be hindering your success in this season of your life?
- If your behavior represents your values, where is your value system taking you?
- In what areas of your life (values, attitudes, lifestyles, choices, etc.) might you be called to resist the values of the culture? Where is your value system taking you? Is it causing you to lead a reflective, productive, and attentive life? Or is it leading to a foolish, wasteful, and destructive life? Take a look at the fruit of your philosophies. If they are ineffective, change them.
- Do you need to recalibrate your inner compass? Note: Never compromise your standards. Just acknowledge when you are having a hard time living up to them and be willing to change yourself, not your values. You often have to clean up former decisions before you make a new decision. Know your values so that you know you're not selling out. Do not dilute your values. As life circumstances become more complex, the values often get lost. What steps do you need to take to bring your actions into alignment with your declared values?
- In this season of your life, what is your integrity calling you to address that might be out of order?
- Values often come from voids we've had in our lives. What values have you had in your life that create personal value?

For additional exercises and tools, see Chapter 3 - Values — *Bridge the Gaps - Lessons on Self-Awareness, Self-Development and Self-Care — Tools for Building a Life that Matters*. Visit www.amazon.com or www.thebridg330.com to pick up a copy.

Virtues roadwork:
Develop the building blocks of character needed to protect the values you establish.

To implement a value into your life takes time and work.

IN THE LAST EXERCISE, WE discussed the integrity of values. You must defend what you build, because the foundation is always under threat of corruption, corrosion, or thievery.

We practice our values by learning the power of virtues, which serve as the building blocks of character. One of the tools used in reinforcing your value system will be the language that mentors use in regular interactions.

In order to hold on to one's integrity, virtues must be practiced on a daily basis. I want to combine the practice of cultivating virtue with the creation of a language-rich environment.

Virtues help strengthen the lens through which we see.

Here are some short phrases describing particular virtues you might want to emphasize:

Virtue Phrases
Embracing the reality of life on its own terms – willingness to take responsibility for every choice – seeing the beauty in life – speaking one's belief with a peaceable certainty – showing attention to things and people that matter to us – having a certainty and confidence after discerning what's right – possessing a generous heart toward those suffering – looking for the good in every situation – pursuing a goal, a person, or a belief wholeheartedly – deep empathy for the less fortunate – feeling capable and certain – carefully thinking about the needs of others – working together for the benefit of the collective – using fear to fuel determination – treating

others with honor – using inspiration to ignite our originality – being firm when making a decision or taking a stand – experiencing our emotions without giving them control over our actions – using the power of focus to drive our ambitions – having a sense of personal worth and respect – showing extreme care and attention to our work – subduing the desire to rush decisions – putting ourselves in someone else's shoes – withstanding adversity and hardship – showing the ability to adapt to change amidst stressful times – letting go of resentments – deeply respecting what's true and right – being oriented toward a better world – possessing modesty and being unpretentious – seeing what's possible and working to make a difference – practicing fairness in all we do – steadfast commitment to ideals and people we care about – being reflective and consciously aware of our actions – keeping things where they belong – trusting the process – possessing the strength to recover from adversity – being content with the basic gifts of life – accepting personal differences and avoiding passing judgment – seeking comprehension of the full truth – choosing the right path at the right time – passion for what we care about

How mentors can use virtue phrases

1. You can use these virtue phrases to compliment your mentee: "You showed attention to the things you cared about and were very generous toward the less fortunate." This shows them that they are capable of good behavior and specifically describes the behavior.

2. You can use the virtue phrases to correct your mentee. Focus more on what you want to happen, not what you don't want to happen. "Jon, when you make a decision to pursue a goal, you must pursue that goal wholeheartedly."

3. When there's improvement, make an acknowledgment: "You have fully embraced the process of pursuing your goal wholeheartedly."

4. You can use the virtue phrase to decide what type of culture you want to create in your environment. You can create a poster or a slogan.

Exercise: Using the virtue phrases above,

1. What three virtues do you want to begin to work on?
2. What three virtues are you already strong in?
3. What three virtues will be needed in this season of your life?

Warning to Mentors:

As a mentor, you must deliberate about what you model. There will most likely come a point in your life where everything you profess to believe and value will be tested. These moments can help you ascertain how much work you've done or how much you have to do on firming up your values.

When you begin to work on being more authentic, you might experience growing pains with friends and family. Your attempt to live in a genuine way might affect them. My source of courage comes from the following pieces of Scripture:

1. The fear of human opinion disables; trusting in God protects you from that. (Proverbs 29:25, MSG)

2. They decided to send some of their men along with the Herodians[a] to ask him (Jesus) this question: "Sir, we know you are very honest and teach the truth regardless of the consequences, without fear or favor." (Matthew 22:16, TLB)

3. The Lord says, "I am the one who comforts you. So why should you be afraid of people? They are only humans who live and die like the grass. (Isaiah 51:12, ERV)

For additional exercises and tools, see Chapter 23 – Decisions – *Bridge the Gaps Lessons on Self-Awareness, Self-Development and Self-Care – Tools for Building a Life that Matters.* Visit www.amazon.com or www.thebridg330.com to pick up a copy.

3: Confidence Toolkit

Without confidence, you lose twice in the race of life. With confidence, you win before you even start.

As American politician and sociologist Daniel Patrick Moynihan discussed in his 1965 report *The Negro Family – The Case for National Action*—specifically in the fifth section, called *The Case for National Action*—the disorganized family structure of black communities has left many young people handicapped in their relationship to the greater community.

Families often have not provided for the emotional needs of children, or have not provided a sense of structure. The effects can be devastating.

Our view of the world is based more on our internal confidence than on our external observation. Anton Lembede, the South African activist who founded the African National Congress and was a mentor of Nelson Mandela, believed that the greatest obstacle to the liberation of black people is the black inferiority complex – this lack of confidence in themselves, which is rooted in the ideology of white supremacy.

I believe that failure is something you feel long before you make it manifest. As Carter G. Woodson, author of *The Miseducation of the Negro* discussed, a feeling of failure has been deeply implanted in the psyche of black Americans by the incorrect and spiritually depleting education they receive on a daily basis, through educational and societal conditioning.

Conversely, success is something you feel long before you make it manifest. From Woodson's perspective, black people must improve their self-regard individually before they can engage in successfully changing the collective condition of black people. How can that happen?

First, you have to believe it's possible. As a mentor, if you are going to believe it for your mentee, you have to believe it for yourself. There's a lot of self-confidence needed to chase a dream and break cycles of failure, and it doesn't come without work.

People assume that confident people have always been confident. That's the furthest thing from the truth. Confidence is a result of both mental/emotional inputs and one's own personal output.

You can have an immediate impact on your life if you make decisions based on *who you know you are* and what you bring to the table—as opposed to what white people allow you to do. A sense of inferiority can be effectively counteracted several ways.

Based on my study of successful black people, there are three main confidence builders:

1. *Emancipate and Guard Your Mind: Be Careful What You Let Influence You*
2. *Stand: Remember Whose Shoulders You Stand Upon*
3. *It's Your Life: Take Responsibility*

In addition to the tools above, confidence is not about seeing yourself as better than others. It's about not having a need to compare yourself at all, because you know who you are; you know what you believe (See Chapter 7 – Be Differentiated – *Book: Bridge the Gaps*); and you know what you bring to the table (Chapter 5 – What Do Others See in You? Reference: *Bridge the Gaps*).

Emancipate and Guard Your Mind:
Be Careful What You Let Influence You

"Whatever is true, whatever is noble, whatever is right, whatever is pure, whatever is lovely, whatever is admirable—if anything is excellent or praiseworthy—think about such things." (Philippians 4, NIV)

IN MAY OF 1987, THURGOOD Marshall, the first African American Supreme Court justice, delivered the Bicentennial Speech marking the 200-year anniversary of the US Constitution. He took a turn in the speech when he commented that he did not find the insights, future visions, and sense of fundamental fairness particularly profound.

According to Justice Marshall, America was born out of a great moral error – the robbery of land of one people, the indigenous people of the Americas, and the enslavement of another group of people, Africans. The government was defective from the start, requiring a civil war, several amendments, and a social transformation to win the respect for freedoms and human rights that we have today.

To find the flaw, we only need to look at the first three words of the Preamble: "We the People." Those words did not include most Americans, including the black people, who did not have the right to vote but had 3/5s of their population counted for representational purposes in 1787 during the US Constitutional Convention.

Justice Marshall's observations make one thing very clear. The history of this nation is riddled with the intent to create a ranked social order and included the belief that black people were inferior. This belief was used to justified slavery, lynching, and segregation. The sinister genius of racial dehumanization made many white people believe black people were inferior, and also made many black people believe this untruth about themselves. If everything around you reinforces the belief that blacks are inferior and whites are superior, blacks will continue to live out the inferiority complex and whites will see themselves as superior, whether unconscious or not.

If black people want to change life for the better, they must change the way they feel about themselves. This requires that the environment reinforce the understanding of the full humanity of black people and the possibility of a greater future.

Steps to Guarding Your Heart and Mind

If you lived in the mud for 400 years, at some point, you have to start cleaning. America has been in the mud. Bryan Stevenson

Changing reality for black people starts with changing the conditioning of black people. Black people were taught to be ashamed of being black. Racist systems are so well designed that some victims do blame themselves.

It's important to note that the stolen Africans were not slaves when they were stolen. African doctors, teachers, builders, astronomers, mothers, and fathers were brought to the US. They were made to be slaves through their conditioning.

One of the first steps to making a slave is enslaving the mind. The most powerful weapon of the slave master is the mind of the slave. As Carter G. Woodson, author of *The Miseducation of the Negro* discussed, if you can control a man's perception of himself, you can control his destiny.

Liberating the mind is just as important, if not more important, than freeing the body because we are not free until we can free our minds. In the 1930s, Negro teachers were powerless to change programs that promoted black inferiority. That is no longer the case. In our day and time, mentors can have meaningful impact.

To reverse the enslavement, you need to re-engineer and heal the mind of the enslaved African by changing the self-perception. As Frederick

Douglass said, you have seen how men became slaves. You will see how slaves became men.

Here are the four steps:

1. Do a Detox
2. Learn to Protect Your Heart and Mind
3. Sharpen Your Perspective to Recognize Miseducating/Inferiority-Producing Content
4. Interrupt Racist Socialization

Step 1: Do a Detox

You become what you think about and what you expose yourself to. Your brain is like a computer program—garbage in, garbage out. Put yourself and your mentees on a detox program.

Unless your business depends on it, start doing a regular detox of social media and television. Start with a day, a week, or a month and see what your life feels like without constant exposure to random sources of media. Young or old, we are all impressionable. What we see and hear informs the direction we take. Be mindful of the character and quality of the content you take in. Be intentional about what you will and will not consume.

Some pathologies are rooted in lies you might have believed. Sometimes you need a change of input to ignite who you are. Emotions and desires are contagious. The higher the stakes are in your life, the more intentional you have to be about your environment and your exposure to it.

A detox will allow you to free yourself from the petty thoughts and concerns that weigh you down. James Baldwin said that it took him years to throw up all the filth he was taught to believe about himself before he believed he had the right to be on this Earth. We should be intentional in getting to that place as well. I strongly subscribe to the principle of new affections possessing expulsive power. In other words, to get rid of darkness, you have to flood it with light. Here's a good Scripture to reflect on.

Solution: Fill Your Mind with Positive and Uplifting Content

"Summing it all up, friends, I'd say you'll do best by filling your minds and meditating on things true, noble, reputable, authentic, compelling, gracious—the best, not the worst; the beautiful, not the ugly; things to praise, not things to curse. Put into practice what you learned from me, what you heard and saw and realized. Do that, and God, who makes everything work together, will work you into his most excellent harmonies." (Philippians 4:8-9, MSG)

Step 2: Learn to Protect your Mind and Heart

The Scripture says, "Above all else, guard your heart, for everything you do flows from it." (Proverbs 4:23, NIV)

An interpretation of this verse is to be careful how you think and what you allow to influence or condition you, because will affect how you move through the world. Be Intentional about the type of media you consume, because "As a man thinketh, so is he." (Proverbs 23:7, KJV)

You must protect your mind as much as you would protect your physical assets. On a daily basis, you have to stand guard at the door of your heart and mind by monitoring the movies/shows you watch, the people you hang around, the music you listen to, and the people you follow on social media. Your deepest perception of you must be self-determined, instead of being automatically programmed by the forces of the various media of communication (TV, social media, etc.)

Everything is conveying a message. The more positive your self-perception, the better equipped you'll be to cope with adversity. The quality of your life is determined by the quality of your thinking. Our acts can be no wiser than our thoughts. Your thinking will affect the decisions you make, the places you go, and the relationships you engage in.

Remember, the higher the stakes are, the more intentional you have to be about your conditioning. I would argue that the stakes are always high when it comes to guiding the young people of tomorrow.

Promote Positive and/or Humanizing Media Depictions of Black People from the Lens of Black People

If you don't like someone's story, write your own.

Blackness is a powerful symbol, because we were taught to be ashamed of being black; to overcome that teaching, you must affirm blackness as a positive trait. Slavery is over. The physical bodies of African Americans have been liberated, but the mind must also be liberated. Our hands and feet were once shackled, but now our minds are being shackled. One of the ways to remove the shackles, aside from learning one's history, is to take in positive media images of black people.

Reflection question: What content choices promote positive depictions of black people that you are familiar with?

Here's a non-exhaustive list of people who are intentional about promoting overall positive and/or humanizing depictions of black people that you can google or learn about at www.imdb.com:

-Ava Duvernay: *13th* (Documentary), *When They See Us* (TV Show), *Queen Sugar* (TV Show)

-John Singleton: *Rosewood* (Movie), *Higher Learning* (Movie), *Boyz N the Hood* (Movie)

-Spike Lee: *Do the Right Thing* (Movie), *Malcolm X* (Movie), *Four Little Girls* (Documentary)

-Ryan Coogler: *Fruitvale Station* (TV Show), *Black Panther* (Movie)

Be mindful that some of these works have serious, intense content. Know your own mind's needs and determine whether it's appropriate for you to take in a certain type of content. That is a judgment call that you have to make.

Step 3: Sharpen Your Radar for Recognizing Miseducating/Inferiority-Inducing Material

If people "put" you in your place long enough, after a while, you never want to leave.

Descriptions belong to the describer; not the described. Based on histories of genocide, a necessary precondition for culturally or state-sanctioned violence is dehumanization, which begins with language. As such, the war that is fought today is more a war of the mind. Marcus Garvey warned that black people would die from the effects of taking in information indiscriminately from Western civilization.

You think and believe according to what you're exposed to, and your life becomes a reflection of what you believe. Generally, your world view comes from the programming received during the formative years of your life. Our friends, families, and communities are influential in forming our self-concept, but the most influential contributor, besides families, is the media.

Unfortunately, some people's spiritual and emotional radar is broken, and they don't know how to guard their hearts and minds. Oscar award-winning actor Lupita Nyong'o, at the Essence Black Women in Hollywood Luncheon, read a letter by a young dark-skinned black girl. The little girl wrote to Lupita that she considered Lupita to be lucky to be successful despite her dark skin. The young girl wrote that she was about to buy skin-whitening cream until she saw Lupita on the screen—a woman who looked like her.

Lupita says she experienced the same thing as a little girl. She prayed to God for lighter skin. She would wake up disappointed that she was just as dark as the day before. She negotiated with God that she would be obedient to her parents and stop doing mischievous activities if he would make her wake up lighter. It wasn't until Lupita saw Alek Wek, the dark-skinned British-Sudanese model, that she began to see herself as beautiful.

Media propaganda has created in blacks a contempt for themselves. Black people have been exposed to decades of miseducation and black inferiority-inducing content. Young people pay a hefty price for feasting on the narrow forms of beauty propagated in the media—and their caretakers might not understand how dangerous these messages are.

It's been said that a slave cannot be bought. A slave must be made. One of the ways that a slave is made is through mental conditioning. We all receive two educations – the one society gives to us, and the one we give to ourselves.

Your mentee will pursue what they are conditioned to pursue. As a mentor, always ask what message is being conveyed in songs, movies, shows, and books that you and your mentees consume. Music and images, in particular, are the messages of the soul. You must look behind the content and understand the intent of the creator. Be aware of the programming behind anything you hear, because you can't deconstruct what you are continually reinforcing.

When you look at the history of black film, feelings of inferiority were intentionally cultivated by depicting black people in stereotypical and degrading ways. Mentors of black children must ensure that children see positive images of themselves on the screen.

You use your mind to plan and chart your course in the world. Don't give anyone else the power to condition you. Don't give your power away. As far as the media goes, we are not required to partake in it, so you must exercise self-control or completely disqualify from the social menu any medium that promotes negative depictions of African American people with no redemptive value.

A black American whose sense of self has been compromised through the legacy of black trauma and ignorance of black history is not who he believes he is. He is not who you think he is, either. He is what *he thinks you think* he is.

The ideology of white supremacy created to justify enslaving black people is the same ideology used to incarcerate black people. It's done in more sinister ways, like labeling certain demographics as "thugs" or "super predators." It's much easier to enslave people if you see them as *less than*. It's easier to lock people up if you see them as destined for prison.

A clear example is an electoral strategy used by the Southern Republican party in the 1950s and 1960s. They increased political support among white voters by appealing to racism against black Americans. The campaign of Ronald Reagan, for example, used seemingly race-neutral words that were actually racially coded rhetoric, such as "welfare queens" to conjure images of black people in the minds of southern whites. The strategy was successful. When lies and myths have been told about you—and then TV, film, and media retell that story—you can end up believing what you hear. You must be on guard to not indiscriminately take in information or let young people do so.

The average black American is a decent, hardworking, faith-based person who wants to live a great life and reach their dreams—but you would not believe that if you watched the 6 p.m. news. Ava Duvernay's documentary, *13th*, did a great job demonstrating the media's use of provocative language and grotesque images to paint a horrific picture of the black man and woman. The dehumanization includes the robbery of complete and factual history. It also includes the use of labels, and/or carefully constructed images that misrepresent, demean, and degrade black people, in an attempt to exonerate America's imperfect and complicated history.

Here are some examples of ways that miseducating/inferiority-inducing content gets created and addressed.

Examples

- Representation matters in the cinema more than ever, particularly at an impressionable age. Of the 1,000 top grossing films made in the last eleven years, more than 90 percent were directed by Caucasian men. The majority of the movies that receive top billing are creations from the mind and heart of white men. Does this mean that all black movies produced by white men are racist? Of course not. A white man, Steven Spielberg, made *The Color Purple*, the story of a black family that had economic independence and the subversion against male dominance.

A white man, Brian Helgeland, made *42*, the story of Jackie Robinson, the first black baseball player

to make it to the major leagues. A white man, Taylor Hackford, made the movie *Ray*, the story of Ray Charles, a legendary black musician who lived an extraordinary life of ups and downs. What makes these movies authentic to the black experience is that the directors were willing to have the texture and cultural feel of the movies be guided and shaped by black people.

But those films are exceptions. Most popular movies portray life from a limited worldview that often does not capture the authentic and true experiences of non-white men and women. DGA (Directors Guild of America) President Thomas Schlamme acknowledges that discrimination is prevalent in the feature film business.

A black actress once said, about growing up when actors were all white and black characters were negatively depicted, that she wanted to love films, but the films never loved her back. To this point, Byron Allen asked a white man if he would be comfortable if Byron Allen, as a black man, controlled all the images of his daughter and how she saw herself on screen and grew up in the world. If a black man controlled how a little white girl saw herself—whether she saw herself as a crackhead, a prostitute, or someone who's not that bright—would the white man be comfortable with that?

The white man said no and Byron replied, "Then why would you expect it from me?"

White-controlled media often exponentially reflects the challenges in the black community without highlighting the precipitating factors, including the historical policies and practices that created those challenges. Media campaigns that promote black inferiority can also be found in music videos and picture books.

As mentors, we must be mindful of how images and stories play a role in impacting people's sense of self. We need to be intentional about our mentees' cell phone access and the TV programs allowed.

- Ava Duvernay, creator of the most-watched Netflix series *When They See Us*, said she believes the news given by a white man goes unquestioned. Her series describes news coverage in 1989 about the Central Park Five. One study showed that 90 percent of the news reports about the five men falsely accused of the Central Park rape never used the word "alleged." Meanwhile, a black man's credentials are constantly brought in question as a means of discrediting. When a white man says something, at best, it's always true and at worst, he's credible without offering evidence. When a black man says something, at worst, it's always a lie. At best, his background and credentials will be investigated thoroughly. President Barack Obama's citizenship denial (sometimes called "birtherism") is one of the best examples of what has been perceived as a racist attempt to discredit a black man.

- With the rise of mass shootings and police killings, US media outlets now have different reporting policies. When an unarmed black person is shot and killed by a police officer, the murdered person's life is often thoroughly investigated and combed through for any infraction that might be used as a justification for the murder:

    - Michael Brown may or may not have stolen cigars.

- Eric Garner sold "loosey" cigarettes. He was a victim of making bad decisions, one journalist commented.

- Trayvon Martin wore a hoodie. This image was used to depict him as a "thug."

- Tamir Rice, who was twelve years old when he was shot by police while playing with a toy gun, was referred to in the media as a "young man."

This kind of reporting creates a sense of comfort in the mind of the viewer that these killings are not a major loss, because the victims had checkered pasts. The danger of this kind of reporting is that it takes away from a person's humanity. Someone's checkered past doesn't exonerate agents of law of enforcement from wrongful death. It's important to maintain a perspective that allows for nuance and calls out manipulative uses of media to soothe society's conscience. People will take up for those who are treated unjustly, but if they don't believe someone is innocent, they won't speak out. The strategy is to kill someone's image, to lessen the public outrage when that person is killed.

On the flip side, when a young white man engages in a mass shooting, the default explanation is one of mental illness. That killer is humanized and is seen as a victim of inadequate mental health services.

- Dylan Roof, who admitted to his white supremacist ideology and intentions after killing nine people at Emanuel AME church in Charleston, SC, was described by an FBI agent as having "mental issues." His stated motive for killing the church members was that black men were raping white women.

- James Holmes, who killed twelve people and injured seventy more in a Colorado movie theater, was described a "regular American kid."

- Adam Lanza from Newton, CT was referred to as a young man of deteriorating mental health after killing twenty-seven people at Sandy Hook Elementary School.

Murders by white people are generally deemed to be based on evil individual intent, instead of a pattern of behavior used to explain crimes by people of color. This exonerates the system from addressing residual white supremacy.

- "The Star-Spangled Banner," America's national anthem, is lauded as a uniting, patriotic song. It was written by Francis Scott Key. In the mid-1800s, Key was a slave owner who used his position as a District Attorney in Washington, DC to suppress abolitionists. The anthem, which was originally composed to have four verses, has a verse that many consider to be racist and anti-black. The third stanza of the Star-Spangled Banner discussed Key's opposition of the Colonial Marines, an auxiliary force for the British Marines and a battalion of runaway slaves. It's ironic that the person who wrote about "the land of free" amassed his own wealth by enslaving men and then endorsed killing these men when they fought for freedom. How should black people feel about this song? Can you redeem the song by only singing the first stanza? When the ugly truth of the song's origin is uncovered, can the song still be considered a unifying symbol of freedom?

- The Declaration of Independence, written by Thomas Jefferson, professes that all men are equal—but then goes on to refer to indigenous people of the Americas as merciless savages. The dehumanization of indigenous people of the Americas provided the white settlers with a moral exclusion that made it possible to kill millions of indigenous people and force many others to relocate. According to historians, roughly 10 million indigenous people lived in the United States before the settlers arrived. By the end of the Indian war, less than 240,000 indigenous people remained.

- In 2016, Princeton University's board of trustees decided it would not remove Woodrow Wilson's name from the School of Public and International Affairs and from a residential college. After a thirty-two-hour sit-in in the President's office, the University agreed to consider removing his name from campus institutions. Why? Woodrow Wilson, who was a Princeton University president, had worked to keep black people from entering the University. He also agreed to screen the D.W. Griffith film *The Birth of a Nation* (1915) at the White House during his presidency, which served to revive the most lethal domestic terrorist organization, the Ku Klux Klan.

Famed journalist Katie Couric discussed how she had a sanitized impression of Woodrow Wilson until she realized Wilson invited members of the Ku Klux Klan into the White House and held other racist beliefs. Couric is not alone. In some states, children grow up to see white supremacists as heroes. For example, in some states, Confederate Army General Robert E. Lee's birthday is celebrated alongside the birthday of Dr. Martin Luther King, Jr.

To black people in general, the Confederate flag is akin to the Nazi flag. It is a harsh reminder of a great struggle to keep a horrific institution (slavery) intact. While some consider the flag a "celebration of Southern heritage," many consider it a symbol of black oppression.

Back in the days of the Confederacy, I, as a black man, would not have had an opportunity to learn about the heritage, because I probably would have been lynched and hung from a tree. It's an interesting intellectual, social, and moral exercise to re-examine history. Doing so has led some institutions and municipalities to take down Confederate statues and refuse to memorialize people who were white supremacists. Only after white supremacist Dylan Roof killed nine members of Emanuel AME Church in Charleston did South Carolina's Capitol grounds no longer allow the Confederate flag to fly.

- This is the simplest example: During Hurricane Katrina in 2005, credible US media outlets reported the white people "found" bread and water while black people were "looting." White people were referred to as "survivors" and "residents," while black people were referred to as "criminals" and "looters." When social conscience is silenced in the minds of the viewers through the use of this language, the viewers can also condone police use of force against certain groups of people.

Step 4: Interrupt Racist Socialization

You may not be able to control what actions are taken against you, but you can decide not to be diminished by them.

As Dr. King pointed out in numerous lectures, those in power who wanted to infect the minds and hearts of people invented a lie: that black people were inferior. The lie was that whiteness is the prototype for all things beautiful and worthy. The lie works like walking in a smoky room. Attempting to avoid these negative media messages is like trying to hold your breath to avoid air pollution. Once you go in and come out, it's everywhere. It's on your clothes, on your skin, and in your hair and your lungs.

Our humanity, worth, culture, intellect, hair, skin, physical features, and morals have been devalued. This lowered sense of self becomes internalized, coloring our thoughts, feelings, expectations, and actions. One of the steps we can take to break down this lie is to interrupt it when it's being spoken. Exercise honor in the moment by interrupting maladaptive behaviors like those you'll read about below. Choose to be the "Rosa Parks" and exercise integrity to stop the negative cycles.

Examples of Racist Socialization

- Black mother to dark-skinned son about dating: Don't bring anyone home as dark as you

- White people have good hair.

- She's pretty for a dark girl.

- She was beautiful / she had good hair.

- Insult: Shut up, you black (blank) (blank).

- Look at those ugly sneakers.

- You sound white.

- You think you better than someone cuz you graduated.

- You ain't better than nobody cuz you go to church.

- You know we gonna be on CP time.

- If you darker than the brown paper bag, you're ugly.

These statements are theoretically incorrect and rooted in racist logic, but the opposition is often cerebral and not visceral. There may be a sense of outrage, but it's often fleeting. These types of situations and messages affect your mentees' perception of themselves, their worth and value, and their place in the world. Sadly, people develop a tolerance for racist ideology, and it becomes a normalized part of the culture. Just being critically conscious that racism has been normalized begins the process of liberation.

A Major Practice Reflecting Racist Socialization

Skin-bleaching. The Number One weapon used against black girls is the perception of beauty. Black women spend more money on cosmetics than other races of women. See Chapter 38 of *Bridge the Gaps: Lessons on Self-Awareness, Self-Development, and Self-Care.*

Reflection
What other forms of racist socialization have you seen?

_____

_____

_____

Stand: Remember Whose Shoulders You Stand Upon

As we work to rebuild our community, mentors have to remember whose shoulders we stand upon. Each generation had had amazing black people who worked tirelessly to accomplish their dreams and serve people. As black people in America, we have issues and times that we think are tough—but when you look at what those who came before us endured, the problems in our time are minimal in comparison. Learning our history is important, because it allows us to see ourselves better and draw strength from our ancestors' triumphs.

When you take time to learn the stories of those who have come before you, you can become a force of nature in your own life. Part of filling up your cup of confidence comes from learning the stories of those who have come before us who faced trials, difficulties, and sorrow with dignity.

Here are some:

1. In 1908, Jack Johnson, age thirty, became the first African American boxer to become a heavyweight champion, despite a hateful white society seeking to dethrone him. His greatness initiated a search for a "Great White Hope." Undefeated boxer Jim Jeffries came out of retirement in 1910 to fight what is called "The Fight of the Century." Johnson dominated the fight and Jeffries threw in the towel in the fifteenth round.

2. Ida B. Wells-Barnett was an activist, investigative journalist and anti-lynching crusader. In 1878, at age sixteen, both her parents and a sibling died of yellow fever. She was left to care for her five surviving sisters and brothers. She rose to national

and international prominence when, after losing several close friends to a lynch mob, she published an editorial exposing that lynching mobs were not motivated by black crime but by black people's success and competition with white people. Her work enraged Southern white men who wanted to assert their power, and a mob destroyed her newspaper press. She was labeled a radical by the NAACP for her unwillingness to compromise any aspect of her vision of justice.

3. After having served seven years in prison, Malcolm X became a human rights activist during the Civil Rights Movement. He was thirty-two years old when he stepped onto the national stage by galvanizing thousands of people to address police brutality in New York City. His life and transformation informed and birthed several civil rights leaders and movements.

4. Mary McLeod Bethune, an educator and activist, was born to former slaves in 1875. She had sixteen siblings and grew up extremely poor. She attended DL Moody's Institute for Home and Foreign Mission in Chicago and returned to the South to work as a teacher and share her knowledge. In 1904, when she was twenty-nine years old, she opened a school for Negro girls in Daytona Beach, Fla. She built the desks and chairs herself. The school started with five girls but ended up with 250 students. The school later merged with another school and eventually became Bethune-Cookman University. Bethune went on to fight for women's rights as the president of the Florida chapter of National Association of Colored Women from 1917 to 1925. Throughout her career, as she accomplished all these amazing things, she was threatened by the KKK. Her life is a testament to improving the lives of others and fighting for equality.

5. In 1955, a twenty-six-year-old Dr. Martin Luther King, Jr. led the Montgomery Bus Boycott that protested racial segre-gation in the public transit system. His work to awaken the consciousness of white America has had a profound effect on America and the fight for equality that continues until this day.

6. Ella Baker was a great civil rights organizer who made room for SNCC (Student Nonviolent Coordinating Committee). She was the valedictorian of her graduating class at Shaw University and was referred to as the "Godmother of SNCC. When Baker heard the story of her grandmother being beaten and whipped for refusing to marry a slave she wasn't in love with, her sense of social justice caused her to become one of the most influential women in the civil rights movement—not only because of her critique of racism in American society, but also because of her critique of sexism in the civil rights movement.

7. Fred Hampton was twenty-one years old when he played an instrumental role in organizing the Black Panther's Free Breakfast Program, which fed more than 10,000 children every day before they went to school.

8. Ava Duvernay started making movies at age thirty-two after listening to 200 director commentaries. For her widely celebrated documentary, 13th, she interviewed each person featured for two hours, carefully demonstrating the legacy and residue of white supremacy in the criminal justice system up until 2016. In addition, she's made two critically acclaimed and culture-shifting pieces of art: *Selma* and *When They See Us*.

9. Harriet Tubman was born into slavery in Maryland. She was twenty-seven years old when she escaped to freedom in the North and later become a "conductor" in the Underground Railroad. She was the first woman to lead an armed expedition in the Civil War, which served to liberate more than 700 slaves.

10. Booker T. Washington was an author, educator, orator, and advisor to multiple presidents. He was one of the founders of Tuskegee Institute, a historically black college. He preached a philosophy of self-help and racial solidarity. His militancy against racism in any form inspired and continues to inspire many blacks.

11. Fannie Lou Hamer was a humanitarian, civil rights leader, and voting rights activist. She was jailed, beaten, and threatened for standing up against state-sanctioned injustice. These stressful events severely impacted her health. She gave a speech at the 1964 Democratic National Convention entitled "Sick and Tired of being Sick and Tired," which changed the course of voting rights.

12. Patrice Lumumba was an Independence Leader from the Congo. He played a major role in transforming the Congo from a Belgian colony to an independent republic.

13. Toni Morrison was a professor, author, and essayist. She received numerous awards, from the Presidential Medal of Freedom to the Nobel Prize in Literature. She is famously known for writing for black people and making no apologies about it. From her perspective, many white writers didn't consider black people significantly in their work. She challenged

that double standard by not considering white people in major ways in her work. Morrison inspired many with her firm convictions.

Exercise: Do Your Googles

I'm not going to do all the work. As a mentor, have your mentee research the black figures listed below. They are to answer two questions:

1. What has been their individual contribution in the role of black progress and/or freedom?

2. What lessons can you learn from them that can inspire your confidence in you?

1. Nina Simone

_____

_____

_____

2. Anton Lembede

_____

_____

_____

3. Billie Holiday

4. Marcus Garvey

5. Michelle Obama

6. Zora Neale Hurston

7. Angela Davis

_____

_____

_____

8. W.E.B. Du Bois

_____

_____

_____

9. Shirley Chisholm

_____

_____

_____

10. Rosa Parks

_____

_____

_____

11. Katherine Johnson

12. Maya Angelou

13. Gwendolyn Brooks

14. Eldridge Cleaver

15. Michelle Alexander

16. Kwame Ture

17. Madam CJ Walker

18. Medgar Evers

19. Josephine Baker

20. Beverly Bond

21. James Baldwin

22. Elaine Brown

23. Geoffrey Canada

24. Septima Clark

25. Nelson Mandela

26. Denmark Vesey

27. Vivian Thomas

_____

_____

_____

28. Cornel West

_____

_____

_____

For additional exercises and tools, see Chapter 35 – Assertiveness in *Bridge the Gaps: Lessons on Self-Awareness, Self-Development and Self-Care*. Visit www.amazon.com or www.thebridg330.com to pick up a copy.

It's Your Life: Take Responsibility

People may feel sorry for you, but they will not feel responsible for you. Discipline yourself so no one else has to.

When you take responsibility for your life, you free yourself from the mental slavery that says someone else is responsible for your life. As a mentor, one of the ways to elevate your mentees is to help them elevate themselves. It starts with giving them a strong sense of ownership and responsibility over their lives.

The most important thing a parent can give a child is a sense of responsibility and accountability. Our job is to take full control of the individuality we were born with and develop it, without being defeated by the harshness of life.

There is no perfect way to measure the social health of a group or a community without error. However, anecdotal evidence can be helpful in assessing prevalent perspectives and mentalities. I have personally observed that, for those born in the "crack" era until now, external service providers and systems of institutionalization have taken responsibility away from black Americans.

Child protection services, foster care, group homes, juvenile correction facilities, jails, and prisons have become tools to address the fragile family dynamics in the black community. As a behavioral consultant and life skills coach in many of these institutions, I have observed patterns of thoughts that don't serve to help the clients' development of self-sufficiency and accountability. Instead, services designed to "help" create a dependent and inferior mentality.

Here are a few examples:

- "My social worker is going to find a job for me."

- "I went on an interview, but the job never called me back."

- "If I go to jail, at least I'll get three hots and a cot."

- "My teacher never taught me/my child to read."

- From a fifteen-year-old black male: "I'm going to live off SSI like my mother and grandmother."

- When asked a question about their future: "I don't know."

From overly religious people who use religion as a drug to run from reality: "Let go and let God handle it."

As a result of a legacy of trauma and institutionalization of black communities during the crack epidemic in the 1980s, many black Americans have a learned helplessness and/or a dependence on systems for aid.

Ralph Ellison, in his book *Invisible Man*, says that a part of the black man's invisibility is irresponsibility. Responsibility depends on recognition. Why be responsible in a world that doesn't see you? Because you are seen, and will be seen, you matter. What you do and don't do matters.

As a mentor, we need to teach young people that what they do matters, and that they can take the initiative to solve their own problems—instead of waiting for Superman to arrive.

Everyone receives assistance along the way to get to where they are going. There's nothing wrong with asking for help or receiving help—but an overreliance on help to get out of your condition is the surest path to stagnation, complacency, and dependence. In order to change the future of black people, we need to face to reality of the negative thinking patterns that they use to make pivotal life choices.

It can be hard to acknowledge the reality, but you cannot change what you tolerate. Taking ownership of your life requires that you live the life that was meant for you to live, and not the script that society hands you. It all starts with responsibility.

As a mentor, the way to teach a person responsibility is to *hold them responsible*. Once they've taken responsibility for their own lives, they can elevate themselves.

Here's a perspective for you to consider.

Solution: The Ant Perspective – The Danger of Being Lazy

"Take a lesson from the ant, you who love leisure and ease. Observe how it works, and dare to be just as wise. It has no boss, no one laying down the law or telling it what to do, Yet it gathers its food through summer and takes what it needs from the harvest. How long do you plan to lounge your life away, you lazy fool? Will you ever get out of bed? You say, "A little sleep, a little rest, a few more minutes, a nice little nap." But soon poverty will be on top of you like a robber; need will assault you like a well-armed warrior." (Proverbs 6:6-11, The Voice)

In this passage, the ant doesn't have a boss, nor does it need a boss. It knows what's necessary to be independent, based on its own needs. The governor of the ant's life is internally based self-sufficiency.

If nothing changes in majority culture, the internal governor of black people must be self-reliance, self-determination, and self-enterprise. These are the same values that the formerly enslaved Africans used to build self-sufficient black businesses or towns like the Black Wall Street in Tulsa, Oklahoma in 1921; Rosewood, Florida in 1923;, Knoxville, TN in 1919' Wilmington, NC in 1898; and East St. Louis, IL in 1917—before these areas were destroyed by white supremacists.

As slaves, black people were made dependent. They had to be productive, but only to satisfy the needs of the slave master. As free men and women, they embarked on a journey of independence to build a life for themselves. Despite being let down time and again, they persisted.

These values will serve as the primary foundation for building and rebuilding the black community. Your job will be to help your mentee find their way to authenticity and self-determination. The way to address learned helplessness is to model self-efficacy and how taking responsibility for one's life can lead to positive changes.

Dependent behavior, which the young person sees modeled, creates more dependency. Responsible and accountable behavior on the part of the mentor can break these cycles. No one should tell another person what he should live and die for. That's each person's choice. But it needs to be a choice they make based on a mindset of independence and accomplishment.

To remind yourself of your purpose, you can create a mantra to keep you grounded. Here's one that I use.

The Responsibility Mantra:

This is my life. I'm responsible for who enters it and for what takes place in it. I determine my life mission, goals, my values, and my pace. I will respect and learn all the different views and opinions from others, but my decisions for my life will be a product of my own conclusions.

For additional exercises and tools, see Chapter 2 – False Self, 7 – Be Differentiated, and Chapter 33 – Boundaries and Safe People, and Chapter 35 - Assertiveness of *Bridge the Gaps: Lessons on Self-Awareness, Self-Development, and Self-Care*. Visit www.amazon.com or www.thebridg330.com to pick up a copy.

4: Community Healing Toolkit

Black people are a nation within a nation, searching for a nationality.

THERE'S A TRIBE IN AFRICA where the warriors would meet one another with a traditional greeting: "And how are the children?"

It's a question that demonstrates a value in that society to protect the children and the vulnerable populations in their community. What would happen if we began demonstrating this paradigm-shifting value in our community?

Well, there was a time when people did demonstrate it. For 381 days—from December 5, 1955 to December 21, 1956—40,000 black people agreed not to ride the bus in Montgomery, Ala. When the US Supreme Court upheld the June 5, 1956 Montgomery federal court ruling that racially segregated seating on buses was in violation of the 14th amendment, they began riding again.

Whenever we see successful historic moves for justice, we should look more deeply at how they occurred. How did the people maintain a commitment for that long?

1. They stayed together and recognized their power. African Americans represented 75 percent of Montgomery's bus ridership.

2. They started the boycott by arranging carpools and getting black taxi drivers to charge the same price as the bus – ten cents.

3. They organized regular meetings to keep people enthused and mobilized. In their time, they worked together because they recognized that their destinies were linked to one another.

Much of our well-being comes from having a high level of trust within our community.

We should also study things that provide insight into the causes of community breakdown, which have been used as tools to divide the black community. Because black people have a specific history in America, the healing needs to be specific as well. The subjugation of African people was aided by broken bonds between and among black people.

As mentors, we must develop an honest view of how we've been separated and a commitment to heal the wounds of the past. In order to heal, rebuild, and adopt culturally uplifting practices, it would serve us well to understand the issues that plague or play a role in creating division in the community.

These are the tools that can help:

Tools
1. *Never Stop Asking Questions*
2. *Is Willie Lynch Real?*
3. *Talented Tenth: Beat the Odds to Change the Odds*

Never Stop Asking Questions
The ones who ask questions will not lose their way.

When I served as a mentor in different correctional facilities, I quickly noticed how disproportionately filled these places are with black males. It was impossible for me to not make the connection of how three centuries years of torture, lynchings, trauma, family breakdown, racist legislation, and political oppression inflicted on black people in America was reflected in a vastly racially disproportionate population in prisons and state-supervised program.

We have work to do to excavate how our shared history is affecting the present. Notable scientist Albert Einstein, who corresponded with the renowned black scholar, W.E.B. Du Bois, said he considered racism America's worst disease. He said most important thing you can do is to refuse to stop asking questions.

If students are not allowed to question, how are they to learn? Children do well when they are around people who let them ask questions. As Dr. Cornel West said, as long as they are asking questions, that's a sign of hope. Questions inspire them to dream, make sense of their place in the world, and begin to think about possible solutions.

Silence in the face of oppression is costly on an individual and collective level. Individually, one loses integrity by ignoring human suffering. On a collective level, when it's left unquestioned, oppression is allowed to continue.

I've heard several questions posed by young people I've encountered around the topic of racism and its effects on the black community:

- Are black people more criminal than white people?

- Can we ever get rid of racism?

- Do people's living situation adversely affect their sense of community?

- Why are black people being unjustly treated by the judicial system?

- How does the legacy of slavery, Jim Crow, lynching, and the assassination of black leaders affect the condition of black people today?

- Are black people less desirous to obtain higher levels of education?

- Has the American government done enough to tackle these problems?

- Is the government responsible, or are the people responsible, to bring healing and solutions—or are both?

- What keeps black people from working together?

- Was integration a good idea for black people?

- Is "color blindness" a good thing?

- Why do black men have a relatively easier inclination to injure one another to the point of murder?

- Why do many black organizations have a hard time organizing because of internal conflict?

- Why do black parents have a hard time complimenting their children?

- Why do black people have an excessive focus on material acquisition in spite of economic lack?

- Why do black people have a hard time supporting one another's success?

- Why do black people have eurocentric beauty standards?

When young people are discouraged from asking questions, they become disengaged. Their questions might spark anger in some people and discomfort in others, which makes people avoid asking altogether, because the reactions are so unpredictable.

Don't be ashamed if you don't have all the answers. It's acceptable to admit that you have to rethink some things. After all, these are big questions and they require deep thought, research, and developing a full picture of how the condition of a community came to be.

Dr. Martin Luther King, Jr. and Malcolm x were both willing to rethink their approaches to gaining civil rights and progress for black people. This is part of what made them great. If these men of tremendous virtue can admit they were wrong and rethink things, why can't we?

If we are going to heal as a people, we have to stay in the room even when things get uncomfortable. We must ask the hard questions, search for the answers, and be willing to change our minds when evidence suggests we might have been misguided. We must also ask: Whose interest is served if these questions are answered a particular way or not answered at all?

I heard a really great piece of advice when I was in high school. If you don't know what you believe about a particular topic, read two books on it and then make up your own mind, because there's a thin line between education and indoctrination. Education opens the mind; indoctrination closes it.

Each person receives two educations – the one given to him and the one he gives to himself. Children are educated within a system to fulfill the desire of a particular system. A noble and worthwhile institution will not only tolerate questions, but invite them. That is the only way any situation can change for the better.

They say that closed mouths will not be fed. The same is true for closed minds. The mind is a womb, and ideas are seeds. When the two combine, a whole world of life-producing insights can be birthed.

At the end of this book, you'll find a list of other books that you can use to answer many of these questions.

Is Willie Lynch Real?
"If a house is divided against itself, that house cannot stand."
(Mark 3:25, NIV)

WHENEVER A BARBERSHOP-TYPE DISCUSSION ABOUT the problems in the black community comes up, someone will inevitably say the name "Willie Lynch." But who *was* Willie Lynch?

Willie Lynch was allegedly a vicious slave-owner from the West Indies who was summoned to the Virginia colony in 1712 to provide the local slave owners with guidance on how to control their slaves. On December 25, 1712, he is said to have delivered a speech which is commonly referred to as the "Willie Lynch Letter" which was entitled "The Making of a Slave."

In the speech, he explores possible methods of control, such as exploiting age and skin tone to pit the slaves against each other and to bring about envy, distrust, and fear. His guarantee was that, if correctly installed, the methods would be effective for 300 years.

The document came into print in the 1970s and gained more popularity in the early 1990s, when it appeared on the internet. According to several historians, the story of Willie Lynch is a hoax. But the reality of what the letter discusses is very much alive and well in the black community.

The Honorable Minister Louis Farrakhan of the Nation of Islam mentioned Willie Lynch in the 1995 Million Man March. Legendary actor Denzel Washington quoted Willie Lynch in the 2007 movie, *The Great Debaters*. The hit TV show *Black-ish* had an episode that discussed colorism in black families and used the Willie Lynch story to illustrate the issue. Prominent music artists have made reference to Willie Lynch in their songs.

Was Willie Lynch real? The fact that the story has survived is an unambiguous indication that it addresses a serious type of tension in the black community. The phenomenon in the black community that the letter refers to exists. Destroying internal conflict, disunity, and generational psychological chaos must be the agenda and assignment for each black person.

As Dr. King said in his last sermon, "I've Been to the Mountaintop," the common denominator for black people in America is the history of racial oppression and its residual effects. King discussed how, in the biblical story of the Jewish people enslaved in Egypt, the Pharaoh's favorite strategy to prolong slavery was to keep the slaves fighting amongst themselves.

Sadly, the reality is that all black people are not in solidarity with each other. We are a people who have faced hundreds of years of racial hostility followed by consistent patterns of injustice across all sectors of society. Solidarity is a tool to protect the future generations from these issues.

However, unity does not mean uniformity. One of the most important tools that we all must learn is to have respectful conversations with people we don't agree with, without allowing our emotions to override our listening ability and reason. At the end of the day, we must be people who seek the truth, no matter where it comes from.

We must also be willing to re-evaluate our positions upon further review, which requires that we think deeply and process our emotions as best we can before we engage in dialogue. To be sure, "There is more hope for a fool than for someone who speaks without thinking." (Proverbs 29:20, NLT)

Aspects of the "Willie Lynch" Curse

We can't heal what we don't reveal and what we don't understand. Slavery had a multifaceted impact on the life of black people. It affected not only how we relate to the world but how we relate to each other.

The social environment created during slavery conditioned black people to be hostile toward one another. It was an artificially created environment that encouraged separation and distance among black people by pitting them against each other. Divide-and-conquer tactics still work today.

Historians tell us that black people separated on the basis of being *house Negroes* vs. *field Negroes*. This is what happens when you strip people of their sense of self by creating an environment hostile to their culture and robbing them of their history. Sadly, social distinctions that existed during slavery persisted after slavery ended. Some slaves even bragged about having white blood.

Unfortunately, until this day, there are social distinctions in the black community that don't serve the purpose of uniting people, but further separation that fuels a sense of resentment and betrayal.

Understanding your condition is half the battle to healing. Once you can look at the issue from a new angle, it loses its power to control you.

In the Willie Lynch Letter, the main method of control was psychologically damaging black people through widespread division, internal conflict, and dependence on white slave masters. Being aware of the ways such divisions have been and are being established is essential to healing the division.

Here are a few strategies of separation to consider and recognize:

1. Meritorious Manumission: Betrayal to pay for freedom. In the early 18th century, slaves were starting to show rogue behavior. In order for the slaves to be controlled, a special set of laws was created. Essentially, slave masters would grant freedom to slaves who would become informants on other slaves who were planning to escape. The Meritorious Manumission Act of 1710 was a legal act of freeing an enslaved African for "good deeds," as defined by the national public policy. Meritorious manumission could be granted to an enslaved African who distinguished himself by saving the life of the white master, inventing a new medicine, or snitching on fellow enslaved Africans planning a slave revolt. This

incentivized enslaved Africans appease their masters and betray their fellow enslaved Africans. Betrayal to appease those in power is not something new.

2. Colorism: Prejudice or discrimination, often among same-race people, based solely on skin tone. Essentially, colorism is the belief that the lighter your skin tone, the prettier and more valuable you are. It stems from the belief that beauty and desirability increase with the proximity to whiteness. Colorism is a spinoff of racism. It involves prejudice and power. Colorism was created and used by white Europeans in power who considered light-skinned people to be more valuable than the darker-skinned people. Often, light-skinned slaves were children born of the union of slaves and slave masters, who would want to keep them close by placing them in service in the house. These families believed that their homes could be run well if those slaves were given an education, so it was more likely that these light-skinned house slaves would be taught to read and taught upper-class tradition in white society. It was also believed by most white people at the time that, if slaves had white blood, they had a greater intellectual ability and subsequently, a greater capacity to be "civilized." Many light-skinned slaves internalized these assumptions and developed a sense of superiority to darker skinned slaves, which eventually lead to distrust and resentment. Colorism was also an instrument used by slave masters to divide and conquer their own enslaved persons by extending more privileges to light-skinned slaves. This would often pit light-skinned slaves against dark-skinned slaves, which made the light-skinned slaves more loyal to their owners in the event of a slave rebellion.

Considering gender issues, generational tensions, and class differences, all groups of people have division. The Willie Lynch Letter, however, does highlight issues that still apply in contemporary America. Light-skinned vs. dark-skinned; Black Sorority Conflict such as AKAs vs. Deltas; debating who has the bigger home; pastors debating who has the larger congregations; fine vs. coarse hair texture; male vs female. Among black people, these distinctions still wield strong influence in the ability to create or destroy social cohesiveness among black people.

3. In the first section of the Willie Lynch Letter, the methodology was to get the slaves to love, respect, and trust only their white slave masters. This work was accomplished through the appointment of black overseers referred to as "Sambo." The term "Sambo" became prominent through the anti-slave novel *Uncle Tom's Cabin*. His character was a slave overseer who served the cruel slave-owner's commands. This is the black person who would hurt you worse than a white master would, just to please the master.

   American politician and sociologist Daniel Patrick Moynihan discussed the Sambo personality in his 1965 report *The Negro Family – The Case for National Action*, specifically in the third section called "The Roots of the Problem." Social researcher Thomas Pettigrew discovered that the conditions of a Nazi concentration camp and American chattel slavery would bring about the personality type that accepted the SS guards and slave masters as father figures. It's important to note that there is no anthropological data to show that this personality type was part of African culture or was an inborn racial type. This personality type was created by the environmental condition of slavery.

Historical Examples of Black Ideological Differences or Monolithic Expectation

Not all black people think alike, nor should they. Being black in America is not monolithic. We can recognize beauty in the diversity of thought as a way to uplift one another, without feeding into silly conflict over size, skin tone, or class. The goal is to think together and to work hard to find the redemptive value in each person's philosophy and perspective.

The sad truth that many of our black elders have shared is that, on the road to making a way for ourselves in this world, black people have to fight two different wars: one against a hateful white society, and the other against our own people.

On the flip side, black monolithic expectation is a form of slavery because it takes away the freedom to think independently. This expectation is a double-edged sword because it's also possible for a black person to share ideas that are harmful and destructive to the community at-large.

There's a lot of friendly fire amongst black folks. There have always been disagreements about how to achieve progress. Representation doesn't mean that all black folks are necessarily in solidarity with each other.

Here are some historical examples of differences that existed:

1. Black educator and orator Booker T. Washington and black activist, sociologist and historian W.E.B. Du Bois had disagreements on the right strategies for the economic and social progress of black people. Booker T. Washington encouraged racial solidarity and self-help. He encouraged black people to accept discrimination for the moment and focus on elevating through cultivating enterprise and economic prosperity, to ultimately win the respect of whites. W.E.B Du Bois believed this tactic would only prolong white oppression. He advocated

for political action and a focus on civil rights. His strategy was to develop a small group of educated black people called the Talented Tenth who would provide the leadership to win full equality for black people. Washington and Du Bois were both exceptionally wise men. Their backgrounds influenced their philosophies. There was no doubt that they both wanted the best for black people. They were not in agreement on strategy, but their works significantly influenced movements that exist until this day.

2. The legendary civil rights activists Martin Luther King, Jr. and Malcolm X had different approaches to the Civil Rights Movement. Malcolm called for a militant approach to achieve equality with a "do what it takes" attitude. Martin had a nonviolent approach to awaken the conscience of white America. Martin believed that Malcolm's philosophy would only end in grief. Malcolm believed that Martin was too slow and too accommodating to white Americans, referring to him as a "20th century Uncle Tom." They met only once, in 1964, when they were on their way to forming a unified front against prejudice, but Malcolm was killed a year later. Even today, these two leaders inspire and challenge many educators and activists to think deeply about the challenges black people face.

Reflection: Learning from historical examples, we can avoid needless drama if we take a step back to recognize how important each person is in the tapestry of black America. Each idea is redemptive, if only we can learn to have healthy dialogue.

1. What lessons can we learn from their lives and examples?

_____

_____

_____

2. How can we avoid unnecessary internal conflict on the road to promoting freedom and equality?

_____

_____

_____

Contemporary Examples of Black Gender Conflict

Before we move forward, we must be aware of the conflict that exists among black people in gender-specific ways. If we want to change, the first step is awareness. We need to recognize how bad behavior is sometimes nuanced, based on gender.

Conflicts Among Black Women

- Black women who reinforce destructive behavior in other black women

- Black women who demonize and judge younger black women instead of guiding them

- Black women who antagonize or degrade other black women out of envy and jealousy

- Black mothers who compete with their daughters for the attention of men

- Black women who are reluctant to acknowledge or be cordial to other black women

- Black women who are reluctant to encourage or help other black women

Conflicts Among Black Men

- Black fathers who compete with and abuse their sons

- Black men who reinforce destructive ways in younger black men

- Black men who are reluctant to encourage or help other black males

- Black men who manipulate/betray other black men out of ego, jealousy, or for profit

- Black men who kill other black men or brag about killing black men

For many black people, this is hard to read. Some will be upset at the mention of these issues. But in order to change, we must first acknowledge what is happening.

In your mentoring of black youth, you have an opportunity to identify and address these behaviors. It starts with your own choice to value black people. Reconsider your conduct on a microscopic level, and see if you can own any of these behaviors. Then you can help the next generation eliminate culturally destructive behavior.

Heal the Division

As American politician and sociologist Daniel Patrick Moynihan discussed in his 1965 report *The Negro Family – The Case for National Action*—specifically in the second section called "The Negro American Family"—several immigrant groups came to America with remarkably strong family bonds and have progressed faster than others as a result. Black people in America did not have that luxury. One leader said that black people in America are like a family coming together, and the common denominator was child abuse. Slavery was the abuse of a nation.

How can we tell if a group of people is doing well? Here are a few ways to determine the health of a people.

1. Their ability and willingness to prioritize goals that heal and uplift the collective community.

2. Their ability to set and focus on collective goals without being sidetracked by minor issues.

3. Their ability to support each other's success without tearing each other down. The first sign of spiritual maturity is the ability to delight in the success of your neighbor. To celebrate the success: "For wherever there is jealousy and selfish ambition, there you will find disorder and evil of every kind." (James 3:16, NLT)

As Carter G. Woodson discusses in *The Miseducation of the Negro*, Christ cannot operate in atmospheres riddled with conflict. One of the greatest weapons used against black people is disorganization. We must learn how to work with and for each other, despite having differences of opinion.

As I drive through the streets of Newark, where I grew up, there are different make-ups and social organizations: Bloods, Crips, Five Percenters, Hebrew Israelites, Christians, Traditional Islam, Nation of Islam, street dudes, conscious people, and semi-conscious people. Each group is likely to have a different opinion about many issues. We have to learn to cooperate with differences of opinion for the common good.

On March 30, 1967, Muhammad Ali and Dr. Martin Luther King, Jr. met for more than an hour. Dr. King referred to Muhammad Ali as "a friend of the cause." Ali affirmed that many black people in America had similar concerns. Despite having different beliefs, they were still brothers. Dr. King and Ali transcended their religious and ideological philosophies for the sake of brotherhood without abdicating their convictions. We have to work hard to help the people we mentor become happy in solidarity with black people without compromising their beliefs.

Here are a few steps we can take to heal our community:

1. Recreate the village. The culture of enslaved African was destroyed when they were torn away from traditional moral and social norms. Historically, black people had the tools of self-respect, a subversive memory, and a deep sense of integrity. (See the tool in Chapter 5 - Code of Conduct: Bring Order Into Your Life) The village supports these deep-rooted values.

2. Choose to find common ground with other black people. You can focus on what's ripping you apart, or you can build on what's keeping you together. Remain mindful and critically aware of who will profit from instigating and magnifying

division amongst black people. When you have a historical understanding of the legacy, force, and depth of the injury of anti-black racism—slavery, Jim Crow, and mass incarceration—you might be more inclined to fight to work together to heal. Black enslavement should serve as a perpetual reminder of the consequences when we lack unity and collective strength. Our enemies exploit our frictions. We should also provide reminders of how far we've come and how beautiful our culture is to motivate us to continue to build. (Chapter 3 – Stand – Remember Whose Shoulders You Stand Upon).

3. Take in content (books, movies, shows, etc.) that promotes black healing and unity. A movie that I think positively affected millions of black people, *Malcolm X*, has an amazing story behind its development. The producers of the movie ran out of money to complete it. In the spirit of self-reliance that Malcolm X preached, Spike Lee called on several black people to help complete the movie, which was successfully done. Culture is the backbone of a community. If a community's culture is acknowledged, respected, and protected, the community's influence will grow.

4. Help heal our standards and hold ourselves to a higher and healthier standard. This will require discipline and, at times, conflict. We sometimes fight publicly over news stations or social media. Bitter infighting creates cliques and draws divisive lines between black people. An example of this is the conflict between black American actor Samuel L. Jackson and British actor Idris Elba.

Samuel L. Jackson criticized the idea of British actors portraying black Americans. He pointed to *Selma*'s Martin Luther King, Jr. being played by British actor David Oyelowo and British actress Cynthia Erivo's performance in the movie *Harriet*. Even in Jordan Peele's *Get Out,* a movie about liberal white America's ignorance and hubris, the main character of Chris Washington—a black American man—was played by British actor Daniel Kaluuya. After speaking with Elba, Jackson took his comment back.

This is a great example of how healthy confrontations can help refine ideologies that place black issues and philosophies on extreme courses with no room for nuance or situational factors.

1. Acknowledge and respect other black people, in spite of conflicting beliefs. If we are going to fight a system designed to undermine our humanity, we can't be at war with each other. Have healthy, constructive conversations. How we speak to each other is just as important as what we communicate. If necessary, remove yourself from involvement in silly comparisons that serve the purpose of dividing. In the Scriptures, we see Paul and Barnabas part ways over a dispute on whether Mark should come with them. They ended up going their separate ways. (Acts 15:39) Sometimes, that is the appropriate course of action.

2. Choose to love. Love is the glue that we need to rebuild our community. Love is not a feeling. It's a disposition rooted in the desire for your well-being and that of your brother. Many brothers don't think about brotherhood until they are chained together in prison.

Change is possible when people put the love of their brother ahead of their own self-interest. We don't want to become brothers because we share a similar pain. We want to become brothers because we share the same destiny.

Healing a community is not always pretty and not always fun, but love is a choice. The way to heal black self-hate is black self-love. I'll close with a verse from the Good Book on humility as a building block for healing.

"Agree with each other, love each other, be deep-spirited friends. Don't push your way to the front; don't sweet-talk your way to the top. Put yourself aside, and help others get ahead. Don't be obsessed with getting your own advantage. Forget yourselves long enough to lend a helping hand." Philippians 2:4 MSG

Reflection Question:

In addition to the suggestions above, what are some effective ways to promote black unity?

Talented Tenth: Beat the Odds to Change the Odds

"Much is required from those to whom much is given, for their responsibility is greater." (Luke 12:48, TLB)

IF WE WANT TO SEE change, we need to aim for specific results. But how can we even imagine something if we've never seen it? We have a tool. This perspective can serve to help heal and rebuild a sense of community.

I was born and raised on the Westside of Newark in the Vailsburg section. My family stayed in Newark until I was about sixteen. At the age of ten or eleven, I started seeing the shifts in the neighborhood that was once family-friendly and safe. Over the course of my childhood, there would be close to or more than 100 homicides each year.

I remember going to Ivy Hill Park, where I was trying to work on my game (basketball). I would be looking for the guys I used to play with. I would ask, "Where's ____?" Reply: "He dead. His brother had beef with dudes down the hill and he ain't back down, so they clapped him and his bro." I was sad, confused, and hurt. At the time, my young sheltered mind couldn't understand the socio-cultural dynamics of the hood. I had to learn fast.

I remember feeling afraid. I tried to look cool and emotionless, but inside I felt a despair that I can still feel today as I reflect on the grey skies over the basketball court. Those days were gloomy. Too many young people died senselessly. Too many black men, women, black kids.

I was raised in an immigrant family with the message that life would be better when we got out of the 'hood and away from black people—and closer to white people.

As one black educator said, black people are always running away from themselves. Carter G. Woodson alluded to a similar sentiment in *The*

Miseducation of the Negro when he noted that the people who should create programs that lead to their people's progress leave their people instead.

That's exactly what happened to me when I was in high school. When our family got into a better financial position, we moved from the hood to the suburbs. There's no doubt that my parents had legitimate reasons to want to move. We left behind the urban violence, drug dealing, murders, and other pathological behavior that they didn't want their children exposed to.

Unfortunately, there are certain things that I can't unsee. This is exactly what American politician and sociologist Daniel Patrick Moynihan discussed in his 1965 *report The Negro Family – The Case for National Action*, specifically in the fourth section called "The Tangle of Pathology." Moynihan said most black youth are in danger of getting entangled in the pathological events of the ghetto. It's true, the risk is there.

At the time, we wanted to escape the hood—but it never made sense to me as a final solution for helping people that you love. If I've made any progress in my life, it is largely due to the social justice organizations that were created in times of hostility toward black people in America to protect and provide an easier path to progress, such as the NAACP (National Association for the Advancement of Colored People), the National Urban League, and the Inroads organization.

These organizations set an example for me on what W.E.B. Du Bois meant when he used the term "the Talented Tenth " to describe the one in ten black people who would become leaders of their communities, serve with their education, and reinvest their gifts and talents to improve the condition of the community.

The true purpose of education is not to help us live as elitists. It's to teach us how to lift up the underserved. As Dr. King said, some black people sailed out of the muddy waters of poverty and found their way into the fresh waters of the mainstream, but they forgot the stench of the muddy waters.

When I was a teenager, kids on my block would have fights with kids from other blocks. One of the worst things you could do was run if your friends got jumped. Loyalty was considered an important virtue.

But many black Americans now run away from acknowledging systemic injustice toward black people because they have achieved their own trappings of success and a comfortable standard of living. They have become comfortable, complacent, and in some ways, complicit with unjust systems and practices. Their fear of what can happen to them personally exceeds their love and commitment for their community. They are looking for their own interests instead of the interests of others (Philippians 2:4, NIV).

As Carter G. Woodson discussed in *The Miseducation of the Negro*, you must cultivate an unselfish concern for your people and sacrifice for their elevation. Black people cannot win if they are willing to exchange the success of their children for their own safety and comfort. I share in Dr. King's philosophy regarding the need to develop a dangerous and radical unselfishness.

Dr. King's social ethic was rooted in his strong commitment to his faith. From his perspective, only a dry religion provokes a minister to exalt the beauty of heaven while ignoring the community conditions that create an earthly hell.

My parents had a strong commitment to their faith and cultural community, so I was also going to church on a regular basis. One of the ethics that stuck out to me was the story of the Good Samaritan in Luke 10. The social ethic of Jesus can be traced to this parable.

In the story, a man has been badly beaten and left for dead on a dangerous road. A priest and a Levite, religious and famous leaders of the day, passed by and did not stop to help the man. But the man of another race stopped to help the injured man.

For many people, when they see people out in public who need assistance, a common sentiment that I hear is, "I can't stop to help this person. Something might happen to me." While there is prudence in this type of thinking, we also have to ask, "If I don't stop to help, what will happen to them?"

- What will happen to the one in three black boys scheduled to go to jail or prison, according the Bureau of Justice?

- What will happen to the seven out of ten fatherless children in American cities?

- What will happen to the one in three women and one in six men who have been sexually abused?

- What will happen to the one in four Americans living with mental illness?

- What will happen to the black families living below the poverty line?

- What will happen to the 10,000 people released each week from a prison population of 2.3 million?

- What will happen to the grade/high school students who are not reading/computing on grade level?

By God's grace, I never saw myself as different from the other young black men on my block who ended up in prison or underachieving. I was blessed and privileged to not have parents incarcerated, drug addicted, or absent. But the problems of my community never left me. It remained dormant as I tried to find my way personally and professionally.

The issue came alive in a new way as I was working on this manuscript. In the winter of 2018, I drove home from a trip to the store. As I attempted to pull into the driveway of my Newark apartment, I saw a black man lying in the street. He'd been shot. The police told me that I wouldn't be allowed to enter the parking lot and would have to find someplace else to park. I drove around and found street parking. As I gathered my bags, two cops stopped me and patted me down. They asked me to stand with my hands visible while they ran my records. Fortunately, I had my brother on the phone through my Bluetooth the entire time, and he heard the whole conversation.

Officer: "Hey. Where you coming from?"

Me: "The store."

Officer: "Do you live here?"

Me: "Yes"

Officer: "Someone got shot."

Me: "I know. I saw him lying on the ground. The cops told me to go around, so I'm headed home."

Officer: "Let me see your I.D.………Did you do it? (He was asking if I shot the man in the street).

Me: (confused look on my face): "…No…no….I didn't shoot him."

Officer: "I have to ask."

Me: "I get it…."

I handed over my I.D. The police patted me down to check for weapons.

Officer: "You know why we stopped you?"

Me: "Why?"

Officer: "Because the suspect is a black man with black hoodie. Light-skinned. Skinny."

I'm not light-skinned and I'm not skinny, which saved me. But because I was a black man wearing a black hoodie, that was enough for the officers to temporarily check to see if I had committed the crime. Fortunately, things ended well, and I was allowed to leave. In all honesty, I was calm and collected and unphased the whole time. This hasn't always been the case. A couple years prior, I immersed myself in the literature of America's history of racial terror and the contemporary issues of disparities and injustice. I decided a long time ago that the only way to live free is to let go of the fear of death. So when I go to work the next day and a white co-worker says, "how are you Jon?" I reply, "I'm fine. How are you?" I really am fine but should I be? In my experience, most black people who live and work in places that are predominantly white feel it's unsafe for them to voice their anxieties about what they experience. Racism is not a disability but mental distress from living and working in environments that are culturally insensitive or violent creates prolonged anxiety and stress that results in illness. I would rather not use the ineffective and unproductive tool of casting blame but rather starting a conversation that can lead to change in our world. If healing occurs when we are no longer accustomed to dysfunction, am I sick for accepting that I should suffer in silence when I leave my home? Do black men have to get comfortable with a sick world to live well? I've made peace with the fact that my presence in this world is going to be viewed with constant suspicion and my peace of mind requires that I get comfortable with that reality quickly. Unfortunately, that mental, emotional, and deeply spiritual development work doesn't happen for every black male who encounters police and the interaction with police demonstrates it.

What stands out the most to me are the number of innocent black boys and men who have been derailed by the system of injustice. One situation in particular comes to mind. Kalief Browder was a seventeen-year-old black minor who was falsely accused of stealing a backpack on May 15, 2010. Police stopped Kalief on his way from a party. The police told Kalief he would be brought to the police station and released. That didn't happen.

He was taken to the precinct and subsequently charged with robbery, grand larceny, and assault. Unfortunately, the first bail amount of $3,000 was beyond his means. Once he was in the system, he was denied bail and transferred to Riker's Island Jail. He was held there for three years before the prosecutors offered a plea deal where he would get credit for time served. Out of a sense of integrity, he rejected the plea deal.

Kalief was returned to prison. Eventually, the prosecutors dismissed the charges, after Kalief denied another plea deal. Two of the three years he served, he was kept in solitary confinement, which caused him significant mental and emotional distress. In addition, jail footage shows that he was abused by correctional officers and other inmates.

Kalief was released, but not without injury. His experience on Riker's Island severely disturbed his mental and emotional health. He committed suicide on June 6, 2015.

This is one of the reasons I go to the local prison and detention center to volunteer. I know many young black men who have been so traumatized by being incarcerated it becomes increasingly difficult to not succumb to stress and fear when engaging with law enforcement. They don't know how to *not* look like a suspect and they don't know how to speak to the police, which can escalate these situations.

Personally, I don't believe that most police officers proactively seek to injure black people—but a presumption of guilt exists for black men in this country. That can make it uncomfortable and nerve-wracking to leave home.

I don't mean to say that every person should physically relocate to a disadvantaged community, but it might be a calling for some people. Remember, the farther away you are from a problem, the simpler the solution appears.

I chose to get closer to the problems, and now these are some of the changes I want to see.

What Do I Want to See Change?

America is better, but it's not good. Nina Simone taught us that the artist is called to reflect the current times. Amiri Baraka taught us that the artist has a job of raising the consciousness of the people. To add to these amazing icons, I believe the role of the artist is to project a new reality. And we must all become artists if we are to create a better reality for our communities.

Our identity is not only rooted in what we know about ourselves, but what we are willing to learn about what we could be. There are things we want to happen that we've never seen before. In our minds, we can be residents of a world that does not yet exist. Here's what I want to see happen:

Financial Literacy/Economic Mobility:

I envision black families with enough disposable financial resources to handle a situation like the one I was in. If I had been taken into the station that evening, I would have had access to the resources necessary to clear my name. Every black person needs to have a community to back him.

According to a 2018 report, the average black family in New Jersey has a net worth of $5,900, while the average white family has a net worth of $309,000. One prosecutor told me that the rich white man's justice when he's guilty is much better than poor black man's justice when he's innocent. This, in part, explains the disparity in the prison population.

New Jersey leads the nation in racial disparity in its prisons. In 2016, for everyone white adult, there are twelve black adults incarcerated. For everyone white youth, there are thirty black youth. Between 90 and 95 percent of people in prison *never had a trial*. Many of them lacked the resources to hire a competent defense. See Chapter 10 – Collateral Consequences of a Felony.

Black Man's Safety Training When Encountering Police

Have I prepared for and do I have the emotional maturity to handle myself under stressful situations involving police officers? Yes. But that did not come without mistakes and close calls. As a black man, I have to compensate for the potential bias of the officer. I willingly hand over my ID. I cooperate, because I know exactly what's going on. Because I serve people affected by the criminal justice system, I have learned to be proactive about encounters with police.

Not every black person is fortunate enough to have that experience. It's my right to stand up for myself and to not allow anyone to violate my constitutional rights. But if a black person attempts to do that, they are often not given the benefit of the doubt. Tragically, in 2014, more than 100 unarmed black men, women, and children were killed by agents of law enforcement. These murders sparked a national dialogue around the black community and police brutality.

The Reform Alliance is a collection of leaders in entertainment, government, sports, business, technology, and art who want to reduce the number of people who are unjustly placed under the control of the criminal justice system. One of the Reform Alliance (www.reformalliance.com) founders, Jay-Z, explained the psyche of many young black men, often fatherless, who have issues with authority and are raised in single-parent homes in inner cities. They experience police interaction more frequently than their suburban peers, and they sometimes encounter police officers who lack a knowledge base and critical awareness of the communities they serve.

The interactions between young men and police tend to escalate into violent situations, reminiscent of slave catchers abusing black men who have been unfairly criminalized. I envision a community of young people who are of rational thought and emotional maturity and can navigate encounters with law enforcement with wisdom and courage, when necessary. I envision law enforcement officers who operate as the most sophisticated civil servants and bear the major responsibility of guarding the values of the community and building trust within the community.

Proactive Brotherhood

There was a time when there was a sense of kinship and connection. But now, we have gotten comfortable ignoring each other.

I become brothers with the men I meet in prison because we share a similar struggle of being cuffed and chained. We should also become brothers because we share a similar destiny and objective.

As Carter G. Woodson discussed in *The Miseducation of the Negro*, the free blacks in the 18th and 19th centuries were counseled to go back to Africa, but they didn't go. Instead, they chose to never separate from the enslaved blacks in America, because they saw themselves as brothers and descendants of the same ancestors.

Woodson also said this spirit has deteriorated. The educated black person now is more likely to have an attitude of disrespect toward his own people. Self-hate and miseducation can cause you to turn your back on people who look like you.

The purpose of education should be to facilitate the development of a mature mind that serves others—not obtaining an elitist status.

Constant visible occupational diversity

I envision a time when black youth are consistently being exposed to diverse occupations and given a pathway to pursue vocational training.

As American politician and sociologist Daniel Patrick Moynihan discussed in his 1965 report, *The Negro Family – The Case for National Action*—specifically in the fourth section, called "The Tangle of Pathology," many black youth are fatherless and grow up in broken homes in underserved communities. Those young men are not seeing examples of men, friends, relatives, or neighbors who prioritize work and education.

One of the unintended consequences of integration is that it took black professionals out of black communities. As a result, young black people didn't see the tangible results of hard work, creativity, and persistence. Unfortunately, the situation is similar today. Things are changing for the better, but black youth still need to see role models who look like them in diverse occupations. Ideally, these professionals can provide mentoring, resources, encouragement, direction, and a clear path to receiving training. See Chapter 9 of *Bridge the Gaps*.

A new identity to promote the positive—getting rid of the notion of "acting white"

I envision a time when black communities, particularly underserved and traumatized communities, will cultivate new identities so that young people are not pressured to underachieve in order to belong.

We are designed to be part of community, and if the community doesn't provide us with a healthy value system, it becomes a dangerous place to live. Harvard professor Roland Fryer discussed this in his research paper "Acting White."

Just as it takes time for individuals to find out who they are, the same is true for communities. It takes a community time to rediscover purpose and find a mission. The process is less about individual success or competence and more about cultural healing and collective success. See the chapter entitled "Courage – Fear of Breaking Rules".

Preference/conviction – 'That's a good idea' vs. 'Here's what I'm going to do'

When things are bad, many people attack each other rather than the problem. Or they point out the problems in hopes that it will spur someone else into action. "Somebody should do something!" is a common phrase people use when talking about the issues of black people. I want to replace that hopeful comment with firm resolve: "Here's what I'm going to do."

Complete this phrase: "Here's what I'm going to do:

_____

_____

_____

If you look at the journey of black Americans who are successful, you will see missteps, failures, and poor judgment at points, as well as relationship breakdowns, regrets, and character flaws. You'll also see a willingness to re-evaluate, apologize when wrong, acknowledge their mistakes, and most importantly, a willingness to seek and accept mentorship—and to in turn mentor others.

I say this because when you take the time to share your successes and mistakes with those coming behind you, you can greatly increase their odds of success. If you have achieved success, your journey has been difficult, but you've survived. As a mentor, the pain you endured on the road to success can become a gift to others.

We are, at all times, both individuals and part of a community. Individualism says, "I want to beat the odds." Collectivism says, "I want to change the odds." Our goal should be to improve the odds for others.

We have to believe for a future that we have not yet seen—and belief alone is not sufficient. We must prepare to act, which leads to the next section on Productivity.

For additional exercises and tools, see Chapter 36 – Community Care in *Bridge the Gaps: Lessons on Self-Awareness, Self-Development, and Self-Care*. Visit www.amazon.com or www.thebridg330.com to pick up a copy.

Part 2: Productivity

As part of their psychosocial development, children develop a perspective on life. Their early years inform how subsequent experiences are viewed, which affects behavior.

The life of a mentee will be affected by the greatly lived, unlived, or poorly lived life of the mentor. As such, in order to teach with integrity, you must teach what you live and earn the right to speak into a mentee's life.

This section is about cultivating the mindset necessary to take efficient and productive action rooted in an understanding of one's purpose in life. Things don't get done because you feel like it. Things get done because you have formed your purpose, established your priorities, and cultivated the right perspective.

Part 1 was designed to make you reflective and introspective. It's important to note that soul-searching is not the goal of life. There are seasons when you have to be introspective, and then there are seasons where you need to be actively engaged in work. This section is about helping you accomplish the latter.

If you want to change your position in life, you have to be willing to review the effectiveness of your perspectives and practices. You must be an initiator of change, instead of accepting life as it is. You can author your destiny or be a victim of your circumstance.

The principles of success are consistent across different walks of life, but the motivations and the nuances of the pursuit vary for each community. Black people created their own success after slavery because of a self-enterprising, self-determined, and self-reliant spirit.

Sadly, black people's success in the early- to mid-20th century could not be sustained, due to white hatred and the subsequent destruction of black success. Self-sufficient black towns were burned to the ground. Black people were lynched all through the 20th century. Black people had to find new ways to succeed in this world, and they often had to relocate to safer places where opportunity could be found.

Millions of black people left the South for the northern communities. Somewhere along the journey, their self-determined spirit was taken captive by learned helplessness, unresolved pain, and fear rooted in past assaults. In addition to the trauma, government policy incentivized the removal of the black father from the home through the welfare system's "man in the house" rule. Mass incarceration of black men, through the misguided war on drugs in the 1980s led by Ronald Reagan, also removed many black men from their homes.

The historical oppression of black people in America has injured the black family structure. Home is the place where children shape their characters and abilities. As American politician and sociologist Daniel Patrick Moynihan discussed in his 1965 report *The Negro Family – The Case for National Action*—specifically in the fifth section called "The Case for National Action"—the disorganized family structure of black communities has made it harder for many young people to cultivate the habits and discipline necessary to become productive members of the community.

As a mentor, your role is to help your mentees develop a level of focus and build a base of self-efficacy rooted in knowledge of their purpose and the attitudes needed to achieve that purpose. This section becomes particularly relevant in our time when young people have access to loads of information but a shortage of wisdom.

We can't change the world with ideas in our mind alone. We need conviction in our hearts. And if we *can* find that conviction and we *can* make a difference, then we have an obligation to try. We can be the midwives of a new America.

5: Purpose Toolkit

You can't do everything, but you must do something.

HUMAN BEINGS OFTEN COMMIT LARGE shares of their lives to either pointless or destructive activities. According to Bronnie Ware, author of *The Top Five Regrets of the Dying*, the most often-named regret of the dying is that they didn't have the courage to live the life that was authentically theirs. Instead of pursuing their own dreams, they settled for a life that other people intended for them.

One of the worst legacies of racial dehumanization in America has been its consistent goal to keep black people from advancing and choosing their own destinies. They couldn't pursue their purpose because they were used for the purposes of others. They had no power.

Power is the capacity to achieve one's purpose. Bringing about change in your life, personally and corporately, begins by acknowledging that you have the power within you to do so. It also requires that you shift your thinking in a way that empowers you to live unapologetically in pursuit of purpose. The beginning of living a truly productive and impactful life is finding your purpose and losing yourself in that purpose.

If you are to sustainably change the condition of your life, you must make the decision to live "on purpose" early in life and manage the decision for the rest of your life. Many young people are not walking in their purpose. If you've been alive long enough, you know that when people don't know what they are here to do, they often find a poor substitute.

The sooner young people can find their greater purpose, the sooner they can let go of lesser distractions that can derail them. Once you know what you were born to do, everything about you will change.

Part of your work as a mentor is to help your mentees develop a sense of purpose that allows them to find their place in the world and organize their life in a tailor-made way. These tools will help you guide your mentee in articulating their purpose, identifying wise principles to protect their purpose, and providing principles of character to promote success.

Tools

1. *Find Your Lane: There's Less Traffic*
2. *Code of Conduct: Bring Order Into Your Life*

Find Your Lane: There's Less Traffic

Don't do things that you think will inspire hope. Do the things that bring you hope, because it can inspire hope in others.

THE MOST FUNDAMENTAL QUESTION THAT people ask children is, "What do you do want to do when you grow up?" This question often asks them to name a particular professional ambition. A better question is, "What do you want your life to be about?" This question speaks to purpose.

In the world of personal development, you often hear phrases like: pick your battle, start with the end in mind, define your success, and identify your desired return on investment (ROI). These questions speak to specific aims or targets. But before you get too specific, I think you should start the mentorship process with a broader intention - finding your lane.

Each person has a lane in life that they are fit to travel. If we don't identify that lane, we run the risk of making premature commitments to certain paths. You don't have to be too specific too soon. The journey to your specific destiny is a funnel.

Far too many people have been derailed by going down a path that they were not meant to travel. As a result, their lives are filled with poor choices, wasted time, and tons of regret. The following exercises can be used to prime the pump of your purpose.

Exercise#1 – Merge your conviction with your vocation

If you only care about your deeply-felt values, you become a narcissist. If you only care about addressing external needs, you become a robot. You want to find the balance between what deeply moves you and what the world needs to have done. This exercise is designed to help you do that.

Every person *knows*, deep inside, what their purpose is. Unfortunately, most people haven't taken the time to discover what it is. As a mentor, you need to give your mentee room for self-discovery. Whether it relates to your family, friendships, workplace, or the world, answer these questions daily.

Journaling is an underutilized tool on the road to finding your purpose. Have your mentee keep a daily journal, because purpose is applied and discerned on a day-to-day basis. Every thirty, sixty, or ninety days, you want to review what their days have been like and identify consistent themes. Ask your mentees to talk about and write about their past experiences. Recollection is likely to turn up some useful information. There are clues in your history that can speak to your destiny. Finding your purpose is often not a *discovery* but a *recovery* of themes from your past.

One of the goals of life should be to identify your deeply-felt desires and values and how they align with the needs you see in the world. The time that this exercise requires is so small and so minimal compared to what's at stake – spending the rest of your life clueless about why you are here. Here's a list of questions that you can use to grow in awareness of your purpose.

What makes you mad?
Anger – Your greatest frustration is a problem you are here to solve.

What makes you sad?
Sadness – Ask the Lord to break your heart with what breaks his heart.

What makes you excited?
Excitement – Don't do things that you think the world needs. Do the things that bring *you life*, because the world needs people who are fully alive.

What makes you afraid?
Fear – What would your life look like if you were not afraid? Name your fears and fight them.

What makes you generous?
Generosity – Where do you find yourself most generous?
Note: If you find yourself giving everything to everyone until you have nothing left, see Chapter 33 – Boundaries in *Bridge the Gaps*.

What do you talk about without being asked?
Unsolicited conversation – What do you know enough and care enough about to talk without being asked?

What makes you feel complete?
Integrity - What is your integrity calling you to?

What suits you best? What are you challenged by but not overwhelmed by?
Suitability – "His yoke is easy, and his burden is light." Matthew 11:30

Who inspires you?
Role models – We can see ourselves better when we can see ourselves in others.

What gives you hope?
Hope is the conviction that doing the work makes sense regardless of how it turns out.

When do you feel most hopeful? Where do you see possibilities while others see hopelessness and despair?
What is your dream job? Beneath this question are the seeds of destiny.

Your feelings can speak to deeper realities that you want to investigate. The purpose of this section is to help find out what you want your life and work to be about. As you study this topic, you will begin to spot trends that will inform decisions about what college major is best, where to work, what type of business to start, or what major issue in the world to address. The goal is not to just gather information but to figure out the main focus.

It's my hope that this process is not just learning about what you need to do. It's also about learning who you are and, most importantly, loving and appreciating who you are and how you're wired.

You are uniquely designed to do *something* for however long you are on this Earth. Your life is tailor-made for you. But you will need to find your purpose and know how to stay in your lane. So much unnecessary drama occurs because people are in the wrong lane for the wrong reasons.

You'll find an additional exercise called "Your Calling Is Your Compass" in Chapter 1 of *Bridge the Gaps: Lessons on Self-Awareness, Self-Development, and Self-Care*. Visit www.amazon.com or www.thebridg330.com to pick up a copy.

Exercise #2 – Simplify Your Purpose

I believe there is power in simplicity. After you've completed Exercise #1, choose three actions from the list below to find the form of your purpose. Choose actions that resonate with you.

Question: What do you want to do?

Action words

Build - Repair - Learn – Destroy - Teach - Fight - Overcome - Restore - Remove - Correct - Prepare - Change Remember – Inform – Raise – Alert – Become – Resolve – Determine – Manifest – Promote – Provide - Protect Encourage – Make – Care – Counsel – Commit – Defend – Ensure – Revive – Break down – Prevent – Instruct Hold on – Leave behind – Avoid – Invite – Evoke - Invoke

If you have any other words you want to include, you can add those words below.

_____

_____

_____

Question: Who do you want to help?

Choose three groups/interest/causes from the list below that you'd like to benefit from your purpose.

Groups/Interests/Causes
Politics – Studies of culture – Business – Animal life – Social justice – Finance – Education – Travel – World history – Great inventors – Family health – Fitness – Airplanes – Faith – African American history – Music – Gospel – Mental illness – Community building – World missions – Human development – Space exploration – Law – Nutrition – Child care – Education – Community development – The incarcerated

If you have any other words you want to include, you can add those words below.

_____

_____

_____

Exercise#3 – Write a Purpose Statement

If we don't find what we're called to do, we'll find a substitute. We cannot productively live in the absence of purpose. We would never start a business without a mission statement and core values. So why do we often skip over identifying a purpose for our own lives and/or the lives of our mentees?

A clearly defined purpose statement can help us chart our course with confidence and resist our need to please others. Unfortunately, many people focus on obtaining a position or material possessions. These are not bad goals, but once the position or the material possessions are obtained, the pursuit may dwindle and enthusiasm is lost. Studies show that an excessive focus on material goals and career is correlated with a decrease in happiness.

When you have a sense of purpose, inner strength is released that allows you to take appropriate risks. You'll be able to hand dull moments or even find interest in menial tasks. You will have a sense of value, because you'll know you are contributing to something bigger than yourself.

As a mentor, you want to get people to walk in their purpose as soon as humanly possible.

A purpose statement is designed to integrate who you are and what you do. It is the way you start transforming your life from a wandering generality to a meaningful specific. Combine Exercises #1 and 2 to come up with a statement of your intention. It doesn't have to be perfect, but it must be honest and grounded in reality.

Here's an example:

"To provide quality mentoring tools to underserved, under-resourced, and vulnerable communities in ways that support sustained social change, a restoration of hope, and an avenue to mental and emotional health."

"To fight against the stigma of mental illness in the black community by inviting people to share their stories in an authentic and safe way."

_____

_____

_____

_____

Exercise 4 – Execute

Your purpose is the job that God gives you. Once you know your purpose, you should always know what to do next: Do your job.

Jonathan Frejuste

Code of Conduct: Bring Order into Your Life
The system is rigged. All the more reason not to help it. Denzel Washington

As AMERICAN POLITICIAN AND SOCIOLOGIST Daniel Patrick Moynihan discussed in his 1965 report - *The Negro Family – The Case for National Action*—specifically in the second section, called *The Negro American Family*—the conduct of adults in society is learned when they are children. Both good and bad behavior are significantly influenced by one's environment.

Nelson Mandela believed that *nurture* rather than *nature* is the main builder of one's personality and character. If that is the case, then our community can foster an environment to cultivate a particular type of character.

I've observed that every organization or group that wants to have a sustainable existence—whether it's a Fortune 500 company or a street fraternity—must have a *code of conduct* to keep from disrupting the main agenda. This principle works for individuals as well.

When you monitor the way you conduct yourself publicly and privately, you have an opportunity to build and improve your character, your confidence, and subsequently, your destiny.

You can tell where someone is headed in their life by what they do on a consistent basis. Achieving our goals and building the lives we want to live will largely be determined by the principles, boundaries, and policies that we incorporate into our lives. On the flip side, we can prevent major problems and avoid pitfalls by putting certain controls in place.

I believe that if Dr. King was alive today, not only would he be addressing issues of injustice, he'd be talking about the black family and teaching black people about the importance of developing themselves to be quality people. He addressed this topic his speech *"What Is Your Life's Blueprint?"*

Many times, mentors lecture their mentees on what they should have known about how to be a wise person—after the fact. Rarely do we see the advice or standards given *before* the fact. But codes of conduct exist for a reason.

I heard a story about a group of young black women who attended a conference where a prominent figure was giving a keynote lecture. At the end of the conference, the young ladies approached the prominent figure and asked for advice. The advice given was to keep from getting pregnant and to educate themselves. They were offended. The advice was construed as condescending.

I often speak with black elders who have a frank and sometimes harsh or even bitter demeanor. I've always wondered why. After speaking with a number of black elders, I realized why.

Many of them, unfortunately, have witnessed tens or hundreds of young men and women sabotage their opportunities by making poor life choices. Others are carrying broken dreams because they were not given the opportunity to manifest, as result of oppression that existed in their time.

These elders don't have time to mince words with young people. Even though their tone may be off, the heart of the message comes from a redemptive place. It's important for young people to recognize that a harsh message may not have anything to do with them, and that if they can find the redemptive elements in the advice, they should take it.

I know several women who were teenage mothers. Their experience occurred at a time when the social shame was strong and relentless. Friends and family derided and judged them. They told them they would not amount to anything, that their lives would be ruined.

Through grace and their own resilience, these women didn't listen to the negative messages. They went on to become successful business owners, authors, executives of major companies, PhDs, etc. Some of them do express regret over the timing of their decision and the person they chose as partners.

One conversation stands out to me. A woman told me that particular things should have been done - in order. In order to keep things from going wrong, you want to do things - in order. It's important for young people to understand how quickly life can spin out of control when you make the wrong choices.

Confidence comes from living your life in such a way that you can reliably predict where you will be in the future. It's been said that you can choose the future by how you act in the present. A young person can change his or her life before it falls apart. For that you need, a code of conduct.

The definition of a code of conduct is a set of moral principles, boundaries, and expectations that are incorporated into your life, which keep you from sabotaging, interrupting, or detouring a life of purpose.

As one black educator said, black people have been turned upside down and inside out. Black people have to turn themselves right side up. In a society that has historically oppressed and prohibited black people from experiencing the quality of life that should be every person's God-given right, we need a culturally uplifting code of conduct to keep us from undermining and sabotaging our success.

Another black educator said, (the world) will provide you with all the resources to destroy yourself. We need moral restraints to keep us from accepting everything that is offered. It's not wrong to be tempted. It's foolish to fall into temptation, when you can put something in place to protect you from you.

What if, as a mentor, you never had a code of conduct to guide your behavior and choices? Forgive yourself. My faith tradition teaches me that God can "restore to you the years that the swarming locust has eaten." (Joel 2:25, NKJV.) The second half of your life can be better than the first half, especially if you have learned the lessons of the first half.

One of the greatest ways to add value to someone's life is to provide them with a structure to keep them on a productive path. We want the next generation to preserve what they have, rather than restore it at a later date, because the pain of regret is heavier than the pain of proactivity.

A code of conduct provides guidance in preventing some of the common mistakes, instead of focusing on a cure. If you don't teach, they'll never learn—or worse, they'll learn the wrong things.

You want to teach young people how to solve problems before catastrophes arrive. You don't want them to sink their ship before it leaves the harbor. It's better to work to keep negative things from happening instead of working to fix the problems that arise.

Your confidence will not be based on who you know in this world, but on what you do day-to-day and moment-to-moment. Low self-esteem comes from not having been productive. We can feel incomplete if we're aimless and misuse our time and energy.

I want to be careful here, because I don't mean to say that you have no value if you are not productive. I mean to say that if you can be productive and are not, you'll feel a nagging sense inside that says, "I know I can do more and do better." Your intrinsic worth and value does not have to be earned, but it can and should be expressed through your actions and endeavors.

As black people, we have been conditioned to see life a certain way and go in a direction not chosen by us. I consider the formation of a code of conduct to be a crucial element of freedom, because it can help you determine the direction your life will go in.

Why not take control and point your life in the direction you choose? As the quote says, you can't buy a slave. You have to make a slave. A free man does what he chooses and goes in the direction that he points.

Bridge the Gaps Code of Conduct
Here's my code of conduct based on the guide

Bridge the Gaps – Lessons on Self-Awareness, Self-Development, and Self-Care.

Culture is something that changes over time. As the culture redefines itself, beliefs, customs, traditions, and ideas change. Yet certain principles need to be honored in order for life to move forward in a positive way. Telling people what they should do right is just as important as telling them what they did wrong.

Human nature tends to lure us down the easiest and most comfortable path, even if it's harmful. In order to have an orderly relationship and community, we must put this human tendency in check. In a world that is rapidly changing and full of temptation to compromise one's calling, young people need mentors who know what really matters.

Here's a code of conduct based on proactivity, prevention, and instruction.

1. Choose your environment and friends wisely.
a. "Do not be misled: Bad company corrupts good character." (1 Corinthians 15:33, NLT)

b. "The righteous choose their friends carefully, but the way of the wicked leads them astray." (Proverbs 12:26, KJV)

c. Read Chapters 22 and 33 of *Bridge the Gaps*

2. A person's greatness is determined by what it takes to discourage him/her.
a. "Dear brothers and sisters, is your life full of difficulties and temptations? Then be happy, for when the way is rough, your patience has a chance to grow. So let it grow, and don't try to squirm out of your problems. For when your patience is finally in full bloom, then you will be ready for anything, strong in character, full and complete." (James 1:2-4, TLB)

b. Read Chapters 26, 27, 28, and 30 of *Bridge the Gaps*

3. Don't venture past your sphere of knowledge until your sphere of knowledge exceeds your venture.

a. "Desire without knowledge is not good — how much more will hasty feet miss the way!" (Proverbs 19:2, NIV)

b. Read Chapters 7, 9, and 16 of *Bridge the Gaps*

4. Work to achieve mastery of yourself and your craft.

a. "Do you see someone skilled in their work? They will serve before kings; they will not serve before officials of low rank." (Proverbs 22:29, NIV)

b. Read Chapters 4, 6, and 24 of *Bridge the Gaps*

5. Cultivate a vision and work hard to bring it into fruition.

a. "All hard work brings a profit, but mere talk leads only to poverty." (Proverbs 14:23, NIV)

b. "Where there is no vision, the people perish." (Proverbs 29:18, KJV)

c. Read Chapters 8 and 20 of *Bridge the Gaps*

6. Talk less. Make fewer announcements and more adjustments.

a. "Like billowing clouds that bring no rain is the person who talks big but never produces." (Proverbs 25:14, MSG)

b. Read Chapter 15 of *Bridge the Gaps*

7. Eliminate distractions and identify your focus.
a. "No one serving as a soldier gets entangled in civilian affairs, but rather tries to please his commanding officer." (2 Timothy 2:4, NIV)

b. Read Chapters 1, 12, 17, and 29 of *Bridge the Gaps*

8. You're not required to be great to get started, but you have to get started to be great.
a. "Do not despise these small beginnings." (Zechariah 4:10, NLT)

b. Read Chapter 11 of *Bridge the Gaps*

9. Manage your priorities wisely.
a. "Teach us to number our days, that we may gain a heart of wisdom." (Psalm 90:12, NIV)

b. Read Chapters 18, 19, 23, and 43 of *Bridge the Gaps*

10. Learn how to love yourself and others.
a. "Let your love abound in knowledge and depth of insight." (Philippians 1:9, NIV)

b. Read Chapters 31 to 42 of *Bridge the Gaps*

The Scripture says that "A principled life can stand up to the worst." (Proverbs 11:4, MSG). When I lead life-coaching courses in prison, I have the sad realization that so many men will never reach and share their true level of greatness because they're spending the best years of their lives behind the wall.

I'm convinced that, for many of the brothers I meet, their lives were derailed because they had no leadership in their lives to provide them with the discipline and accountability we all need to live our best lives.

As the Scripture says, "A refusal to correct is a refusal to love." (Proverbs 13:24, MSG).

One of the main, painstaking lessons that I've learned is that the greatest threat to freedom *is* your freedom. As a leader, you want to use your freedom to cause the right and best things happen and to keep the wrong things from happening.

Many of the men I meet were never taught to have consequential thinking. They didn't consider the penalties of their actions, which is part of adolescent thinking.

Part of being confident comes from knowing that you have put the controls in place in your life to keep negative things from happening. These controls serve as a kind of referee. With your code of conduct, you're mapping your behavior to what you want your life to look like for the next twenty years.

What might be some of the negative things you want to keep from happening? Let me give you a list. These are the consequences of having no code of conduct.

- Poor sexual/relational practices can lead to: STDs, unwanted pregnancies, child support battles, lifelong relational drama

- Poor eating/sleep/exercise habits lead to: preventable diseases, low energy, poor mental/emotional/physical health

- Poor self-control/due diligence of your financial life leads to: unmanageable debts, relational conflict due to unpaid personal loans, foreclosures, property repossessions

- Poor relationship choices lead to: long-term relational turmoil, community breakdown, and misguided choices, including breaking the law

- Poor emotional habits lead to: Using addictions to cope with your emotional pain, impulsive actions

- Poor time management: Missed deadlines and opportunities leading to life-altering circumstances

There can be no change without truth. The truth listed here is in no way meant to shame you. It's hard to face certain realities, but if we are going to build a great life, then that's exactly what we need to face.

When you don't have a good code of conduct that you live by consistently, the older you get, the worse your life will be. When you have a code of conduct that aligns you with who you want to be in the future, it helps you project a strength of character that inspires trust in others.

At this point in my life, I've seen enough to say that putting together a code of conduct, sooner rather than later, is the smartest thing to do. No one talks about the foundation of a house until the house is falling apart—yet the foundation is the hardest and most important part of building a house. Your code of conduct is the foundation to your life.

Sample Code of Conduct

Here's a sample code of conduct that one person gave me:

1. I will read two books a month based on my personal and professional developmental needs.
2. I will arrive everywhere I am scheduled to go on time and adequately prepared for my responsibilities.
3. I will offer my seat to women if limited seating is available.
4. I will show respect and honor to all those I encounter on my journey.
5. I will budget my money properly every week in order to live below my means.
6. I will not loan money to others unless I am prepared to not have it paid back.
7. I will foster healthy relationships.

8. I will preserve the preciousness of sexual intimacy within the context of marriage.
9. Serious interpersonal conflict, especially with other black people, needs to be settled privately, personally, and peacefully.
10. I will commit to eating healthy food and working out at least four times a week.
11. I will refuse to gossip, slander, or speak of someone in a negative way.
12. I will keep my commitments. Otherwise, I will refrain from committing in a way that exceeds my limits.

Personal Code of Conduct

Take some time to come up with your own code of conduct based on who you want to be and the kind of person you want your mentee to become.

1. _____

2. _____

3. _____

4. _____

5. _____

6. _____

7. _____

8. _____

9. _____

10. _____

For additional exercises and tools, see Chapter 25 – Habits and Systems in *Bridge the Gaps: Lessons on Self-Awareness, Self-Development and Self-Care*. Visit www.amazon.com or www.thebridg330.com to pick up a copy.

6: Process Toolkit

You lose sight of your plan when you get punched in the face.

In a few centuries, historians will reflect on our times—not only on the technological advances that we have made as a society, but on the vast number of decisions that we had to make and how we were ill-equipped to handle them.

Some forces in the world have a vested interest in people remaining distracted. When you are unable to focus, you become your own worst enemy. When you're in a season of life where you have to execute at a high level, you must learn how to cultivate a certain level of focus. Focus is the ability to concentrate and apply oneself to a target.

Most people live a life without focus because they never learn how to develop it. To have a purpose requires that you have a set of commitments. Purpose requires time, discipline, vision, and limits. Whatever holds your attention will control the course of your life.

But how can you teach a distracted mind to focus? Many effective people give advice that contradicts what they actually did! What I want to do is de-mystify their process, so you can replicate it in your own way.

As you read about this, it might seem like common sense, but it's not always common practice. As a mentor, you want to hold mentees accountable for where they choose to place their attention, because that will determine the course of their lives. Their productivity in life will come from intentionality.

The activities that matter most don't always make the most noise and are not always readily identifiable. Because we have a variety of competing interests, we need a framework to establish a focus rooted in purpose.

In the spirit of being productive, these three tools are the most important:

Tools
1. *Define Your Success: What Do You Look Forward to Achieving?*
2. *Dreams to Reality: What Will You Do to Get There?*
3. *Expertise: Greatness Takes Time*

Define Your Success: What Do You Look Forward to Achieving?

Never change one brush stroke on your canvas because someone doesn't like what you paint.

People buy things they don't need with money they don't have to impress people they don't like. In the same sense, people do things they don't like to impress people they don't respect to get things they don't want. We live in a world where people buy homes, cars, and clothes they can't afford to give the impression that they are successful. They work long hours to climb the corporate ladder so they can be successful. Sometimes, if they can't do it, they enlist their children.

As I'm writing this book, several wealthy American parents have been charged and convicted of bribing school officials and coaches to have their children admitted to the top universities. The million-dollar question everyone asks is, WHY? Why did these parents do this?

The answer is their definition of success. One journalist commented that the bribes were not made to benefit the children but to benefit the *parents*. The consensus is that it was about "bragging rights." The cultural value placed on a certain perception of success led these parents to violate the law and a sense of fundamental fairness—in other words, to cheat.

Their crimes were rooted in a dangerous version of the American dream where someone can set goals, work hard, become successful, and do better than their parents. The problem with this version is that it doesn't take reality into account.

This self-centered and individualistic view of success can lead to much unhappiness, and it tends to be passed along to future generations. This cycle needs to be broken. Many of these celebrities' children didn't even know their parents tried to bribe their way into the school or into programs associated with the school!

One productive outcome of the exposure of the college bribery scandal is that it forced many people in America reflect on what success looks like and re-evaluate their own personal definitions. Before you chase success, it would serve you well to define what your personal definition of success looks like to you. When you don't define what success is, society will tell you what success looks like, and it might not be a definition that serves your personal and community well-being. In fact, if you don't define your success, someone else's definition can become your prison.

Popular opinion shapes mindsets, but they should never be the driving force behind them. If your definition of success is unfulfilling and/or detrimental to you and your community, you must work to redefine it. Most people don't get what they are going after because they don't take the time to determine exactly why they are pursuing it.

In Chapter 5 – Purpose Toolkit, it was established that each person has a unique, tailor-made purpose. If a purpose is unique, then the accompanying definition of success must be unique as well.

Here are a few thoughts and reflections on success and failure that have their own unique implications and applications to life. Take note that these definitions may vary and even contradict each other. That's why each of us must develop our own unique definition/understanding of success—because each of us has been uniquely designed. Success is as unique as a fingerprint.

Meditate on who you are and what you want. Develop clarity of intention. Then live it out.

When you uncover the rationale behind a goal, you'll be more motivated. Defining what you believe success is will be important in determining how to organize your efforts.

Here's a list of different definitions/ideas of success to consider:

1. Success is running the race uniquely designed for me. Nothing is worse than crossing the finish line only to realize that you were in the wrong race.

2. Success is not about where you are in relation to the person next to you. It's about where you are in relation to where you started and what you started with.

3. The greatest fear we should have is in succeeding at things that ultimately don't matter.

4. Success is being respected most by people who know me best.

5. Success is not about starting well but finishing well.

6. Success is not about standing with the greats but sitting with the broken.

   While Jesus was having dinner at Levi's house, many tax collectors and sinners were eating with him and his disciples, for there were many who followed him. When the teachers of the law who were Pharisees saw him eating with the sinners and tax collectors, they asked his disciples: "Why does he eat with tax collectors and sinners?" On hearing this, Jesus said to them, "It is not the healthy who need a doctor, but the sick. I have not come to call the righteous, but sinners." (Mark 2:15-17, NIV)

7. Success is doing things that are important, even if they are not impressive.

8. Success is never allowing my ambition to become greater than my gratitude.

> *I'm glad in God, far happier than you would ever guess—happy that you're again showing such strong concern for me. Not that you ever quit praying and thinking about me. You just had no chance to show it. Actually, I don't have a sense of needing anything personally. I've learned by now to be quite content whatever my circumstances. I'm just as happy with little as with much, with much as with little. I've found the recipe for being happy whether full or hungry, hands full or hands empty. Whatever I have, wherever I am, I can make it through anything in the One who makes me who I am.* (Philippians 2:12-13, MSG)

9. Success is refusing to conform to the standards of the people who are "in charge" but submitting to the One who has ultimate authority.

   Am I now trying to win the approval of human beings, or of God? Or am I trying to please people? If I were still trying to please people, I would not be a servant of Christ. (Galatians 1:10, NIV)

10. People say they want to do things that matter and then measure themselves against things that don't matter.

11. Success is having more ability than visibility in order to avoid questionable credibility.

12. Your greatest responsibility is to invest in yourself to become absolutely clear about what it is you want.

13. Success is making decisions with eternity in mind.

14. Success is contributing more than you criticize.

15. Success is glorifying God by living in a way that makes sense in light of eternity.

16. It makes no difference how fast you are in the first 100 meters if the race is 400 meters long.

17. Collective progress is just as important as individual accomplishment.

18. Success is being relevant to your center instead of adopting mainstream notions of success.

19. Success is holding onto your principles in the midst of pressure. No amount of applause can dictate success. Otherwise, one can be controlled and compromise on what's right.

20. Success means you replace the words "bigger" and "well-known" with "effective" and "better."

How do these thoughts and reflections resonate with you?

_____

_____

_____

Which one(s) motivate you? In what way(s) do they motivate you?

_____

_____

Do you have your own personal definition(s) of success? It's been suggested that the ideal definition of success includes four elements: contentment, achievement, happiness, and other people.

___

___

___

Black Success—What Does It Look Like?
One definition of success is about gradual materialization of a worthy goal. What defines worthy? Does your personal background determine what worthy looks like? Does your ethnic background determine what worthy is? How should black people's definition of success be informed in light of the legacy of racial hatred and hierarchy?

As black scholar and professor Amos Wilson would ask, are your desires and wants being produced by white society, or did you choose them yourselves?

When a black person leaves their community and goes to white-run institutions, they can become accustomed to definitions of success that don't take into account the well-being of people who look like them. It's a delicate dance. My only caution is that you approach everything with a self-sustained definition of success, so that you know what really matters *to you* as you rub shoulders in societies that are ignorant or apathetic to the plight of black people.

I will not attempt to answer these questions here. I do believe that they set the stage for important conversations in this and the next few generations of black people in America.

If you're ambitious without reflecting on the source motivation of what you're pursuing, you're setting yourself up as a pawn.

This guide was written to address provide mentoring tools that acknowledge the legacy of racial dehumanization and white supremacy and this might be the most important tool: defining your success.

As American politician and sociologist Daniel Patrick Moynihan discussed in his 1965 report *The Negro Family – The Case for National Action*—specifically in the fourth section, called *The Tangle of Pathology*—white America broke the will of the Negro people by destroying the Negro family.

The resurgence of the will reasserted itself over time, but from my vantage point, the idea of success was still distorted by white supremacy. The legacy of white supremacy at it relates to success says that white people should always be in charge, black exploitation can be used for white profit, and the aspirations and thoughts of black people have no merit.

The 1952 book *Invisible Man* by Ralph Ellison was written at a time when racial attitudes in America were in flux. It was one of the most important voices in the civil rights movement. Many black people, including Ellison, had been taught that there were only three ways a black person could be successful: Be like white people. Please white people. Separate from white people.

In *The Miseducation of the Negro,* Carter G. Woodson comments that if you can control a man's perceptions, you don't have to be concerned about his actions. The same goes for a man's standards and expectations for his life. Miseducation leads to mis-leadership.

Everyone has a definition of success based on their conditioning. I was taught that success was moving out of the 'hood (which we did), successfully imitating sophisticated white people, and no longer associating with lower-class black people.

A contrary definition of success is to invest in your neighborhood, provide community building resources, make a commitment to value the beauty of the culture, understand the culture in order to bring healing, and stay intimately connected with the lower class and those on the margins, to create grounded solutions.

The struggle for every black person in America is deciding which path they want to take in the world. Sometimes, the path is given based on the opportunities available. Other times, there is conflict based on the differing ideologies around success.

The decision-making process concerning black people has an ugly history. A phrase that was common in the south is that "blacks should know their place." Some have interpreted this to mean that, if black people diminish themselves in front of white people, they will somehow achieve equality. When this happens, which is fairly often, it encourages the notion that black lives don't matter unless white people say so.

I believe the phrase "black lives matter" needs to be directed at black people more than anyone else, because what we think about ourselves is more important than what anyone thinks about us. If we have our own definition of success, we can wake up every day and make choices based on who we know we are, as opposed to what someone allows us to do.

When you define success for yourself, you're saying you do know your place and you have also chosen it. You're saying that you choose to live the life you were meant to live, not the life that was given you—even if you fail. What's more frustrating than achieving in a life that you were never meant to live is failing to achieve in a life you were never meant to live.

Examples of Black Success: What Does Success Look Like in My Color?

The great South African anti-apartheid activist, Steve Biko, explained the black consciousness movement. One of the main points of his ideology is that black people must participate in articulating their ideals and aspirations. He realized that we have a lot of great black history, but it was also important to craft a great black future rooted in the self-determination of black people. Biko said that if white people determine whether black people are free or enslaved, there is never an opportunity for the black man or woman to choose his or her own destiny.

One of the legacies of black oppression was the destruction of the desire to be concerned with one's own destiny and the wholesale adoption of the oppressor's ideas and values about what life should look like. Even after slavery, black people were held captive—culturally, economically, legally, and academically. It's not rare for people being held as captives to think like their captors.

When you have a group of people with a history of marginalization and oppression who have been cut off from their culture, customs, and family traditions, they will often sit in the shadows and wait for an opportunity to imitate the oppressing party, because their oppressors have modeled what "success" looks like. They might even believe wholesale what the oppressing party dictates about life.

It's important that we have this conversation as often as necessary, because people who are unaware of their condition often attempt to become something other than they are. As Dr. King said in his last sermon, "I've Been to the Mountaintop", we must straighten our backs, because no one can ride you unless your back is bent.

What can be done to elevate the aspirations of black people? One thing we can do is to review the history of black people who aspired to do great things and were successful. Here are two great examples:

1. The Harlem Renaissance, also known as the "New Negro Movement," was a powerful turning point in black cultural history. In the 1920s, the movement helped writers and artists gain control of the representation of black culture. The movement worked to help bolster and redefine black people as a force in American life. They were guided by the principles of self-definition, self-reliance, self-expression, and self-determination. The Harlem Renaissance helped to redefine how Americans and the world understood African American culture. It integrated black and white cultures and

marked the beginning of a black urban society. The Harlem Renaissance set the stage for the civil rights movement of the 1950s and '60s.

2. In 2019, Tyler Perry launched one of the biggest movie studios on a former Confederate army base in Atlanta, Georgia. He endured a long journey to get to this place. He had realized that no institution will give you a space to articulate a vision of the world that undermines their power at their expense. Years prior, Perry had been picked up by a major network to do a show, but the notes from the studio said that he wasn't allowed to say "Jesus" in the sitcom. How many people would have compromised that to secure an opportunity to work with one of the largest viewerships on television? What happens when your dream is a threat to someone else's reality? In his case, he was ignored. So he ultimately purchased a studio whose size now is a combination of Disney, Paramount, and Warner combined. At a time when black people were praying for opportunities to be given, he created his own opportunity by building a studio. Despite his success, he is ignored in Hollywood. Black people have always had to engage in a world where, at best, those in power didn't look like them and were non-responsive to them—and at worst, were hostile to them and wanted to marginalize them. Tyler Perry's example shows you can't lose at their game if you don't play. Perry made his own lane. One journalist called him "the most successful mogul that Hollywood has ever ignored." But Perry's definition of success is ownership. When someone asked him if he would let his son play football, he replied, "If he owns the team." Black people in America have managed to do great things, in spite of America's climate of racial hostility.

We have great examples historically and contemporarily of black people who didn't allow racial hostility to change their intention and ambition. They defined their success. You can, too.

For additional exercises and tools, see Chapter 12 – Define Your Success in *Bridge the Gaps – Lessons on Self-Awareness, Self-Development and Self-Care*. Visit www.amazon.com or www.thebridg330.com to pick up a copy.

Dreams to Reality: What Will You Do to Get There?

Dreams will remain dreams unless they generate a clear vision of what you want to happen.

AT THE HEART OF A dream is change. A dream is a cherished aspiration, ambition, or ideal. Our dreams and visions push us forward, mandate our focus, spark creativity, and stir a sense of urgency and toughness. They keep us motivated and persistent.

One of the ways to turn dreams into reality is with information and reflection, because you will bring to fruition what you have the most clarity on. That's why education is so vital. You want to relentlessly search for models and systems that can help you get to where you want to go and accomplish the purpose you have in mind.

"Hope that is put off makes the heart sick, but a desire that comes into being is a tree of life." (Proverbs 13:12, NLV) Real pleasure comes from seeing what you envision in your mind become reality. It all starts with the dream.

Human beings, through the imagination, have the remarkable ability to finish something before we start it. Everything you see in the man-made world began as a thought in someone's mind. You can, in your own way, become a resident of a world that does not yet exist. When you experience the realization of your vision, there is a joy like no other, particularly if you put in hours, days, months, and even years to reach it.

When I reached major goals in my life, I realized how athletes who win championships, people who pass difficult tests, and people who get accepted into their school of choice feel. As a mentor, you must identify and cultivate your own dreams and demonstrate your commitment to achieving them and your joy when they are attained.

Someone during prison ministry mentioned to me that they wanted their kids to dream big, but that first, they would have to realize that they were dreaming too small. Before we can teach young people to dream big, we must do so ourselves, and we must include others—because if your dream only includes you, it's too small.

Bryan Stevenson is the author of *Just Mercy, A Story of Justice and Redemption* and the founder of the Equal Justice Initiative (www.eji.org), a human rights organization in Montgomery, Alabama. Through his work as a public interest lawyer for the incarcerated, the condemned, and the poor, he has saved dozens of people from the death penalty.

In short, Stevenson's work is a miracle, because he didn't meet a lawyer until he got to law school. By God's grace and his tenacity, he stuck to his ideals and tried to become something he'd never seen.

When he got to Harvard's law school, he was tempted to compromise and settle for a life that he was not meant to live. In school, he didn't hear anything that addressed race, poverty, and inequity—the topics he cared most about. But he refused to become well-adjusted to injustice and pursue the corrupted American Dream of peacocking and posturing.

His dream went further than the American Dream. He had a dream of justice. Believing the dots would connect, he followed his convictions, though it led him off the well-worn path. I believe that God gives us lamps, not flashlights, so that we can take the next step even though we can't see the road ahead.

As a mentor, you are like a midwife for people's dreams. When someone tells you their dreams, it's almost like they are letting you hold their child. The best ideas can only be born with very trusting midwives. You want your mentees to feel safe telling you their dreams. (See Safe Leader Assessment)

All of us are capable of having big ideas about what life is and should be like. Unfortunately, many of us were not given the space to express our unique ambitions. Lerone Bennett, Jr., a black scholar and social historian, was a student at Morehouse College in 1945 with Dr. Martin Luther King,

Jr. He admits that he knew Martin would go on to do something great, but he didn't know that he would turn the world upside down.

The moral that Bennett draws is that there is no way to tell about the mystery of the human personality. As a mentor, regularly remind yourself that you may feel sure of who the mentee is today, but you don't know who they will become tomorrow. When you give your mentee attention and validation, you let them know that their ideas are valuable, and you give them permission to operate within the context of the dreams they have of themselves.

Unfortunately, many mentors question the visions their mentees share because they don't line up with their own script. As a matter of safety, *never* criticize the dream of your mentee. Your job is to help them ground their dreams in reality and a positive direction and to find out if the dream is a possibility or just a fantasy. That grounding takes place in the goal-setting process.

As Proverbs 28:19 (NIV) says: "Those who work their land will have abundant food, but those who chase fantasies will have their fill of poverty." A dream is rooted in reality and backed by work. A fantasy is rooted in fiction and laziness.

When you focus on what's possible instead of what's difficult, your dream becomes attainable. You see the opportunity instead of the obligation. Bryan Stevenson's dream was justice and social equality. He was willing to wake up early, stay up late, and allow his life to be animated for this dream. Each day contributed to the dream he had of justice for the most broken people in society.

When you make space for your mentee to make their own choices after laying out the options (including the options you suggest), they will be more inspired to move forward, because they'll have a heightened sense of control and autonomy.

Remember, *your* excitement about a goal is irrelevant. It's about their excitement and more importantly, their self-sustained motivation. One of the most frustrating things as a mentor is having bigger dreams for people than they have for themselves. But with wisdom, you can coach your mentee to dig deeper.

Here are some exercises to help you do that:

Exercise 1: What is your dream for what life could be?
After completing the first section and getting a sense of your purpose, you now want to begin to identify what dream (cherished aspiration, ambition, or ideal) moves you in this season of your life?

_____

_____

_____

Exercise 2: Practical Dreaming: Write Your Vision
And then God answered: "Write this. Write what you see. Write it out in big block letters so that it can be read on the run. This vision-message is a witness pointing to what's coming. It aches for the coming—it can hardly wait! And it doesn't lie. If it seems slow in coming, wait. It's on its way. It will come right on time. (Habakkuk 2:2, MSG)

The greatest pull on your life should be the pull of your dream. Your life is unique, so the manifestation of your dream must unique as well. Once that dream is well-designed, you can face the future with anticipation instead of apprehension. When the future gets clear, the price seems easier.

It is my hope that the uniqueness of your purpose will transform into practical, time-stamped goals. Acknowledging and celebrating the past is great, but without a vision of how to improve on the past, we will never move beyond it.

The first thing that you want to bring into focus is your mental picture of your goal fulfilled. That's where the improvement begins, because you can only hit what you aim at. Writing down your goals speaks to your belief that you are worth taking the time to give your life structure. With each action you take, you're painting the picture of the vision you possess.

It's been said that we overrate what we can do in a year and underrate what we can do in ten years, so let your goals reflect long-distance vision as well as short-term. What goals can you accomplish over the next six months, one year, three years, or five years to bring your dream into fruition?

As a mentor, just because you're excited about a certain goal or course of action doesn't mean your mentee will be, and vice versa. Ask yourself what you will be doing five or ten years from now and write it down.

Six-month goal(s)

_____

_____

_____

One-year goal(s)

_____

_____

_____

Three-year goal(s)

_____

_____

_____

Five-year goal(s)

_____

_____

_____

Ten-year goal(s)

_____

_____

_____

Exercise 3: Prime the Pump of Your Dreams

We have to create environments where people feel safe to stumble, crawl, and walk to their greatness. We often become so goal oriented that we neglect the process of creating a vision and bringing it into fruition.

Even more important than a job, young people need a vision of their purpose manifesting in their life—because vision without execution is just hallucination. You may not be able to do all that you find, but at least find all that you can do. What can you do in the next six months to bring your vision into fruition?

Suggestions

1. Get proximate to the places that will animate your purpose and allow your dream to develop its own footing.
   a. While in law school, Bryan Stevenson eagerly signed up for a class on poverty and race litigation, which required him to spend time at a social justice organization doing justice work. Through this experience, he met a black man on death row who was the same age he was. This led him to fight harder to learn the laws and doctrines that shape policy and criminal procedure.
2. Create a list of books you can read in the area of choice.
   a. Stevenson made a list of the courses he would take on the death penalty and extreme punishments, to understand how to approach the issue. Most people don't succeed in what they are going after because they don't take the time to research; they ask for things and then see if they want them.
3. Identify whom you can connect with and learn from, to discover exactly what it will take to realize your dream. (Proverbs 20:18, MSG): Form your purpose by asking for counsel. Also see Chapter 9 – Models and Mentors in Bridge the Gaps.
   a. It's difficult to accomplish a goal when you're not accustomed to seeing people do it. When you do see someone like you become successful, you don't count yourself out.
4. What classes/conferences/workshops do you need to attend?
5. How will you, as a mentor, hold the mentee accountable for their goal?
   a. Will there be regular check-ins?

6. What resources will need to be made available to the mentee to reach his/her goals?
7. If there were no limits and it was impossible to fail, what dream would you wholeheartedly go after?
    a. We have to believe in things that we haven't seen, particularly as it relates to black people, because creativity and imagination are integral in creating change.
8. Count the cost. (Luke 14:28, NLT). Many people want to accomplish different things. Most simply have no idea what it's going to cost them. People want great things, but they have no idea what the price will be. Every dream takes longer than you want it to.

For additional exercises and tools, see Chapters 8 – Models and Mentors; Chapter 15 – SMART Goals; Chapter 11 – Why You Should Set Goals; and Chapter 23 - Decisions in *Bridge the Gaps – Lessons on Self-Awareness, Self-Development and Self-Care*. Visit www.amazon.com or www.thebridg330.com to pick up a copy.

Jonathan Frejuste

Expertise: Greatness Takes Time
Each of you as a good manager must use the gift that God has given you to serve others.
1 Peter 4:10, GW

BEFORE ROSA PARKS REFUSED TO give up her seat on that Alabama bus on December 1, 1955, young men were carving out a path of excellence in their own right. Those men were the Tuskegee Airmen. They were the first black military aviators in the US armed forces.

During WWII, despite being subject to Jim Crow laws, these men served the US faithfully. By 1945, it was reported by the *Chicago Defender* that the 332nd Fighter Group—which escorted bombers and defended from enemy planes—suffered no losses of bombers after 200 missions.

These black men were excellent in their work. Their talent to fly helped to eradicate the stereotypes of black inferiority and restore a sense of pride in the black community. These men had a collective sense of purpose and developed their craft to help uplift their people.

As one black educator said, the rescue of a people can only be done by exceptional men. The Tuskegee airmen were those exceptional men. The freedom that black people took back was even sweeter when the talents, skills, and abilities of black people were developed to such a great level of excellence.

From the last section, I discussed Bryan Stevenson's dream of justice. His dream could not have been realized unless he had constantly developed his craft. His purpose started with his frustration about the justice system and evolved into a focus on developing the skills necessary to get a job done.

After meeting with the young man on Death Row in the days before he was an attorney, he was motivated to learn more. He took many courses on litigation, federal courts, constitutional law, appellate procedure, and collateral remedies. His desire to sharpen his abilities was based on his acute sense of purpose, which was afforded to him by his proximity to the problems. Simply, he got close to what he cared about and saw what he needed to do.

Many young people know their passion and their purpose but lack a process to become proficient at something. Part of having a fulfilling and productive life is finding a talent and then turning it into a strength. Accessing human talent and ability is too unique to be confined to a formula, but there are some overarching elements for achieving mastery of your chosen craft:

Connect your purpose with your gifts and talents

Identify your gifts and talents. See Chapter *4 Gifts, Talents, Skills and Strengths* in *Bridge the Gaps*. The eye can't see the eye. Have your community provide you with feedback. See Chapter 5, *What Do Other People See in You*.

Help your mentees find the gift and talent that they can become world-class at: mindset. Here's a hint. Whatever you can do obsessively is what you have the potential to be world-class at.

It's rare to find someone who had clarity in advance about how their talent would connect with their purpose. That takes time and often, trial and error. You must fight to remind yourself that each person has genius and an enormous level of talent, but both often remain dormant.

Ava Duvernay used her gifting to create movies and series, including *When They See Us*.

Dr. Martin Luther King, Jr. used his keen spiritual insight to highlight the immorality of segregation and awaken the conscience of a nation.

Lebron James used his gift for basketball to create new entrepreneurial models for inner-city youth. He also went on to start a school.

Robert Smith used his gift for business to pay off the debt of the graduates of Morehouse College in May of 2019.

Reflection: What untapped gifts do I need to acknowledge?

_____

_____

_____

Have a standard of performance consistent with greatness

It's hard to be what you've never seen. It's hard to aspire to heights that you've never seen reached. This requires that you identify who is a master of their craft and commit to practicing consistently, reaching toward their level.

"Observe people who are good at their work. Skilled workers are always in demand and admired; they don't take a backseat to anyone." (Proverbs 22:29, MSG.) "Iron sharpens iron." Proverbs 27:17, NIV. Identify your craft and put the 10,000 hours in. See Chapter 24 of *Bridge the Gaps – Lessons on Self-Awareness, Self-Development and Self-Care*.

Time and work are the price you pay for greatness. I'm a big believer that when you study all the great people in your craft, it's impossible to not be inspired. You automatically start drawing from people who have done it before.

Expand your exposure. Teach your mentees to trace the steps of those they look up to and see what positive habits or action steps fit their own journeys. Listen to those who are farther along the same path, and learn from their successes and failures.

Rather than being a fan, be a student of great people. Find the person who is the best at their craft and then prune their philosophy to fit the context of your purpose.

Submit to a process of development
"Give yourselves to disciplined instruction; open your ears to tested knowledge." (Proverbs 23:11, MSG)

When you first get started, the size of your dream probably outweighs your mastery of the craft by tenfold. While it's true that "a person's gift makes room for him, and leads him before important people," that gift will not nurture itself (Proverbs 18:16, NET). This is where structure becomes important.

Many people have passion, but they need a *process* to give their gift time to mature. Pay your dues with preparation and education Desire without knowledge is not good. (Proverbs 19:2, NIV)

All people who intend on growing and learning will, at some point, go through the feeling of incompetence. That's part of the learning curve. It's usually a two-step process. You realize you want to do something, and then you realize your abilities are lacking—not because you lack talent, but because your gift hasn't yet been cultivated.

Your power of choice includes the choice to work on being better. Adults have a harder time at this than young people. If you want to improve, old or young, you must learn to be comfortable with the feeling of incompetence that comes with learning something new.

Don't skip steps. Go through the process. You'll be better for it. Don't be afraid to go slowly. Be afraid to stand still. Ignorance cannot be an excuse when the resources are available. If you want to make a difference with your craft, your free time isn't free. It belongs to the craft.

It's been said that post-season success in sports comes from pre-season practice. You can't control how long the game is, but you can control how long you'll practice for the game.

Tools of Development

1. Repetition in the dark—Repetition is the road to turning talent in strengths. If you don't see greatness in rehearsal, you won't see it in recital. Can you play without clapping? Quantity leads to quality. Develop memory within your specialty. Experts develop indexes of information that they can relay to you at any point in time. Constantly working on your craft keeps you from being obsolete. Professionals strive to do things until they can't get it wrong.

2. Reading—This is the greatest piece of advice I've ever heard. Read more books and do more personal development than anyone in your profession.

3. Focus—Learn how to engage in your work with no distractions. Cultivate distraction-free concentration and work with intensity to hone your cognitive abilities. The process of developing mastery of your craft will have its share of complications, so focus is vitally important. As our world changes, this skill is becoming increasingly important. A simultaneous phenomenon is that the number of potential distractions is increasing. Many people live in a state of partial inattention. Practice giving one thing at a time the priority of your focus.

4. Embrace failure. Keep failing, and fail better. Feeling bad about your performance of a particular skill is not only a good thing—it's a necessary prerequisite to improving and eventually achieving mastery.

5. Develop a great work ethic. It's been said that you should think of rest as a necessity and not a destination. For many

people, natural talent and ability can sustain their success in life, but at some point, the returns will diminish. Only tenacity, commitment, and hard work will yield high achievement. Stay within striking distance of excellence, because you won't have to get ready if you stay ready. Some opportunities do not become available unless you are fine-tuned to get that shot. When you work hard to become an expert, you let your work do the talking. Don't miss out on something that could be great just because it could be very hard. Great opportunities are usually disguised as hard work. Young adults have to push through a sense of entitlement that urges them to leapfrog over the hard work that those who came before them did to provide them with a potential to do more. Mastery requires not just effort, but sustained effort. To achieve a standard of excellence and accomplish anything extraordinary means aiming high and being disciplined and willing to devote long hours to the task at hand.

- Olympic athletes train for years just to experience the thrill of one winning moment.

- Virtuoso musicians practice endlessly just to keep their skills at peak performance.

- The scientist who wins the Nobel Prize has experimented and refined his theories over the course of a career.

6. Iterate. You develop expertise by repeating the same action again and again. You developed a skillset by repeating a set of actions iteratively. Nothing happens overnight. You pick up gold one nugget at a time.

7. Value obscurity. The cost of notoriety is safety, because you can lose credibility when your visibility surpasses your ability. It's harder to take risks when people are watching you. Anyone who became great at anything became great by first criticizing their own performance. It's not a great feeling to be criticized about your performance, but it is necessary to get honest feedback. If you sweat more in practice, you'll bleed less in the battle. The best time to perfect your gift is when you're out of the public eye. Then you can prepare yourself emotionally and mentally for the exposure. You can make low-cost mistakes when the lights are not on you or the audience is smaller.

8. Find your element. This work is too hard to only be concerned with the results. There has to be an element in the work itself that aligns with something you derive enjoyment from. See Chapter 6 – Work Styles. A Word to Parents: When you, as a parent, invest in your child and that investment doesn't produce the desired result, don't stop investing in your child, as many parents do. As a parent, you can encourage vocational experiments/investments without recklessly spending money. Continue to encourage freedom for a young person trying to find their niche while understanding that there will be false starts.

9. Respect the process. Be faithful. In football, receivers are taught to catch the ball, secure it, and then make a move. They practice this over and over again. Start with the basics until you can't get them wrong. Focus on being deliberate and clear on the process of developing your skill. Part of respecting the process is being open to discoveries about yourself.

10. Focus on getting better, not just being good. A perspective that focuses on progress rather than perfection will help you maximize your talents. Fortunately, there's no time frame on practice. You will become a life-long learner in your area of expertise.

See Chapter 24 – 10,000 Hours in *Bridge the Gaps – Lessons on Self-Awareness, Self-Development, and Self-Care*. Go to www.thebridge330.com to pick up a copy.

7: Permission to Be Courageous Toolkit

We give up our power when we choose to believe we don't have any.

THE STORY ABOUT INVESTMENT—"IT'S ALSO *like a man going off on an extended trip. He called his servants together and delegated responsibilities. To one he gave five thousand dollars, to another two thousand, to a third one thousand, depending on their abilities. Then he left. Right off, the first servant went to work and doubled his master's investment. The second did the same. But the man with the single thousand dug a hole and carefully buried his master's money. After a long absence, the master of those three servants came back and settled up with them. The one given five thousand dollars showed him how he had doubled his investment. His master commended him: 'Good work! You did your job well. From now on be my partner.'* "The servant with the two thousand showed how he also had doubled his master's investment. His master commended him: 'Good work! You did your job well. From now on be my partner.' The servant given one thousand said, 'Master, I know you have high standards and hate careless ways, that you demand the best and make no allowances for error. I was afraid I might disappoint you, so I found a good hiding place and secured your money. Here it is, safe and sound down to the last cent.' The master was furious. 'That's a terrible way to live! It's criminal to live cautiously like that! If you knew I was after the best, why did you do less than the least? The least you could have done would have been to invest the sum with the bankers, where at least I would have gotten a little interest. Take the thousand and give it to the one who risked the most. And get rid of this 'play-it-safe' who won't go out on a limb."* (Matthew 25:14-29, MSG)

In this story, the third servant with a thousand dollars was not reprimanded for being afraid. He was reprimanded for not confronting his fear and doing the best he could to be productive. Refusing to confront one's fears to use the gifts given insults the giver of the gift.

This story demonstrates that trying to avoid and/or mitigate every risk is the riskiest thing you can do. The essence of this story is that living too cautiously keeps you from fully taking advantage of every opportunity given and can even cause you to lose what you had in the first place.

We could say that the third servant in the story has been victimized by a "learned helplessness." Instead of taking the money and taking a risk to capitalize on what he had, he buried it and lost out on any opportunity to multiply it, because he feared the potential wrath of the master.

I wonder who taught this man to bury the money instead of invest it? Who taught him to fear failure, disapproval, and/or loss? Where did he learn to act helplessly and hopelessly? From his parents? His society? His community? His friends? His culture?

Unfortunately, many people were raised in homes where they were taught—intentionally or unintentionally—to be and feel helpless and hopeless about their future possibilities.

As a person who was raised in a black community and who now works with a predominantly black audience, I recognize the same behavior pattern of the third servant in some of the people I work with. For many black people, fear is the dominant emotion. You might say being black in America and being afraid go hand in hand.

In the days of slavery, there was inculcation of fear that was so deep that some slaves would adopt the master's ways wholesale, just to be safe. After slavery, thousands of black people were lynched by the KKK and other racist whites. The survivors moved to safer parts of the nation in search of work.

Black men in the North and Midwest who wanted jobs as steel workers, plumbers, carpenters, or electricians did not have access to the union jobs and were denied because blacks were not given union cards. This discrimination limited their income, their chances of success, and their hopes of a better life. Eventually, many of them gave up their dreams.

This emotional reality evolved over the course of black American history until today. In the black community, the legacy of trauma has been fear. Fear has put them in a psychological and emotional box, where they feel hopelessness and defeat.

I need look no further than one of the most insidious forms of trauma that black people have faced – Post Traumatic Slave Syndrome (PTSS). The phrase was coined by Dr. Joy Degruy, the author of *Post Traumatic Slave Syndrome*. PTSS is a condition of trauma that exists as a consequence of hundreds of years of chattel slavery followed by decades of lynching and institutionalized oppression, followed by the mass incarceration of black men and the institutionalization of the black family.

One of the effects of PTSS is learned helplessness. Learned helplessness is a condition in which a person suffers from powerlessness as a result of trauma and/or a persistent reality of personal failure and witnessing the failure from those around them. Learned helplessness wastes the time and potential that should be used to accomplish one's purpose in life.

Fortunately, anyone who views life with a learned helplessness can unlearn it and begin to take steps toward living courageously.

What does learned helplessness look like?
Passivity, giving up, lack of effort, failure to ask for help, procrastination, poor motivation, and negative thinking.
How do you solve learned helplessness?
Through learned self-efficacy. Whatever you want people to become, you must become yourself first. You have to show them what it looks like to execute. Often, mentees won't do what you say, but they will do what they see modeled. They learn how to move through the world through the people in their environment.

You must provide mentees with a new script for pursuing their purpose, starting with your own example. Why? Because it's hard to impart lessons that you don't live. It's hard to teach someone to courageously pursue his or her purpose if you're not in courageous pursuit of yours.

Far too many people opt for a life of fear, but it's important to "not lose your courage, then, because it brings with it a great reward." (Hebrews 10:35 GNT)

Courage is not the lack of fear, but the conclusion that something else matters more than your fear. Another helpful definition of courage is knowing what to fear and what not to fear. You'll never reach your destination if you consistently acknowledge the wrong fears. You will be successful to the extent that you eliminate the wrong fears, embrace the right ones, and keep them in check.

Left unchecked, the wrong fears can infiltrate every corner of our lives, break down our confidence, increase our anxiety, and take us down a path of comfortable and cautious mediocrity and self-sabotage. We can't change destructive patterns of underachievement and failure with rationalization. It's changed with courage.

Courage won't guarantee your success in breaking cycles, but it always precedes it. When you're ready to be productive, irrational fear can creep up on you. Before you can take control of your life outwardly, you must do so first inwardly.

Fear will always be present, but we want to have the right fears. To change a community, you have to tell them what their real fears should be. If we as mentors want to change the world around us, we must take control of the world within us. That starts by acknowledging and facing your fears.

Here are three fears to address:
1. *Fear of Reality: Denial and Procrastination*
2. *Fear of "Breaking the Rules": Conformity and Dependency*
3. *Fear of Raising Expectations: Mediocrity and Self-Sabotage*

Fear of Reality: Denial and Procrastination
If you tell yourself a story long enough, you will begin to believe it.

THERE WAS AN AMERICAN PRISONER of war who was housed for almost ten years in a POW camp. He was repeatedly tortured and kept isolated from the other POWs. In an interview he did after he was released, he was asked which of the POWs didn't survive the torture and abuse. His response was *the optimists*.

From his perspective, the optimists were the ones who thought they would be released sooner than was likely. They didn't take full stock of the reality of the situation. As a result, they didn't prepare themselves for the harshness, and subsequently folded under pressure.

There's a fine line between faith and folly, between positive thinking and being delusional. The surviving POW's approach while in the prison was to face the harsh facts of the situation at hand without losing his unwavering faith that one day, he'd be free. He accepted the reality of your situation without capitulating to it.

The psychology that saved his life is also used by successful Fortune 500 companies and world leaders. It can be summed up in two statements: Face the Facts and Hold On to Your Faith. How good are you are assessing the reality of the situation you're in and the goal/dream/purpose you're pursuing? Let's do some reflection.

Reality-Testing Reflection

Below is an exercise to get a sense of your ability to stay grounded, be accurately tuned into situations, and see things as they are. In order to put reality to work, you want to reflect on whether your bias has affected your performance. Don't feel rushed to complete this process. Take your time and engage with reflection.

1. I always see circumstances as they truly are.
2. I know what resources I need and what resources are available to help me achieve my purpose.
3. I understand when I need to be more impartial.
4. I know when my biases get in the way of my perception.
5. Even when I'm angry, I stay aware of what's happening to me.
6. I have a good feel for what is going on in my environment.
7. I fully utilize my skills and talents to serve my purpose in the world.
8. I do my due diligence to get all the information I need to make the most informed decision.
9. I acknowledge when a strategy needs to be adjusted to accomplish my purpose.
10. I put controls in place to keep me from making biased decisions.

Reviewing your results in light of your current circumstances should give you an indication of whether you have made decisions rooted in reality and where you can grow and improve in your ability to face reality.

Self-assessment is hard for many people. If your mentee allows you to see that he is struggling, you need to honor, respect, and protect them for their courage and effort in the process. That's the work we have to do.

It takes courage to be able to evaluate whether our thinking is consistent with reality, for better or worse. We also need to be comfortable with nuance in our planning.

The older I get, the more I realize that things are not always black and white. In spite of ambiguity, we have to be able to set goals and adjust them accordingly as circumstances change. That might be one of the hardest lessons that I learned over the year. A fearless inventory of where you are on the road to being productive in your purpose is vital, but it's not easy.

Quit Faulty Thinking—Challenge Your Assumptions

Faulty thinking is basically telling yourself something that is not true. It is a prison of self-deception. When you tell yourself something false about a situation, you run the risk of suffering more in your imagination than in real life, because we tend to interpret things negatively than positively.

To be empowered, we must remember that we can choose what story we tell ourselves, and we have the ability to see if those stories are true. It starts with checking your ego.

Give up being right about the way you do and see things, and be willing to investigate your assumptions. We make assumptions because we don't have the courage to ask questions. The type of faulty thinking to address will be type associated to the feeling of learned helplessness.

Common Faulty Thinking Patterns of Learned Helplessness

1. Things will never change. Allowing the past to predict the future is one idea that demonstrates learned helplessness, as addressed in the introduction to this chapter. When you're in the middle of a troubling situation, your emotions can make you feel like it will never end. But you always have control of your response.

2. It's all my fault. Not everything that happens to us happens *because of* us. On the flip side, we tend to remember our actions and experiences to our advantage. You have some control about how you will react to what happened, but it starts with acknowledging the reality. It's been said that we can see what we prepare ourselves to see. When we are/remain unwilling to

confront the version of the story we have taught to ourselves, we often and either give ourselves too much or not enough credit.

3. Everything is ruined. When something goes wrong in one area, it doesn't mean that all areas are negatively affected. Recognizing the other aspects of life that remain positive can help you cultivate an attitude of gratitude, which allows you to approach the negative situation with hope.

Here are some questions to get to the bottom of these thought patterns:

1. What beliefs do I have about the situation I'm facing? Psychologists found that we sometimes actively ignore information that flies in the face of our own views, and we actively seek out information that supports it. This is referred to as confirmation bias.
2. Am I allowing unsubstantiated beliefs to affect my decisions about a situation?
3. Do my beliefs about my current position in life expand or diminish my possibilities?
4. Can I find evidence to contradict my beliefs?
5. Have people in similar situations accomplished what I feel like cannot?
6. In what ways have I, as a black person, cast people (mainly white people) as antagonists and made myself feel incapable and powerless? Many black people I've worked with need to diagnose why they are not making progress. This question is always relevant.
7. What beliefs could I adopt to shift my negative views to positive views, without becoming delusional?

8. If I change my beliefs, what will the tradeoff be? Sometimes we feel powerful when we perceive ourselves as victims. Sometimes misery is comforting because it feels so familiar.

Reality Assessment and Adjustment Tools: Curiosity and Calibration

We can replace faulty thinking in two steps: curiosity and calibration. It's been said that to foresee is to rule. Here are some questions to help you identify opportunities and threats to you and your purpose.

Curiosity—Be Eager to Learn/Investigate Each Situation

Think of each of the positive and negative things that can happen with the goal you're pursuing. Reflect on and answer these questions.

1. What's the likelihood of said event or circumstance?

2. Can delay cause me to lose an opportunity or face avoidable obstacles?

3. What am I refusing to fully take control of and responsibility for that I have power over?

4. Are there inevitable situations that I need to prepare for? You can't change the inevitable. You can only postpone it.

Calibration—Adjusting Yourself to the Situation You're Facing

If you take your head out of the sand, strip away all the noise, and ask the pivotal questions, you'll be able to calibrate your perspective to the situation correctly. The sooner you can surrender to what you can't change, the sooner you can create the change you want.

1. What opportunities exist in my present situation that can help me achieve my purpose, now or in the future?

2. What can I do to prepare to increase my chances of reaching my goal?

3. What steps do I need to take to prevent errors?

Embrace the Givens and Inevitables of Your Situation While Projecting a New Reality

Two of the most dynamic leaders in black history were Malcolm X and Dr. Martin Luther King, Jr. Both were thoughtful, intelligent, and charismatic leaders who seemed to have opposite perspectives on progress for black people in America. Malcom X wanted us to fully embrace where we were in the struggle for freedom, while Martin Luther King, Jr. focused on projecting a new reality through leading with ideals rooted in his dream.

To deny reality is to miss the chance to expand your sense of reality and a deepened sense of purpose. When you refuse to face reality, you become your biggest enemy. Whether it's preparing for an exam, considering going back to school for retraining, facing your finances, facing mistakes in your career, or taking charge of your health, the challenge won't determine how productive you are—but the way you face it will.

I often encounter people who are quick to tell me all the things that can go wrong. They often see themselves as wise guides, when in fact, they are wolves in sheep's clothing. A wise person who recognizes the finite nature of life will, of course, advise you to be prudent—but they will also make you aware of the opportunities available and point you in the right direction.

We must keep two perspectives in balance: strategic optimism and defensive pessimism.

Strategic Optimism vs. Defensive pessimism
Another way to say this is: You want to aspire for the best and anticipate the worst. Perspective becomes especially important as you pursue your purpose. You want to stay grounded in reality, but also inspired to act.

Strategic optimism is a perspective that lends itself to high expectations for the future, which contributes to a sense of well-being and abundance in the present. Certain goals require a vitality and energy that transcend obstacles that you may face along the way. In addition, when you are motivated, you increase the likelihood of taking action to reach your goal.

But how can you increase your optimism? According to the expectancy value theory of motivation, your motivation to do something is correlated to the likelihood of success and also the value of the benefit you'll receive. You can manipulate both factors to increase the likelihood of your success.

- Take time to develop yourself personally. It's amazing how your picture of the future changes when you begin to develop skills. See Chapter 16 – Personal Development in *Bridge the Gaps*.

- Identify role models who inspire you to be and do more in life. See Chapter 9 – Models and Mentors in *Bridge the Gaps*.

- Develop a framework for problem solving. See Chapter 26 – Problem Solving in *Bridge the Gaps*.

- Work on your confidence. See Chapter 13 – Self-Regard in *Bridge the Gaps*.

- Monitor your self-talk. See Chapter 27 – Obstacles in *Bridge the Gaps*.

- Learn how to deal with failure. See Chapter 28 – Failure in *Bridge the Gaps*.

Defensive pessimism is a strategy in which we use anxiety to increase productivity. With this strategy, the worst scenarios are anticipated and planned for. We mentally rehearse things that could go wrong in a given situation. This perspective sounds depressing, but it actually helps some people to anticipate and regulate their emotions to act effectively. Ironically, accepting reality paradoxically reduces its intensity and increases your ability to commit.

Can you use defensive pessimism to your advantage? This mindset can help you be more realistic about all the factors in a situation, which might provide valuable clues.

- Carefully consider all the conceivable negative outcomes if you go in a certain direction.

- Ask yourself how you might prevent those outcomes or decrease their likelihood.

- Think about how you would address any issues that occur and who you might reach out to for help.

- Consider the cost of inaction emotionally, physically, and financially.

Both perspectives can be helpful. As you move toward your purpose, holding these two perspectives in tension will be important. It's easy to become imbalanced according to your natural personality trait. Personally, I lean on the side of being a defensive pessimist. When the imbalance happens on the side of defensive pessimism, I tend to excessively and unhealthily concern myself with the details of the goal and miss the big picture and the possibility that things may go wrong.

On the flip side, if you are a strategic optimist, you have to be careful that you don't engage in delusional thinking. Research shows that people who believe they will succeed easily are less likely to engage in the activities necessary to reach their goals. Motivation is determined in part by how hard you think the task(s) will be. So while it's great to believe it's possible, you also must anticipate how challenging it will be. For maximum results, hold both mindsets in balance.

Jonathan Frejuste

Fear of "Breaking the Rules": Conformity and Dependency

One Sabbath, when Jesus went to eat in the house of a prominent Pharisee, he was being carefully watched. There in front of him was a man suffering from abnormal swelling of his body. Jesus asked the Pharisees and experts in the law, "Is it lawful to heal on the Sabbath or not?" But they remained silent. So taking hold of the man, he healed him and sent him on his way. Then he asked them, "If one of you has a child or an ox that falls into a well on the Sabbath day, will you not immediately pull it out?" And they had nothing to say. (Luke 14:1-6, NIV)

IN THIS STORY, THE PHARISEES insist on the overriding importance of the rule of law, while neglecting the *spirit* of the rule of law. The basic dignity and genuine needs of human beings are more important than following rituals and practices for their own sake. When a rule undermines its intention, it should be reconsidered, or the act should be an accepted deviation because the greater principle was upheld.

The worst thing we can do is follow a rule just because it's in place, when there are more effective and honorable alternatives. Geoffrey Canada understands this all too well. He is the black anti-poverty reform advocate and founder of the Harlem Children's Zone, a pioneering nonprofit organization committed to ending generational poverty. His organization has served more than 10,000 children over the last twenty years.

Based on Canada's experience in the 1950s and 1960s, in order for the black people in his mother's generation to get a job, they had to be subservient to their white bosses. Racial dehumanization was so ubiquitous in workplaces that black people were forced to bow down and compromise their dignity to put food on the table. They had to know their place. They couldn't speak up, or they would be fired.

Because of white dominance and subjugation, many black people were forced to bow down symbolically. They realized how hard the fight against racism would be and acknowledged that life was already hard and short, so they acquiesced to the unfair, racist society.

Unfortunately, black parents passed these survival practices down to the children. Their children also inherited the accompanying perceptions, interpretations, opinions, assumptions, and beliefs about the world—and in many ways, the mindset disempowered them.

I am thankful for those who came before me who made it possible to exercise a greater level of courage in the fight for justice and progress of black people in America. Slavery survival practices were appropriate in adapting to a hostile environment, but they could not be a final solution for people living in a just society.

Acquiescing to injustice also is contradictory to brain science. A person's mind needs to be stimulated to progress and develop in a healthy way. The brain requires active exploration, feedback, challenge, and creative work to get the most out of the educational experience. Essentially, many black parents were teaching their children to be afraid, mediocre, and subservient.

Most parents give their children advice based on their experience. If the dynamics of their experience is anything similar to the type mentioned above, the advice will often be disempowering. If an oppressive, racist system signs your paychecks, passes laws, creates policy, and interprets the world, that system influences your culture.

When those in power are indifferent to the way they harm those subordinate to their authority, they force their subordinates to capitulate to the system, fall into despair, possibly pathology, or rebel and revolt by any available means. This has been my observation.

Refusal to play by the wrong rules means breaking the rules. Something may be a prevailing practice, but that doesn't mean it's moral, useful, or necessary. We have been trained by explicit and unwritten rules on how to live, achieve, and ultimately, who to become. But what happens when rules (explicit and societal) don't serve the best and highest purpose? What happens when social/cultural rules and standard professional practices keep you from doing your best and most honorable work?

Then you must break the rules.

What Does Breaking the Rules Look Like

As American politician and sociologist Daniel Patrick Moynihan discussed in his 1965 report *The Negro Family – The Case for National Action*—specifically in the third section, called "The Roots of the Problem"—he acknowledged the way American chattel slavery differed from the types of servitude in ancient or modern history.

One important aspect of American slavery was that the slave could not practice any religion unless their master granted them permission. The master would have to determine if the slave was being taught the "right" way to practice the faith. The "right" way, in the eyes of the master, was the way that kept them ignorant, disempowered, and continually subservient to the system of slavery.

The rules represent what you've been conditioned to believe is "the right way." According to Carter G. Woodson in *The Miseducation of the Negro,* some enslaved black people were against emancipation and condemned abolitionists. A few free black people actually went back into slavery after emancipation, and others didn't even try to be free because it would disconnect them from their "masters."

This practice highlights one of the legacies of Post-Traumatic Slave Syndrome: looking for the permission of white people to succeed in a chosen path or the desire to remain subordinate to white people to be safe. I heard a minister who started a ministry serving homeless people reflecting on the interactions he had with those he served. He realized that the religious traditions he was accustomed to would render him ineffective in his purpose of effectively serving the people.

From his perspective, either you're going to honor your traditions or you're going to reach the world. To be effective, you can't be more loyal to your traditions than you are your purpose. You must be willing to be the driver of new ideas in a world that is designed to make you conform.

Unfortunately, people living on purpose can unwittingly become part of systems that put pressure on them to compromise their purpose, out of fear of making others uncomfortable or calling into question the values of the dominant culture.

Some of us get stuck in the context of society's opinions, ideas and established patterns of thinking and operating, particularly in group settings. If we are to combat the legacy of the racial dehumanization of black people, we have to be able to allow deep reflection to lead the way in breaking out.

As the Word teaches, "Desire without knowledge is no good." (Proverbs 19:2, NIV) Instead of going down an established path, you may have to go where there is no path and establish a new one with your own values and principles.

There are times and seasons when you have to break the protocol of the day to achieve your purpose. World-renowned actor Denzel Washington told a story about an IQ test where a piece of paper has a box with 9 dots marked within and outside the box. The instruction is given to connect the 9 dots on the page without lifting the pencil. The only way to do it was to go outside the box.

The box represents manmade constructs and ideas. Some people live in so much fear that when you step outside of their box—to pursue a purpose or manifest a dream—they will criticize you, because you remind them that they are living for less they were made for.

Far too often, I see people who, in good faith, give their mentees advice to live safe and secure lives without risk. Of course, I think prudence is advisable, but as you can see from the introductory story, living without taking risks is actually the greatest risk.

I was taught that, in order to be successful, I should not make any mistakes. I should try to get everyone to like me. After some years of observation and reflection, I concluded that this type of thinking will rob you of your destiny and lead you to a life full of compromises.

Of course, this is not suggesting you be obnoxious—but you should never let anyone place you in a box. When you set out for a path where there are new concepts, values, and principles being applied, don't be too concerned with the "right" way. Let the task take you where it may. The rules that you follow will be determined by the purpose you've been given.

Instead of thinking "this better work," think "this might work." Many times, we are deeply entrenched in a particular system. You might need to break small rules in service of your purpose before you develop the courage to break big rules that shift your culture.

In basketball, it's a bad shot until you make it consistently. You might be the only one who knows you took a bad shot. You need to have just as much sense as you have courage.

If what you're going to do will needlessly hurt someone or significantly derail you from your life's path, you need to refrain from acting impulsively. You can go after what you're called to do, but you don't have to deny or hurt anyone else.

If the rules you're following violate or stifle safety, morality, common decency, cultural sensitivity, or effectiveness, you have a duty to reexamine and choose a better way.

When you follow rules to achieve validation from white society, you need to break the rules. Just a heads up—when you're pioneering, you'll be criticized, ridiculed, and condemned by some, and if you succeed, you'll be celebrated. You can normalize the confusion and pain and in a weird way, be thankful for it. It's a blessing and a burden to be the first at anything.

If you can live with the controversy and the people whispering about you, you stand a much better chance of being effective. Recognize your progress so you don't lose hope. Learn from those who have pioneered other ways.

We must frequently question the rules we adhere to. Otherwise, we become servants to the rules, instead of the rules serving our purpose. Ensure that you understand both the letter of the rule and the spirit of the rule.

Examples of Rule-Breakers
Because the greater society avoids acknowledging and addressing controversial racial issues, there is a level of hostility that black people endure culturally, judicially, academically, and economically. One of Carter G. Woodson's main messages in *The Mis-education of the Negro* is that black people have been conditioned to operate under white society's prerogatives for so long that they have been lulled to sleep and have not identified why they do what they do.

Many black people are so used to the manmade sense of prison that the notion of freedom feels like bondage. When someone is constantly victimized, passive living becomes the default response. There's something that happens to a person when they know they are more than their opportunity allows them to be.

What makes it worse is that the black people who had the greatest ability to galvanize the masses of black people to action were ultimately killed, rendering the community hopeless and in disarray. Other black people, out of fatigue or hopelessness, drifted toward compromise. They lost moral courage and acquiesced to the powers that be.

American politician and sociologist Daniel Patrick Moynihan discussed in his 1965 report *The Negro Family – The Case for National Action*—specifically in the third section, called "The Roots of the Problem"—commented that the condition of enslaved Africans did not provide incentive for developing enterprise and initiative. Instead, slavery depressed the need for personal accomplishment and placed the slave in a completely dependent role.

Dr. Martin Luther King, Jr. saw this problem up close. He believed that black people must set themselves free. He said we must reach down into the depths of our own souls, sign our own Declaration of Independence, and refuse to let anyone take our humanity. If we are to achieve freedom, we must no longer wait for someone to validate our vision. We must desire to create our own.

The reality is that you can't change the "rules" until you break the "rules" in your own heart and mind. You can't change the accepted norm until you make a new normal, and that doesn't come without some disruption. Game-changers break "rules."

After slavery was abolished, violent racist attacks continued. It was like black people had a sword in one hand and a shovel in the other. How could we fight and build at the same time?

Whether the threat is real or imagined, it's a real fear that's present in the minds of many black people. There's a sense that the game is rigged when you play by the rules of your conditioning. If that applies to you, you will have to rewrite the rules.

Many significant changes are occurring today, and they need to continue. Everyone's task is as unique as his specific opportunity to implement, so I think it's important to identify relevant examples and highlight. Here are a few.

a. On September 27, 2019, Governor Gavin Newsom signed bill SB 206 (Fair Pay to Play Act) into law allowing NCAA players to accept endorsements. California is the first state passing the law that allows college athletes to be paid for the use of their image, name, or likeness. The governor was urged to veto the bill by several university presidents who feared it would destroy the purity of amateurism. On the flipside, $14 billion goes to the universities and $1 billion revenue goes to the NCAA. The players who support the system receive no financial compensation. Long after some of the college stars graduate, their jerseys are still for sale, but they receive no compensation for their likeness. This includes players like Diana Taurasi from the University of Connecticut, Jason Williams from Duke University, and Andre Iguodala from the University of Arizona. California Senator Steven Bradford commented that, for forty years, black athletes have been exploited for their labor and talent. This bill is an opportunity for them to monetize their image and likeness, which gives them an incentive to stay in school longer.

The person who put significant spotlight on the issue was Ed O'Bannon, the black retired professional player who decided to become the lead plaintiff in the *O'Bannon v. NCAA* antitrust class action lawsuit. O'Bannon, a former UCLA basketball player, saw his likeness from his 1995 championship team on the NCAA Basketball '09 EA Sports game. His likeness was being used without his permission.

The case resulted in a ruling that allowed schools to offer full cost-of-attendance scholarships to athletes and to place as much as $5,000 into a trust for each athlete per year. But under this ruling, the athletes could receive no compensation. SB 206 changed that. This started with people who decided to break the "rules" in order to create fairness and equity.

    b.   Bryan Stevenson, author of *Just Mercy, A Story of Justice and Redemption* and the founder of Equal Justice Initiative (www.eji.org), recognized that it was absurd to have traumatized youth certified to stand trial as adults. From his perspective, if a judge can make you into something that you're not, the judge must have magic ability. In one of his cases, he was representing a fourteen-year-old black male. He wrote a motion asking the court to treat his fourteen-year-old black client as if he were a white, privileged, seventy-five-year-old corporate executive.

The court was upset. Stevenson began to engage in an argument with the court about the nature of his motion and about race, inequality, and poverty. A black custodian came into the courtroom and sat behind Mr. Stevenson. Although the deputy sheriff rebuked him for being in the courtroom, the black custodian told Stevenson to never lose sight of the prize and to hold on. Bryan Stevenson and his staff have won reversals, relief, or release from prison for over 135 wrongly condemned prisoners on death row and won relief for hundreds of others wrongly convicted or unfairly sentenced.

    c. John Singleton made the movie *Rosewood* when he was twenty-six years old. *Rosewood* is a movie about a 1923 racist lynch mob attack in an African American community in Rosewood, Florida. Singleton wanted to ensure that black people had the ability to tell their own stories. He wanted to ensure that the falsehoods of black people being benign during their persecution was eradicated. His intention was to uncover the untold history of black people fighting back against their oppression in the South. Few movies have been made about black Americans' experience with white terrorism, partly because it goes against Hollywood's function to create movies wrapped in heroism. Singleton was pressured by Hollywood executives to change his movie's messaging, but he refused. He didn't work for four years after its release. *Rosewood* was not commercially successful, but his movie now sits in the Library of Congress. Its release sparked tremendous dialogue about the race riots in the 20th century. Instead of trying to make more money, Singleton chose to do something important. He brought to light the undercurrent of a progressive and healing paradigm for black America.

    d. Dr. Joy DeGruy, author of *Post Traumatic Slave Syndrome*, served as a therapist in Portland, Oregon. In her work with people of color, she continued to get written up for violating the ethical standards of psychology as it relates to her work in mental health. Ironically, she had one of the highest success rates of any case manager at any point in the city of Portland. But her work, particularly with black patients, was sometimes deemed inappropriate because she believed that, to be effective, you have to be willing to break the "professional" rules.

The black community has a long history of being mistreated by social workers and social services. Their lack of success in working with people of color was not acknowledged, because the root causes were not validated. Because of DeGruy's willingness to break the rules, she started a national dialogue to speak to unaddressed pain and trauma in the black community. Dr. Joy's work on Post Traumatic Slave Syndrome is being used to shape programs all over the country. It helps to explain maladaptive behaviors in the black community.

e. In January 2019, SB 188—also known as the CROWN Act—was introduced in California by Senator Holly Mitchell. The act was signed into law by Governor Gavin Newsom on July 3rd. CROWN stands for Creating a Respectful and Open World for Natural Hair. This law prevents discrimination based on hairstyles by extending statutory protection to hair texture and styles in state Education Codes and Fair Employment and Housing Act (FEHA).

In 2010, Chastity Jones, a black woman, was offered and accepted a job at an insurance claim-processing company. Jones was told by a white Human Resources employee that she would need to modify her hairstyle. When she refused, the offer was rescinded. Ms. Jones brought a lawsuit against the company, which was dismissed by the district court. The court ruled that dreadlocks are not an unchangeable characteristic of black people. SB 188 serves to correct the profound misunderstanding of ethnic hair by amending section 12926 of the California Fair Employment and Housing Act. As a result of SB 188, there has been a proposal of a federal Crown Act bill to ban discrimination against black hair. The passage of the bill at the federal level would be a watershed moment for black people, especially black women, who have historically been shamed and directed to conform to Eurocentric beauty standards.

Reflection Questions
Unfortunately, many black people are conditioned to believe that speaking the unadulterated truth to white people about what they see and feel is a kamikaze mission. Black people's reticence to speak freely and honestly in front of white people is a result of the memory of violence against black people. This is where we need healing as a people.

Each of us has a certain way of looking at the world, acquired from our early conditioning and our experiences. We face the same choice as the enslaved Africans in the 1700s: develop a way of looking at the world that gives you permission to transcend the "right" way, or be a force of nature in your own life. The more often you act in a certain way, the more habitual the behavior becomes.

What social/cultural rules and standard professional practices are you following that do or do not serve your best and most honorable work?

_____

_____

_____

What can you do to bring about a new, healthier, more effective practice to your work?

_____

_____

_____

Jonathan Frejuste

Fear of Raising Expectations: Self-Sabotage and Mediocrity

God is solid backing to a well-lived life, but he calls into question a shabby performance. Proverbs 10:29, MSG

MAHERSHALA ALI, TWO-TIME OSCAR AWARD winner, said that the difference between black and white men is that black men have to move through the world playing defense, continually looking for the moment when we will be disrupted. He understands this more than most, as a one of the few successful black men in Hollywood.

Others say you have to be twice as good to have half of what white people have. This might or might not be true, depending on what arena you're in and its respective rules. Frankly, living life afraid of this boogeyman called *racism* is exhausting.

American history clearly shows that black people's suspicions are not unfounded. After the end of American chattel slavery, the ambition of black people led them to build great, self-sufficient towns. Unfortunately, several of these black towns were burned to the ground by white racists because of economic competition or because the notion of black success cut the heart out of the white supremacist foundational belief: that black people were not smart and ingenious enough to do anything great on their own.

The sad reality is that the black families who endured this oppression had their dreams crushed. It is not uncommon for this type of experience to lead to a psychology of learned helplessness. Over the years, the process of disenfranchisement, disempowerment, and dehumanization shows up for many black people in self-defeating behaviors. This behavior was adapted and modeled to the next generation of black people, and the cycle continued. In order to end the cycle of low expectations that shows up in self-sabotage and mediocrity, we need to identify the symptoms and provide tools for change.

The reality is that raising expectations carries a physical risk, but also an emotional risk. Another way to describe raising expectations is to *dream bigger*. Before anything can be brought into fruition in the physical, it begins in the mind.

Here are four tools you can use to begin to raise your expectations:
- *Deepen your purpose and values*
- *Create an independent educational tradition*
- *Align your work ethic with your deepest desires*
- *Address your methods of self-sabotage*

Deepen Your Purpose and Values

When constructing a building, the higher you go up, the deeper you have to go to lay the foundation. It's the same way with your life's purpose. In order to raise expectations and aim higher, you'll need deeper self-awareness, deeper levels of courage, and deeper levels of focus.

The anchor for these elements is your set of personal values. It's been said that to know what you truly want is the beginning of wisdom. But you must decide what you actually want, instead of what you've been told you should be pleased with.

As life gets more complex and responsibilities pile up, knowing what you truly want will be an invaluable advantage. Children instinctively try to stay close to their true natures. But when more is demanded of us, we tend to stop doing the things children do. We surrender our high expectations and stifle our imagination about what's possible. Imagining other possibilities for our lives reminds us of the uncomfortable gap between who we truly are and our role in the world.

At some point, we all find ourselves in the midst of some assignment or commitment and ask ourselves, "What am I doing here?" Unfortunately, many people choose to stay in that place of confusion.

Ultimately, they choose mediocrity because it's safer. They end up living lives of quiet misery instead of lives of inspiration.

Perhaps the true reason for your work was blurred because you couldn't connect the value of your labor to your reward. That leaves you open to misuse of resources. When your efforts align with what you truly value, you can access more drive and inspiration. Study the lives of high achievers, and you'll find that their goals aligned with their highest values.

Areas to go deeper

Your Purpose—Re-write the purpose from Chapter 6. How would you change it now to make it more compelling and/or condensed?

_____

_____

_____

Your Values—Go Back to Chapter 2 and choose two values that, in this season of your life, drive you to work hard. Discuss why they are important to you.

_____

_____

_____

Virtues

Go to Chapter 2. Your virtues are tools to help you live out those values. Which three virtues do you need to practice in order to go deeper in your values and your purpose?

1. _____

2. _____

3. _____

4. _____

This section is not about learning new lessons, but being reminded of the old lessons. In doing so, you will cultivate a self-sustained motivation.

Create an independent educational tradition

In the 2004 Democratic National Convention speech, then-Senator Barack Obama gave a powerful keynote address. He brought into the national consciousness a term that is used to refer to academically inclined minority students who allegedly conduct themselves in snobbish ways: "acting white."

In a culturally pluralistic society, one of the main variables for success or the lack thereof is the culture of the group. Within the study of educational habits of subcultures, a theory emerged in the 1980s called *oppositional culture*, which attempts to explain the black/white achievement gap in education. This theory suggests that the gap is a symptom of the sub-culture's rejection of the prevailing norms and values of the dominant culture—not just nonconformity within the educational system. In the case of black students, it meant acting white.

The theory accounts for the differences between black and white students in several ways:

1. White educators tend to provide black students with inferior education and handle them differently than white students.

2. Because of the "glass ceiling," defined by the Department of Labor as an invisible and impenetrable barrier that keeps women and minorities from rising on the job ladder, white society fails to reward black people in a way that is commensurate with their educational achievement.

3. Black people often develop self-defeating behaviors that limited their ability to achieve academic success.

The research indicates that the phenomenon of acting white has greater social sanctions in integrated schools than in segregated schools. In other words, when black students conduct themselves in ways that are perceived as "acting white." they lose popularity and the motivation to do well academically. However, this phenomenon seems to be most prevalent in racially integrated environments.

The entrepreneur, educator, and hip-hop artist, Killer Mike, in a 2019 interview, suggests having black children attend school with only black children until they are thirteen years old. His reasoning is based on anecdotal evidence. He attended all-black schools, lived in all-black communities, and only knew black politicians, police, and clergy. The majority of the public schools in his area were named after prominent black figures.

From his perspective, this experience instilled a pride in him that all black children should have before they encounter white society. Coincidentally, his experience is consistent with the research done by Harvard professor Roland Fryer and described in the paper "Acting White." The researcher of the theory of oppositional culture, John Ogbu, suggested that white America's traditional refusal to acknowledge the potential for black intellectual achievement instills doubts about black American's intellectual ability, which produces an inferiority.

In the days of slavery, anti-literacy laws were put on the books because literate slaves were the ones who spread ideas about insurrection.

Examples include Gabriel Prosser, Nat Turner, and Denmark Vesey. An educated mind cannot be enslaved.

According to one historian, black people went from being completely illiterate in the mid-1800s to being half-literate by 1900. One of a slave's main attractions to freedom was reading and writing, in addition to family rebuilding and land ownership.

In *The Miseducation of the Negro,* Carter G. Woodson comments that if you can control a man's perceptions, you don't have to be concerned about his actions. He contends that the modern education given to black people doesn't help black people, because it's designed to conform to the needs of their oppressor. The same goes for the standards and expectations for a black person's life.

With education that is culturally uplifting and healing, black people have an opportunity to adopt new sets of standards and expectations. This type of change can happen when more black families adopt independent educational traditions.

An independent educational tradition is a model of education that does not solely depend on the school system for learning tools. Such a tradition is especially vital for communities where the school system is not adequately meeting the needs of the students.

The most important part of my education was sitting at the kitchen table and reading while my mother supervised me. That literally saved my life and is responsible for the work that I'm doing today. Because she gave me a higher knowledge base of what is possible, I developed higher expectations.

As a mentor, you want to be deliberate about what you model as far as your focus on reading and personal development, because the education of the children begins with the education of their teachers. There is always room to improve as a student, a leader, a businessperson, in your relationships, and in your finances.

What caused black people to develop an academic sluggishness? Malcolm X had an answer. From his perspective, the cause was years and years of being oppressed after slavery, Jim Crow, redlining, and white discrimination. In addition, the educational system that black people matriculated through was designed to cause the young people to lose interest in school.

In addition, many parents who have formal education but saw so many barriers thought it fruitless for their children to reach higher. This ties in with the concept of learned helplessness, which occurs when someone suffers from a sense of powerlessness arising from trauma or a persistent failure to succeed. It occurs when someone attempts to pursue a goal and has that goal blocked.

If every time I go to open a door, someone hits me—and if everyone I know goes to the door, and someone hits them—eventually, we all stop going to the door. Vicarious learned helplessness happens when you see those above you—your parent or your hero—try to open the door, and then get hit. Then I won't even try to open the door.

After a while, even if the door is open, no one bothers to go through it. Whether it's a promotion on the job, a business venture, or the desire to access financing for a house or a business—things that were commonplace a few decades ago—people who are affected by learned helplessness don't pursue opportunities available to them, because they feel powerless.

People who experience having goals repeatedly blocked also can be prone to outbursts of anger and potential violence. The 1967 race riots all across America, which left eighty-three dead and almost 2,000 injured, occurred in part due to discrimination that African Americans faced. President Lyndon Johnson established an eleven-member panel called the Kerner Commission to understand what caused the riots. The commission determined that white racism was the underlying cause of violence.

Did we, as a society, learn from the Kerner Commission? We did not. Instead, we saw white backlash to black assertiveness. The anger persists until this day. Many societal barriers have been broken, but many black people still have an emotional and psychological wall from their experience of racism.

I believe that when your culture limits or restricts your ability to fulfill your purpose, you have to find ways to transcend the limitations. Whether you had a baby out of wedlock, went to prison, got divorced, or filed bankruptcy, you can go on to live a great life. I've been blessed to see people recover from all these situations and prosper through hard work, perseverance, and having high expectations of themselves. They were actually better for what they had to endure, because it made them tougher and more resilient.

The barriers restricting you are within you. People will hold you to your limitations, so don't hold yourself to them. There's always something in life that can cause you to bury your hopes and dreams, but the people who fulfill their purpose face their fears, take risks, maybe fail several times, and get back up.

Malcolm X advised that leaders of black people instill within young people the desire to further their education. How can this be done? Hopefully, by this point in the book, you've reviewed the tools on developing a sense of self and identifying your purpose, which should invoke/restore a self-sustained motivation.

More specifically, there are two things that I believe we need to look at in order to close the achievement gap: Increasing time on tasks in academic study and Creating a culture of high expectations.

Increasing Time on Tasks in Academic Study

Black educational consultant Jawanza Kunjufu has been working for thirty years to reverse the achievement gap. Kunjufu is best known for this book series *The Conspiracy to Destroy Black Boys*.

Here are some statistics about the study habits of the races, based on Dr. Kunjufu's research with SAT scores (which range from 0 to 1600):

The average SAT scores for Asian students was 1600.

The average SAT scores for White students was 1582.

The average SAT scores for Hispanic students was 1371.

The average SAT scores for African American students was 1291.

Upon further investigation, it was discovered that the score differential did not correlate with the parent's education level, income level, or the number of parents in the home.

Here's what the research showed about study habits:

Asian students study twelve hours per week.

White students study eight hours per week.

Hispanic students study three hours per week.

Black students study one hour per week.

What were the black students doing besides homework? They watched thirty-eight hours of television, spent eighteen hours listening to music, eleven hours playing basketball, and nine hours texting/talking with friends. My experience confirms this is an accurate picture of how many black youths spend their free time.

Kunjufu suggests that, for every hour of TV, telephone, or video game usage, students should study for one hour. I can't articulate how important this would be to closing the achievement gap. SAT results are not based on ability or luck. They are based on effort.

How a young person spends his or her free time is something that can be controlled. We can level the playing field. As a mentor, your question should not be whether your mentee is passing all their classes, but whether they are exceling and living up to their potential.

Spike Lee, the director of the famous film *Malcolm X,* commented that Malcolm X would be turning over in his grave if he saw the state of education of black children today. Something is wrong when ignorance is championed over intelligence.

The first step to change is truth. The next step is action. As a mentor, put a reading list together of all the books pertaining to their and your future life experience. Make a plan to work through all the books over time.

Creating a Culture of High Expectations
Do you truly believe the future can and will be better than the present?

In her book *Becoming,* Michelle Obama talks about the white flight that started in her Chicago neighborhood when she was in the first grade. She talks about feeling the disinvestment in the first grade, and how children have an intuitive sense that they are not being invested in.

When we look at young people today, we have no idea where they are going to be as adults. Mentees are at the mercy of the standards of their mentors and the environment those mentors create. You can demand excellence of the children, but if you don't change the atmosphere in their house, they won't be able to meet those demands.

This begs the question: Does a child fail school, or does the school fail the child?

We have a lot of great black history to learn and reflect on, but it's also important to craft a great black future. For that, we need to set high expectations. If we operate under the belief that all children can learn, we can help them best by having high expectations. Children tend to rise to the level of expectations of their mentors.

Unfortunately, many students are surrounded by people who have low expectations for their students, based on their circumstances. Julian Weissglass, Professor Emeritus at the University of California, Santa Barbara, believes that tremendous harm occurs in institutions where people are conditioned to take on values, assumptions, and practices that inhibit the learning of students of color and lower socioeconomic classes.

From Weissglass' perspective, class and race are significant causes of the achievement gap. Class and race are closely correlated with poverty, teachers with unconscious bias, single-parent homes, and students who are disinterested in learning.

But these issues are no excuse for a child not learning. When the mentor has a high expectation for the mentee, it gives the mentee added confidence that their circumstances will NOT determine their potential greatness, and there is no ceiling on their potential.

How do we heal our expectations?
A. Belief in their Potential

> *The one who thinks he can and the one who thinks he can't are both right.*

Your role as a mentor is to help young people break out of that negative thought pattern by promoting a belief in their ability to develop and become better than their present situation may reflect. As simple as it sounds, you can make a choice that you will live the life you were meant to live—not the life that was given to you—simply by believing that you can.

Extensive research has shown that a major factor in fulfilling your potential is belief in your ability to improve. Unfortunately, many people believe that their destiny in life is predetermined and that they are limited, partly because of negative messages they've received from friends, family, and/or society.

Positive expectations can change their perception of a situation just as dramatically as negative expectations. Fixed mindsets hold people back.

What happens if you think that your personality and intelligence is something you can develop and improve? Research shows that with education and consistent practice, you can change your memory, judgment, and attention. Your ability is not like a hand you're dealt in a poker game. It's something you can cultivate through your efforts, although it can take years of passion, toil, and training.

The main factor in achieving expertise is meaningful engagement.

Your opinion of yourself profoundly affects your life. How does the power of belief transform your psychology?

Growth mindsets free people to pursue what they value, with passion and resilience. People can learn these mindsets to break out of self-defeating patterns.

There are five factors that operate in mentors that have high expectations of their mentees.

1. Warm environment—Mentors create a warm climate for the mentee through what they say verbally and non-verbally. They are nicer to them than they are to people of whom they expect less.

2. Added input—Mentors teach more to mentees from whom they expect more, compared to those for whom they have lower expectations.

3. Chance to respond—Mentors give mentees for whom they have higher expectations a greater opportunity to speak and more help to shape their thoughts and perspectives carefully.

4. Thorough feedback—If more is expected of the mentee, there is greater praise when a satisfactory response is given and also a more distinguished response when an unsatisfactory answer is given. One of the ways that mentors demonstrate low expectations of someone is by allowing them to get away with a low-quality answer or low-quality performance.

5. This is the most important piece: accountability. If we don't hold the mentees accountable when they fall short of expectations, then there is no point in having expectations.

Align your daily work ethic with your deepest desires

Do you have the courage to live the life that you've designed? If you want to manifest your destiny, you have to think more about the opportunity available to you than about the work it will take. You also have to choose the environment that's optimal for your progress.

Recognize the opportunity available to you, and teach your mentee to do the same. In the Scriptures, it says, "Ask, and it will be given to you. Search, and you will find. Knock, and the door will be opened to you." (Matthew 7:7, NIV)

In other words, you can't get what you're not pursuing.

Tools to Improving Your Work Ethic
If you want to lead others to higher ground, you must be the first to go there. Regardless of the position you hold, your capacity to inspire others to do more, dream more, and become more starts with your capacity to do so yourself. Here are few thoughts:

1. Don't celebrate prematurely when you are trying to break cycles and raise the standards. Proportionate celebration means you celebrate to the extent that the ultimate goal has been reached, while staying engaged in the process. Don't cel-ebrate until you are content with the progress made; enjoy that celebratory moment when you have reached a goal, and then work to make it better.

2. Never hope for more than you are willing to work for. Consistent with raising expectations is the improving your willingness to work hard. When you find yourself daydreaming of what could be, ask yourself what you could be doing at the moment to bring the dream into fruition.

3. Value obscurity. The cost of notoriety is safety, because you can lose credibility when your visibility surpasses your ability. If you want to raise your expectations and break cycles, you will probably stumble. It's easier to do when there are not as many eyes on you. When you are more visible than you are ca-pable, you'll no longer be credible. How many times do we see

the "overnight success" who, upon arrival, has stories of years and years of toiling away? Instead of constant self-promotion, they spent a tremendous amount of time quietly honing their craft and building a solid foundation. This is what leads to staying power.

"Don't work yourself into the spotlight; don't push your way into the place of prominence. It's better to be promoted to a place of honor than face humiliation by being demoted." (Proverbs 25:6-7, MSG)

4. Do the autopsy of your past failures. I believe that the second half of your life can be better than the first half if you take the time to learn the lessons. This can only occur when you reflect on your past and come to some new conclusions.

5. Recognize when you are not living in a manner worthy of who you are. Your worth and value is not predicated upon your performance, but if your performance is not in line with your potential, you are selling yourself short. There are some glo-ries you don't get through association; you can only get them through dedication.

6. Find the standard of work needed to accomplish your goals. If 5 percent of people survived a terminal illness, we have to study those people to see what they did to survive. Regardless of the possible outcome, give yourself the best chance to succeed. It's not about running with people who break cycles. It's also about modeling their work ethic.

7. As a mentor, it's important to recognize that providing gen-eral feedback reinforces shortcomings. Showing specifically where improvement can be made will keep the mentee feeling

empowered. Pointing out exactly what he can do to improve performance will keep him empowered. Be mindful that those with low self-esteem are more likely to overgeneralize for the feedback they receive, so be mindful of your words.

Reflection: Prime the Pump of Your Desires:

1. What advice would you give to your best friend about how to approach this situation?

___

2. On your last days on this Earth, what would you wish you had done? Envision your funeral. Will you be thinking, *I wish I had* or *I'm glad I did?*

___

3. Imagine standing before God. What do you want to the final judgment of your life's choices to be?

___

Address your methods of self-sabotage

One black educator tells a story of a high school student she worked with. The young lady was a brilliant student who demonstrated remarkable potential. The educator took her under her wing and helped her along her high school journey. She began to show the girl all the possibilities for her future.

Unbeknownst to the mentor, the young girl was afraid. When she was ready to leave for college, she got pregnant. She suffered the painful experience of a miscarriage. Six months later, she got pregnant again. She had a son.

The educator, along with the high school principal, wanted to see what they could do to help the young lady move past this situation and continue her academic journey. The young lady was so bright, she was able to test out of her senior year of high school. She ended up going to college and successfully completing her bachelor's degree, while being a parent to her son. Then she received a full scholarship to get a master's degree.

The educator wanted to figure out what had caused the roadblocks when she got pregnant. The young lady simply said, "They didn't let me grow there. My friends and family pulled me down. I had to get away from them in order to grow."

The young lady realized that no one in her environment could help, encourage, or support her, because she was moving into a world that they didn't know about, and that frightened them. Logically, she knew she had a choice—but emotionally, she didn't know how to break away. As a result, she sabotaged her success with poor choices.

When you walk around with people who are losing, you normalize losing. That's what environments can do. Many people choose to remain unseen because if they do, people can't criticize, condemn, and ridicule them. That's the reality of what will happen when you raise your expectations and pursue a greater dream.

Unfortunately, when you decide to change your life, everyone else doesn't decide to change theirs. When people don't want to see you change, they might undermine you and your goals or even try to sabotage them.

Some people are hard to encourage because they don't want to break up the routine that they have created around low expectations. Sadly, these people influence others who are impressionable and relegate them to a life of mediocrity. These are people who have not engaged fully in life. They've failed to honor the opportunities life presented to them.

When your own life operates at a consistent level of mediocrity, you can feel bitter toward people who are operating in excellence and walking in purpose. But when you start to move out of a state of complacency, you start demanding more for yourself, and you no longer resent those who have accomplished something.

You might have to move to environments that expose you to success, because your environment will determine the level of your thinking. This young lady made it out—but initially, she sabotaged herself because of her fear of success. The deeper part of the fear was the fear of losing those she loved.

Our role as mentors is to help people take control of their lives externally and internally, by helping them fight against the voices that would embed a sense of failure in them. Because they are looking to us, we need to be deliberate about what we are modeling for them.

Methods of Self-sabotage/Maintaining Mediocrity

1. You focus on too many options, which lends itself to divided focus and then inefficiency and wasted effort.
2. You quit when it gets hard.
3. You let other people monopolize your time. In other words, you don't maintain healthy boundaries with others.
4. You run from the most important tasks to do trivial things. You find yourself "majoring" in minor issues.
5. You don't take full responsibility.

6. You buy into the lie of shame.
7. You believe you have to be perfect in order to have value.
    a. You don't take a risk. In life, you will miss 100 percent of the shots that you don't take.
8. You procrastinate.
9. You see a problem for every solution instead of a solution for every problem.
10. You trust the wrong people.

In what ways have you sabotaged your own success?

_____

_____

_____

Many people fear success. I wrote about it in *Bridge the Gaps* – Chapter 29 – Fear of Success. But there's one thing I didn't mention that I would like to here. It's the power of faith.

Regardless of what you think or believe, faith and religion is a very important part of black life and thought. One educator suggests that, if you took all the people who have been healed of mental distress or depression by the theories of reputable psychologists (Jung, Freud, Rogers, etc.), it would not equal a fraction of the number of people who have been healed of mental distress by faith.

Regardless of what you believe about faith, many people have been able to move through depression and sadness, outside of any biological or organic issue, through faith. Even if you are not religious, if it's effective for the person you're mentoring, you need to develop the skill set to point them in the right direction.

I started TheBridge330 Mentoring Program because I believe that the power of faith has the ability to address sociological and psychological issues. Faith is not demonstrated when you get what you hoped for. Faith is proven while you wait for what you hoped for to materialize.

This is worth repeating: God is giving you a lamp and not a flashlight, so you have just enough illumination to take the next step. As you become productive and break cycles, faith is going to help you to take steps even when you can't fully see what will happen. Faith will bring about things you haven't seen.

You will discover that, when you're under pressure, poise and grace are more important than talent. Once you've mitigated the important risks and have done your due diligence, you need to exercise your faith.

Fear and faith cannot live together. Personally, when I encounter situations with constantly changing variables that could knock me off balance and cause me to lose focus, I try to focus on things that don't change. Others have accused people of using faith as a crutch. But when used correctly, it's a weapon to break through the glass ceiling of limiting beliefs and self-doubt.

The young lady in the story above was afraid to lose love. I don't want to lose anyone's love, but the most important love is the love of God. The only person you need to co-sign your purpose is the creator of that purpose: God. Personally, my faith anchors in my willingness to endure harsh treatment from people, knowing God's opinion matters most.

Here are the Scriptural references that I use:

1. Jesus became like these people and died so that he could free them. They were like slaves all their lives because of their fear of death. (Hebrews 2:15, ERV)

2. To live in Christ and to die is gain. (Phil. 1:21, NIV)

3. Even if my father and mother abandon me, the Lord cares for me. (Psalm 27:10, NIV)

4. He will never leave nor forsake you. (Deuteronomy 31:6, NIV)

5. Whoever trusts the Lord is kept safe. (Proverbs 29:25, NIV)

6. You are a man of integrity who is not swayed by people's opinions. (Matthew 22:16, NIV)

7. Am I now trying to win the approval of human beings, or of God? Or am I trying to please people? If I were still trying to please people, I would not be a servant of Christ. (Galatians 1:10, NIV)

8. Walk by faith, not by sight. (2 Corinthians 5:7, NIV)

9. And without faith it is impossible to please God, because anyone who comes to him must believe that he exists and that he rewards those who earnestly seek him. (Hebrews 11:6, NIV)

10. People who always want more stir up conflict. But those who trust in the Lord will succeed. (Proverbs 28:25, NIRV)

11. I have told you all this so that you may have peace in me. Here on Earth you will have many trials and sorrows. But take heart, because I have overcome the world. (John 16:33, NIV)

12. Do you not know that in a race all the runners run, but only one gets the prize? Run in such a way as to get the prize. (1 Corinthians 9:24, NIV)

13. Trust in the Lord at all times. Lean not on your own understanding. In all your ways, acknowledge him and he will direct your paths. (Proverbs 3:5-6 NIV)

14. Do you see what this means—all these pioneers who blazed the way, all these veterans cheering us on? It means we'd better get on with it. Strip down, start running—and never quit! No extra spiritual fat, no parasitic sins. Keep your eyes on Jesus, who both began and finished this race we're in. Study how he did it. Because he never lost sight of where he was headed—that exhilarating finish in and with God—he could put up with anything along the way: Cross, shame, whatever. And now he's there, in the place of honor, right alongside God. When you find yourselves flagging in your faith, go over that story again, item by item, that long litany of hostility he plowed through. That will shoot adrenaline into your souls! (Hebrews 12:1-3, MSG)

Part 3: Emotional Health

WITHOUT A DOUBT, THE LESSONS in Part 2—Productivity are straightforward and direct. They also assume a certain level of emotional health. The reality is that many people have emotional hurdles that they must overcome in order to effectively implement these lessons.

The byproduct of addressing your emotional life is that it can aid you in your professional life. It rarely works the other way around.

Far too many people enter into the workforce or take on entrepreneurial endeavors with unresolved/unaddressed emotional issues that adversely affect their effectiveness. This section will introduce tools to help improve emotional health. It might give you more fortitude to walk in purpose and execute your plans at a higher level.

Emotional health is a positive state of wellbeing in which an individual is able to function in community and meet the demands of daily life. Here was a question that stopped me in my tracks: Do you want to feel better, or do you want to get well?

Feeling better and being well are two different things. Feeling better is a temporary state of emotional appeasement. Getting well is a sustained state of healthy living. Trying to feel better has its limits and can actually work against getting well.

Getting to a place of health, particularly after living an unhealthy life, can be difficult, but it's worth it. Rather than confronting the need to care for themselves first, many mentors attempt to keep driving on fumes. Don't let your ego plan your life or keep you from healing.

As a mentor, the best way to help others get well is to see to your own healing and help yourself get well. That way, when you are needed, you are available.

In my experience, nothing affects the mentoring relationship more than the unlived life and unhealed trauma of the mentor. Your life has the ability to greatly influence life for those you serve.

There's a common analogy we hear about self-care. Prior to take-off on an airplane, the flight attendant explains the emergency process: When the oxygen masks fall, you have to put the mask on yourself first before you can put it on anyone else. Otherwise, you are not going to be of any use, because you will have passed out.

But what does "putting on your oxygen mask" look like? It might involve changing the way you think. It might even require that you take a season of your life to focus and/or refocus on sustainable, healthy living.

The institution of American chattel slavery did not care about the personhood of black people, only about their production. Since slavery has ended, we can take time to learn how to care about ourselves. With love, we can heal from the pain of what occurs in the course of living life.

Some narratives told about black people depict us as superhuman. To be sure, when you look at the history of black people in America, you'll clearly conclude that black people are some of the most resilient people on the face of the Earth. Even American politician and sociologist Daniel Patrick Moynihan in his 1965 report *The Negro Family – The Case for National Action*—specifically in the fourth section, called *The Tangle of Pathology*—comments that the fact the black Americans has survived at all is amazing, and that a weaker people would have perished, as others have.

Yes, we survived—but black people have aches, pains, traumas, and emotional needs, like everyone else. We should not feel shame about that. If black people are as free and equal as everyone else, we should be free to take the necessary time to heal from past hurts, to set appropriate boundaries, to create a structure in our lives to support our growth, and to learn how to relate in healthy ways.

In this section, you'll find tools to inspire you to think more deeply, to challenge unhealthy/toxic cultural norms, and to learn how to better love yourself and others.

8: Well-being Toolkit

IN THE DAYS OF AMERICAN chattel slavery, the most important aspect of life for black people was their productivity, not their personhood. A slave's feelings were never taken into account. Slavery is over but unfortunately, many black people still maintain a culture of silence and don't talk about the hard stuff.

As black people, we have learned to suppress deeply felt emotional pain to be able to function in society. Ironically, the silence that kept folks relatively safe in the days of slavery cause major emotional and psychological harm today.

Just because someone is silent, that doesn't mean they are okay. Too much is at stake if we remain quiet about our pain, our limits, and our areas of vulnerability—because the pain often shows up in unhealthy ways.

Freedom says you matter and you get to choose the life you want to live. As a mentor, it is important that you maintain your productivity but also your personhood, because the state that you're in is the state you will give to others.

Children develop a perspective on life in their early years, and those years inform how their subsequent experiences are viewed, which affects their behavior. As mentors, we must work to cultivate a positive sense of well-being, not only for ourselves but also for those we lead.

You can't bring change to the world until you've committed yourself to healing and creating change within yourself. As someone who has gone through and continues to commit to this process, healing doesn't mean that you have to disengage from life. It does mean that you have to organize your life in a way that promotes your well-being, which will serve your future productivity.

As a young adult, I recall hitting a certain point where I had serious emotional challenges rooted in past pain that I could not fix using the outdated or insufficient tools I learned growing up. Fortunately, I am part of a generation that has the luxury of thinking about emotional healing, because mental and emotional challenges have been largely destigmatized.

Implementing these tools saved my life and reliably led to me healthier living. They've proven useful in the lives of many others.

Here are a few ways you can "put the oxygen mask on first":

Tools

1. *Grieve Your Losses: Fix the Hole in Your Bucket*
2. *No More Shame: Write Your Own Story*
3. *Be Present: Limit/Eliminate Social Media and Phone Use*

Grieve Your Losses: Fix the Hole in Your Bucket

Laughter can conceal a heavy heart, but when the laughter ends, the grief remains.
Proverbs 14:13, NLT

THOMAS JEFFERSON, ONE OF THE founding fathers of this country, wrote in *Notes on the State of Virginia* a very insidious thought about the emotional make-up of black people. Aside from his beliefs that black people could handle more heat and required less sleep—which justified the egregious conditions of slavery—he also believed that black people don't grieve for long.

Unfortunately, this belief seems to have taken on a life of its own. Slavery created a culture of silence in which demonstrating any vulnerability, especially difficult emotions, was prohibited, because that type of emotional vulnerability made the slaves less productive.

Sadly, without an intentional approach to change our mindset, dealing with grief will continue to be suppressed in the black community. Of course, there are pockets of progress—but wholesale permission for grief and emotional expression has not been granted to black people, and it needs to be.

The cause of depression for many people is untreated trauma, unprocessed emotions, and unresolved grief. One of the worst forms of emotional pain is the inability to communicate one's suffering.

In 2008, my cousin—who was more like my little brother—died at the age of seventeen. About a year later, I was arrested for DUI (driving under the influence).

For whatever reason, I couldn't make the connection between the two events. As I reflect on that time in my life, I didn't know how to properly grieve the loss, so I was thrown out of equilibrium mentally and emotionally. Due to my lack of awareness, I made foolish choices rooted in a painful confusion and inattention.

The fallout, though it could have been worse, was ugly. This was the first time in my life that I had a loss so deep that it would be part of the fabric of my future choices. I was just starting my career, and unfortunately, I experienced several other losses in the same season.

An obvious but major truth is that, in these moments, "No one can know your sadness" (Proverbs 14:10, NCV). It's safe to say that I was experiencing a deep depression. I hid my emotional baggage, which was pretty easy—unfortunately, visible injuries get the most respect. Deep, internal sadness goes unrecognized.

I was taught that sadness is weakness, and men are not allowed to be weak. Sadly, many others have also experienced this attitude. It took a few years and a lot of experiences working with people for me to realize how many other people carry deep unspoken and unaddressed pain rooted in their losses.

I learned the hard way that emotional wounds and underdevelopment are not always obvious when you first meet people, but they cause those people to struggle. It's hard to pursue and live a great life when you are emotionally wounded and stuck.

A major, and often unaddressed, part of emotional development and emotional well-being is learning to grieve our losses. If you or your mentees suffer a serious loss, you can help guide the grieving process.

Guide to Grieving

1. **Identify your losses.** A loss is defined as the often-unanticipated, unrecoverable removal of something or someone in your life. Some things are not problems to be solved. Some things are truths that have to be accepted. Unfortunately, the truth doesn't always come without pain. As a mentor, you will

more than likely have opportunities to walk through difficult moments in your mentee's life. It will help if you first expand your world view of pain and tragedy. Grieving your own losses allow you to grow compassion for others. One thing I've learned in my time as a mentor is that time will *not* heal all wounds. There are some wounds you must face head on with full acceptance, or they will insidiously interrupt your life forever.

Considering that one in three children grow up without a father; one in three women and one in six men have been sexually abused before the age of eighteen; and one in five Americans are dealing with a mental illness. In addition, more than 10,000 people are released from prison every week, oftentimes, without adequate skills or tools to build or rebuild their lives.

Many black Americans have received unhealthy and untrue information about their skin color and their place in the world. We can help counteract this by providing safe places for young people to heal. In *Bridge the Gaps – Lessons on Self-Awareness, Self-Development, and Self-Care*, I addressed several common losses in our culture that people endure. You might even understand them from personal experience.

All people have the capacity and the right to take time to heal themselves. See the chapters below. Learn more about this in these chapters from *Bridge the Gaps:*

1. Mental Illness – Chapter 37
2. Colorism – Chapter 38
3. Sexual Abuse – Chapter 39
4. Fatherlessness – Chapter 40
5. Mass Incarceration – Chapter 41

2. **Identify your common defenses against grief.** Many people overestimate how well they control their emotional pain. A lot

of us have learned to live with it for so long, it takes an outside event to force us to deal with the pain. For me, the outside event was a DUI. In many ways, these events can be a gift that opens up a pathway to change.

Some of the common defenses we use against experiencing grief include:
- Blaming
- Becoming hostile
- Intellectualizing
- Denial
- Distracting
- Rationalizing
- Over spiritualizing
- Minimizing
- Medicating

I recently watched an interview of a man who suffered tragedy in his life. Part of the conversation went like this:

Interviewer: "Did you take time to grieve?"
Guest: "Not really. I numb when it gets hard."
Interview: "Is that healthy?"
Guest: "No, but it's practical."

This was an honest response to the way many people have been conditioned to process grief. Sometimes, due to the circumstances and demands of life, we have to "put our pain in a drawer." We might not be intentionally running away from it, but we know dealing with it will take more out of us than we can give at that moment. It's not for me to tell you when or in what precise way to feel and process your grief. I simply want to emphasize how important it is to do so, to live more fully and freely.

3. **Take time to regularly process your emotions**. There is no such thing as an unexpressed emotion. Everything you feel will affect you in some way. We often find ways to compensate for the void in our souls, through emotional triggers, overre-action, holding grudges, instant replay, insecurity, relationship issues, unhealthy patterns with inappropriate relationships, overspending (often on beauty and physical appearance—clothes, jewelry, etc.), over-exposure on social media, or illness, which allows us to attract attention. Why? Because if you don't deal with the pain, it will deal with you. Talking about our emotions is probably the easiest and most effective way to process them—but most people were not raised in environments where we could comfortably talk about emotions. We have a very limited emotional vocabulary and library. See the list of emotions in the Tool – No More Shame in the next section.

4. **Give people permission to grieve their losses**.
Dysfunctional environments teach us not to talk, feel, or trust—yet to grieve, you must be able to do all three. See Chapter 31 – Grieving in *Bridge the Gaps – Lessons on Self-Awareness, Self-Development, and Self-Care*. Go to www.thebri-dge330.com to pick up a copy.

5. **Learn to forgive**. Forgiveness requires that you let go of the desire to change the past or wish it was different. The opposite, unforgiveness, locks you in a prison with no chance for release. See Chapter 32 – Forgiveness in *Bridge the Gaps – Lessons on Self-Awareness, Self-Development, and Self-Care*. Go to www. thebridge330.com to pick up a copy.

6. **Talk to a therapist.** Working through some of the previous tools alone will be a start, but it might not be enough to process all the losses you've experienced. We can't heal what we don't reveal. Sometimes, we think we're over things that have happened in our lives, but we're still showing symptoms that impact us in ways we don't even realize. Unresolved issues in your life will inevitably be exposed and will affect different aspects of your life. They often come from secrets. Holding on to secrets becomes a form of trauma. Revealing your secrets—or allowing someone to reveal their secrets to you—is often the first step in healing.

When I went to therapy and started to work through my emotional life, I came to realize I was sitting on a mountain of pain. As I spoke with a therapist, deeper levels of truth would emerge, and I was able to find a new sense of emotional freedom. It's not easy to do, but it's worth it. You might encounter a stigma in the black community concerning therapy. The only way to break the stigma is to tell our stories of life before and after therapy. Therapy will help you develop a recovery style that fits you, your temperament, and your situation as you pursue your own journey of healing.

No More Shame: Write Your Own Story
Love requires that people know they are not alone.

SHAME IS A PSYCHOLOGICALLY AND emotionally crippling social issue. Shame is defined as a feeling of being broken, shoddy, and unfit for connection with or love from others.

Shame says, "If you knew the truth about me, you would no longer love me." Sadly, the feeling of shame has become a public health issue, as it is correlated with depression, anxiety disorders, and addictions—to name a few.

As mentors, we want to raise young people who won't have to recover from their upbringing. That means we'll have to address our own upbringing.

Shame arises out of false beliefs about ourselves and the world around us. It requires that we buy into the belief that we are alone. When we get to the root of the beliefs behind our shame, we can start to question them, using our logic and reason. Once we start questioning beliefs, we might realize that we don't actually agree with them, and from there, we can deconstruct them.

We don't have to be held hostage to the failures of yesterday, the sins we've committed, or the sins committed against us. Our struggles can keep us stuck in a cycle of self-doubt, shame, self-centeredness, and guilt. Yet all of us have experienced career missteps, poor life and relationship choices, wasted time, and/or emotional and mental pain.

Many of us have learned life lessons the hard way from these experiences, but others never learned them at all and are living lost, confused, and disillusioned with life. If you feel lost, please have compassion for yourself, because it's unloving and unkind to expect to be good at something that you were never taught how to do or that you had no template to model after.

Many of us have were never taught how to live. We might have been taught how to survive, how to get along without causing any trouble, and how to protect ourselves. But we were never taught how to live wholeheartedly, even after experiencing a deep pain, struggle, or disappointment.

Fortunately, healing is always possible. It's never too late to heal, grow, and reposition yourself to live your life wholeheartedly. The first step is to forgive yourself.

Some of us carry guilt from things we've done in our past: things we may have come to terms with and paid for, or things unseen by the world at large. We have to fight through the mistakes we've made. One of the ways you can know if you're in shame is if you hear tapes playing in your head that say, "You're not good enough" and/or "Who do you think you are?" Without disclosing the names of individuals, here are some specific internal messages that others have told me they hear repeatedly:

- You failed the CPA exam five times. You're not really smart. You just got lucky.

- Who are you to write a book? You didn't go to school for this.

- You had a baby out of wedlock. You can never have a better life.

- Your child is in prison. You must not be a good parent.

- You've been used and abused. No one will want you.

- Why are you going back to school now? Will you even be able to keep up? All you did before was fail. What's going to change?

- You dropped out of school. You're not educated. No one cares about your opinion.

- Now that you're married, why can't you have a baby? What's wrong with you?

- You had an abortion. This mistake can never be erased. This will haunt you.

- You are not married yet. Something must be wrong with you.

- You can't have a child. You are defective and worthless.

- Why are you crying? Real men don't cry.

- Why are you still unemployed? You should've finished college.

- You're a felon/ex-con. No one will hire you.

Re-writing the story

As a mentor, I encourage you to review the list above and think about situations you've experienced. Try to identify situations that are similar to situations your mentee may encounter. As a mentor, you can send shame—consciously or unconsciously—to your mentee based on how you react to situations that arise in their life. Our woundedness reflects itself in our choices, understanding, morals, and judgment. Most people I know have had painful, emotional, shame-filled moments in life that might have made their internal lives inaccessible. We want to guide children through their experiences so they won't have to start healing themselves as adults.

I recommend mentors go through this process with their respective situations. When you decide to feel your own hurt, you grow compassion for yourself and others. You can become an example of how to courageously confront pain. Here's a process to help you get in control of painful words and/or situations, like the ones mentioned above, that perpetuate cycles of shame, doubt, and guilt.

1. When a tough emotional experience or conversation happens, it is probably going to take some courage to get curious about your emotional state. Our emotions get the first word when we go through situations in life. Feelings are real, but that doesn't mean they are always the truth or that they have the final word in your destiny. There are a whole host of dysfunctional responses to these emotions, including blaming, overeating, looping thoughts, violence, excessive niceness, etc. Many of the responses are an attempt to numb yourself from the pain. We have a numbing issue across the world. The problem is that it shows up in ugly ways: depression, anxiety, insomnia, etc. Before moving forward to mentally understand, take time to understand what's going on, physically and emotionally. Using the list of emotions at the end of this tool, what emotion are you feeling? What is happening in your body: stomach ache, stiff neck, back pain?

_____

_____

_____

2. When something happens, our brains are designed to tell us a story that keeps us safe. When we embrace the story, it affects our thinking and behavior. Ask yourself: What am I thinking? What's the consistent thought process in my head? What story

am I telling myself about my future? My destiny? My ability to get back up? Name the lie. What lie am I believing?

I am not (*blank*) enough. What story am I telling myself?

_____

_____

_____

Note: Avoid comparing your suffering to someone else's. Comparative suffering helps no one.

Example of comparative suffering: One person says, "I just got fired after fifteen years of being on the job." Another person says, "That's nothing. I got just divorced after twenty-five years of marriage." Another person says, "That's nothing. My child just died in a car accident." Who does it help to compare painful situations like these? It's not a contest. Each person experiences pain in their own way, and all are equally valid.

3. Go back to Chapter 2's Values, Reflection/Meditation, Virtues Roadwork and Chapter 6's Calling Statement and ensure that you have memorized and internalized this information. List the top five values and the calling statement.

_____

_____

_____

4. Rewrite the story by using your virtue phrases in Chapter 2's Virtues Roadwork and incorporating your values and calling statement.

Example:

"I might not have gone to school for this, so I will use the power of focus to drive my pursuit of information that is relevant to serving my community and fulfilling my mission—to provide quality mentoring tools to underserved, under-resourced and vulnerable communities in ways that support sustained social change, a restoration of hope, and an avenue to mental and emotional health. I am anchored by my faith and constant pursuit of personal development. I don't care if I fail as long as I did everything I could to succeed."

_____

_____

_____

Statements of Resilience

- I might have made a mistake, but I am not a mistake.

- I might have done what they said I did, but I am not what they say I am.

- My failure or struggle will not become my identity.

- I don't care if I fail, as long as I did everything I could to succeed.

- I am not ashamed of what happened to me. I am ashamed that I was ashamed. I did nothing wrong.

Here's my favorite Bible verse regarding shame:

> *"Do you see what this means—all these pioneers who blazed the way, all these veterans cheering us on? It means we'd better get on with it. Strip down, start running—and never quit! No extra spiritual fat, no parasitic sins. Keep your eyes on Jesus, who both began and finished this race we're in. Study how he did it. Because he never lost sight of where he was headed—that exhilarating finish in and with God—he could put up with anything along the way: Cross, shame, whatever. And now he's there, in the place of honor, right alongside God. When you find yourselves flagging in your faith, go over that story again, item by item, that long litany of hostility he plowed through. That will shoot adrenaline into your souls!" (Hebrews 12:1-3, MSG)*

List of Emotions

Joy – Tenderness – Defeat – Rage – Cheer – Sympathy – Powerlessness – Boredom – Outrage – Contentedness – Adoration – Dread – Rejection – Hostility – Pride – Fondness – Distrust – Disillusionment – Bitterness – Satisfaction Receptivity – Suspicion – Inferiority Hate – Excitement – Interest – Caution – Confusion – Scorn – Amusement Disturbance - Grief – Spite – Shock – Overwhelm – Helplessness – Vengeance – Enthusiasm – Exhilaration – Discomfort – Isolation – Dislike – Optimism – Dismay – Guilt – Numbness – Resentment – Elation – Amazement Hurt – Regret – Trust – Delight – Confusion – Loneliness – Ambivalence – Alienation – Calm – Stun – Melancholy Exhaustion–Relaxation – Interest — Insecurity – Insult – Relief – Intrigue – Disgust – Indifference – Hope – Absorption – Sadness – Pity – Pleasure – Curiosity –Revulsion – Confidence – Anticipation

– Hurt – Contempt – Bravery – Eagerness –Weariness –Hesitancy –Safety – Fear – Depression – Preoccupation – Happiness – Anxiety Anger – Love – Worry – Sorrow – Jealousy – Lust – Terror – Uncertainty – Envy – Anguish – Annoyance –Disappointment – Humiliation – Compassion – Self-consciousness – Irritation – Caring – Alarm – Shame – Aggravation – Infatuation – Shock – Embarrassment – Restlessness – Concern – Panic – Grumpiness – Trust –Disgrace – Awkwardness – Liking – Nervousness – Exasperation – Attraction – Disorientation – Neglect – Frustration

For additional exercises and tools, see Chapter 34 – Survivor or Victim in *Bridge the Gaps – Lessons on Self-Awareness, Self-Development and Self-Care*. Visit www.amazon.com or www.thebridg330.com to pick up a copy.

Be Present: Limit/Eliminate Social Media and Phone Use

One of the most detrimental weapons against young people's emotional health is social media.

TECHNOLOGY EXISTS FOR THE PURPOSE of making life simpler. Unfortunately, for many people, that's not how it works. Whether we're chronically checking to see how many likes or followers we have on a Facebook, Instagram, or Twitter, or text messaging in group chats, the use of technology consumes a lot of our time, attention, and ability to pay attention.

According to research, we now have a generation of adults who are less aware and have poorer mental health due to their excessive social media usage. Rising rates of depression, anxiety, and sadness can be directly correlated to social media usage, especially with young people.

In some ways, technology can make a young person's life more complicated and stressful. Miscommunications or emotionally charged dialogue in text messages or on social media can affect relationships for the worst. Many young people overthink situations, worry, or misread someone's feelings, which can lead to relationship drama.

In addition, studies have also shown that the dependence on technology undermines our self-awareness, weakens our ability to self-regulate, reduces our ability to show empathy, and diminishes our social skills. This should be alarming to all of us, given the shift toward technology our society has taken.

Here are a few suggestions/considerations to keep you or the people you know from getting absorbed by a culture of technology and social media:

1. **Be aware of your technology use.** Be mindful of how reliant you are becoming on your cell phone and how tied up your well-being is with the number of followers you have or likes you receive on social media.

Here are some questions to consider:

- Assuming it's not essential to your work or school, how hard would it be to leave your phone in the car when you go to work or class? Would you have a difficult time staying away from social media for a day, a week, a month? How hard would it be? If, because of work or school, avoiding social media is *not* even an option, that might be a problem.

- What else should you be doing with that time? Is social media getting in the way of things you should be doing that will affect your future—such as professional development or academic studies—or even enjoyable hobbies and quality family time?

Take some time to reflect, journal, or talk this out to figure out how technology is affecting you and your life's direction. There are features on several smart phones that allow you to see how much time you've spent looking at that screen. Remember, you cannot change that which you don't acknowledge, so be courageous enough to face this reality.

To take it a step further, you need to be courageous enough to *quit* it if it gets in the way of your productivity or even worse, your self-worth. Social media posts are often people's carefully curated images of themselves in their best moments. Due to our constant inclination to compare ourselves to others, we need to seriously consider getting rid of the option to do so. I know a few people whose phones I want to break.

2. **Cultivate healthy and trusting friendships with *actual face time*** (not cell phone "face time") with people you care about. Be sure that your only or main form of communication is not through technology. The canary in the coal mine is college life. Anxiety among college students is rising, largely due to excessive social media usage on campus. Students don't interact with one another as often. Many students are looking to technology to provide what human contact should. A simple piece of advice is to *talk* more than you *type*. The problem is that many people have not cultivated the social skills to talk. One of my long-held assumptions is that people know what a healthy and trusting relationships look like. I no longer make that assumption. Here are a set of characteristics that you can use to evaluate and set a standard for your close and intimate friendships. I refer to them as CASUAL friends. I developed this concept based on the idea that casual friends are friends who provide a sense of comfort and safety for you to be yourself. See Chapter 33 – Boundaries and Safe People in *Bridge the Gaps*.

3. **Decide if you need to detox from social media**. Has your cell phone been more of a blessing or a curse? Do you find yourself using your phone when you know you'd be better off not using it? If you can't get rid of it for a week, you're addicted, and a detox would help. The world will continue to offer outrageous events and entertainment—but you will temporarily not indulge, to protect your well-being. Here are some of the emotions you may demonstrate over a one- to two-week social media detox. I share this list so you can normalize what you'll probably experience:

Fretful, confused, anxious, irritable, insecure, nervous, restless, crazy, addicted, panicked, jealous, angry, lonely, dependent, depressed, jittery, and paranoid.

I've done this. I found that life after the detox is amazingly peaceful, positive, and productive. Constantly breaking attention to check social media keeps you from being present with yourself, others, and any meaningful activity that requires focus. Detox from this addictive behavior, and life will seem simpler.

4. **Monitor your child's phone use.** For parents/guardians who allow their children to have free access to cell phones, I want to give you a scenario. Imagine a perfect stranger entering your home unannounced, going into your child's room, closing the door, and staying there for several hours while you have no knowledge of what's taking place. In a sense, that's what happens when you allow your children to have unfettered access to their cell phone. If you can't be sure your child is unable to interact with strangers on the phone, it's not safe for them to have a phone.

5. **Incorporate meditation into your lifestyle.** As a mentor, you want to maintain a non-anxious presence. Part of mental health is learning to live in the present. Research shows that if you meditate for twenty minutes a day for six weeks, you'll not only reduce stress, but you'll actually change your brain chemistry. Anecdotally, a meditation practice shows that you have more empathy and compassion for others and more patience in interpersonal relationships. Silence and solitude allows you to be absent from the mental "voices" that distract you from focusing on what's relevant and important in your life.

For a more detailed discussion on healthy relationships and cultivating self-awareness, which will help to be proactive against and offset the negative effects of social media, you can check out the book *Bridge the Gaps – Lessons on Self-Awareness, Self-Development and Self-Care*. Visit the website www.thebridge330.com.

9: Healthy Relationships Toolkit

The righteous choose their friends carefully, but the way of the wicked leads them astray. Proverbs 12:26, NIV

ONE OF THE KEYS TO building healthy communities is having the skills to create emotional safety and recognize our personal flaws. This was challenging for me. I know from experience, most people have not learned the skills they need to have emotionally healthy relationships and therefore to build a healthy community.

Those who raised us imprinted certain ways of behaving into us that might be deeper than we realize. If we ignore the effect of the past on the present, it can be very costly. The cost is born particularly in our leadership and our relationships with others. The following tools will help us to focus on understanding how our family backgrounds have shaped us as well as how we can create emotionally safe communities.

Tools
1. *Do the Work: Understand Your Family Background*
2. *Emotionally Safe Communities*

Supplement: Work on Your Love

"And this is my prayer: that your love may abound more and more in knowledge and depth of insight." (Philippians 1:9, NIV)

MANY OF US MEAN WELL, but don't know how to do right. This Scripture is about learning how to love. We are socio-emotional beings, which means we have the capacity for trust, self-confidence, and empathy. Socio-emotional development can't happen apart from relationship. We spend hours, days, weeks, months, and years preparing ourselves for our careers, but we don't spend much time learning how to love well.

In our culture, we prioritize individualistic achievement more than community health, and as a result, we suffer from an inability to give and receive love. The purpose of life is more than connecting, but it can't be achieved apart from connecting.

One piece of advice given by a black educator: "The road of life is long and hard. You'll need good people along the way to help you."

Unfortunately, a lifetime of education has failed to educate us about healthy relationships. It's been said that it's not good to be alone, but it's also not easy to be together. I've seen these two situations fairly often: We attract people who don't know how to love us and then we either push them away or we stay connected to them, despite their bad behavior and even toxicity, because we fear loneliness.

Learning to love well takes intentionality in developing the right perspectives and skills. A more detailed discussion of these skills can be found in *Bridge the Gaps – Lessons on Self-Awareness, Self-Development, and Self-Care*. Go to www.thebridge330.com to pick up a copy.

Relational Tools from *Bridge the Gaps – Lessons on Self-Awareness, Self-Development, and Self-Care*

1. Grieving Losses—Chapter 31

2. Forgiveness—Chapter 32. You can't move on until you let go. Many of us remain stuck in consistent patterns of hurt because we either haven't chosen to forgive and/or we don't understand what forgiveness is.

3. Boundaries and Safe People—Chapter 33. Just because someone is friendly, that doesn't mean they are your friend. Unless you're discerning, you might rush into a relationship that creates big liabilities.

You also want to be a safe mentor. Not everyone should be privy to every aspect of your development. When we trust the wrong people, the implications are vast.

One of my mentors would constantly say that Jesus had twelve disciples, but in his most vulnerable moment at the Garden of Gethsemane, only Peter, James, and John came with him. (Mark 14:33) Jesus only had three people in his inner circle. For that reason, it's important to know how to pick who will be in your life and be willing to evaluate the level of health of your relationships. At the base of every solid bond is friendship, and at the core of a strong friendship is trust.

Trust is the product of a relationship where you know you're safe and unconditionally loved—and trust is fragile. You can lose it and not even realize what you did to lose it. This chapter breaks down the anatomy of trust.

4. Survivor or Victim—Chapter 34.

   Why do people hide their pain? The enemy will use pain to intimidate you, to humiliate you, and to disgrace you as you learn to deal with shame and process/share emotions. Shame is highly correlated with issues like aggression, depression, violence, addiction, and bullying. As a mentor, when people say things like, "I've never told anyone this," it's often the result of shame. Shame is fed by secrecy, silence and judgment. On the flip side, it's destroyed by compassion and empathy when it is exposed and has words wrapped around it. This chapter walks you through the process of deconstructing shame.

5. Assertiveness—Chapter 35

Over the course of life, you are bound to run into a person or two who demonstrate unhealthy relational practices. You are better off learning to stop "mind reading" and to clarify your expectations. You are entitled to your emotions, but you are not entitled to invalid expectations. As a matter of fact, some of the heaviest yokes we carry are the assumptions we make about and the expectations we have of others. When you must disagree, don't fight dirty. Start clean fighting (negotiation). Before confrontation, work through any anger and hurt you feel. Then stand up for yourself. In my experience, most adults have never learned to deal with conflict in a healthy way.

6. Listening—Chapter 42

One of the most loving things we can do for someone is listen to them without interrupting.

Do the Work: Understand Your Family Background

"Jesus is in your heart, but grandpa is in your bones."
Pastor Pete Scazzero

Your family of origin is the most powerful group to which you will ever belong. They become part of your makeup and wiring as a person. A family creates a map for life. It's as if we are all born with an unformatted disk on our hearts and souls. Our family writes the programming to tell us how life should go and how to respond. They also show us how to relate to others and form our values.

Sometimes, your family's lessons are spoken and other times, unspoken. As you grow older, you realize that more is caught than taught. People may look like players acting alone, but they are larger players in a system that goes back generations. Unfortunately, many families and cultures are more committed to their scripts than to actually changing negative legacies in order to support a more positive future.

Human nature conditions us to stay with what's familiar, even if it's unhealthy. We fear the unknown and we'd rather not venture there. The process of unlearning wrong ideas and relearning truths about ourselves in order to change our programming for the better is very difficult. We often hold beliefs, values, and assumptions that we have never examined. One of the best places to start is cultivating a level of awareness about your own beliefs.

Exercise 1 (Reflection): How would you describe the family atmosphere you grew up in? Try to use just a word or two (ex.: *affirming, complaining, critical, approachable, angry, tense, cooperative, close, distant, fun, serious*).

_____

_____

_____

Exercise 2: What messages and scripts has your family passed down to you?

Below is an exercise to get a sense of what scripts and messages your upbringing gave you. Family patterns from the past can show up in our present relationships, often without us being aware of it. Most of us never examine the scripts handed to us by our past.

As we grow older, we recognize the depths of the influence of those who raised us and how their messages affect our behavior and self-esteem. As children, we may have seen or experienced things that intuitively struck us as inappropriate or wrong. But because we were children, our perceptions were often dismissed as naïve or uninformed.

As a result, many children think that something must be wrong with the way they see things—or even with them. Let's take an assessment to identify the scripts/messages you've been given. Take your time when reviewing this questionnaire. Don't feel rushed. Engage with patience and reflection.

Sample Messages

1. Family: My family or those who raised me deposited seeds of fear, obligation, and guilt instead of love, respect, and independence.

"You owe your family until you die. You have a duty to family and culture that supersedes everything else. Never share your family's dirty laundry, even if unhealthy and/or abusive things are taking place in the family."

2. Emotions: Feelings are not important. "You are not allowed to have feelings. You can react based on how you feel without processing your emotions."

3. Attitudes about culture: Don't have friends from outside of your culture. "Our culture is better than other cultures. Don't marry someone from outside your culture."

4. Money: Material wealth is most important. "The more money you have, the more security you have. The more money you have, the more important you are. Money and wealth prove you 'made it'."

5. Anger: Don't show your anger. "Anger is a bad and dangerous thing. Sarcasm is a way to show anger. Explode in anger to make a point."

6. Relationships: Relationships are dangerous. "Don't trust anyone. They will hurt you. Never let yourself be vulnerable."

7. Grief and sadness: You're not allowed to feel bad. "Sadness is a sign of weakness. Don't be depressed. You need to get over losses quickly."

8. Conflict: You are not allowed to respectfully disagree. "Avoid conflict at all costs. Loud, angry, constant fighting is normal.

Don't get people mad at you. Physical altercations are prime options to resolve a conflict."

9. Sex: It's wrong and dangerous. "Don't talk about sex. Men can be promiscuous. Women have to be chaste. Women are only worthy of love if they are worthy of sexual desire."

10. Success: Nothing matters more. "You have to get into the best schools and make a lot of money. You get married and have kids."

Sample scripts

- You exist to keep everybody else happy.

- You don't have a right to enjoy your life.

- It's not okay to make mistakes.

- Your worth and value is based on what you do not who you are.

- No matter what happens, don't embarrass the family. Make us look good in public.

- Don't trust your intuition. Trust what we tell you.

- Don't assert yourself. Submit to our authority indiscriminately.

- Don't tell. Keep EVERYTHING quiet.

- Always be nice.

- Don't feel what you feel.

- Don't have fun.

- Don't ask questions. You don't have a right to your own opinion.

Do any of these messages/scripts resonate with you? Can you add to this list? This might be the first time you have taken a deeper look at the scripts your family handed you. Rest assured that this list places all people on level ground. This exercise is breaking, but also uniting. None of us come from perfect families.

This exercise exposes the issues and negative legacies common to all cultures. We all want to be perfect but know that we fall short.

The point of this assessment is to make you aware of ways that these legacies might have shaped you and point out where you need to heal/grow/change. Family messages die hard and can be very subtle. Part of the journey isn't so much about learning, but about unlearning everything that isn't healthy. Then you can be who you were meant to be in the first place. See Chapter 7 – Differentiation in *Bridge the Gaps – Lessons on Self-Awareness, Self-Development, and Self-Care*. Go to www.thebridge330.com to pick up a copy.

Exercise 3: What Type of Family Did You Come From?
Family relationships can be sources of strength or systems of dysfunction. A parent's choices, fortunately or unfortunately, can decide life for everyone else. Often, their ways of operating don't serve a healthy family life and emotional well-being.

You are responsible for your adult life, but that life was shaped by what your parents/guardians did and didn't do. Unfortunately, as children, we don't have the emotional wisdom and maturity to recognize if the environment we were raised in was toxic. So in order to get along, we just went along.

As an adult and mentor, take some time to identify the level of family health you experienced during your upbringing. Here's a framework of family health. Where do you fall in this framework?

Family Health Level
Level 5 – Severely troubled family. This a very confused family where there is no clear leadership, no clarity or coherence, and a constant sense of danger. It's full of unresolved conflicts and ungrieved losses, similar to a picture of a nation at war with itself.

Level 4 – Dictatorship. Instead of anarchy, there is a rigid system of rules enforced by intimidation and threats. Financial abuse is a common form of control. There is no room for diverse perspectives and no patience with ambiguity. The perceptions are black and white.

Level 3 – Average. At this level, there is no chaos or dictatorship, but the rules of the family are seen as more important than the people. You must follow the rules in order to feel loved. The words "should" and "ought" best define the family. People's emotional lives must be bottled up for the good of all. The chance of true emotional intimacy between one another is limited at this level.

Level 2 – Suitable. At this level, there is flexibility around the rules when the situation calls for a wise revision. Family members sometimes experience real delight and feelings of love and trust. There is a good capacity for growth in intimacy.

Level 1 – This level is similar to Level 2, but to a greater degree. There is a strong sense of security and trust. If there is a difference of perspective, there is either a strong chance that it can be worked out or that the alternative viewpoint will be respected.

What level was your family? Who made the rules, and what were the consequences of not following them? What can you add to the description for your family's level?

_____

_____

_____

How did your family handle important decisions that needed to be made? How did your family adjust to change?

_____

_____

_____

Family Pathologies
It's been said that a family is where a life makes up its mind. Patterns of sin and brokenness can be transmitted through the generations. To change, you must identify the sins of the family, because when you can see the patterns, you can then make a conscious decision to interrupt or break from those patterns.

We shouldn't disrespect or betray our parents, but we need to see them objectively. Just because you love your family doesn't mean you have to be like them.

My time on this Earth has taught me that sometimes life is not fair, and we reap what we have not sown. You may not have created the problem, but it's yours to heal. It can be helpful to establish *generational patterns* and *earthquake events*. Generational patterns are incidents that tend to recur throughout the generations. You can decide to follow the pattern, or decide you will not follow it. Earthquake events are usually one-time, extremely disruptive incidents that change family life.

Generational themes of families: Out-of-wedlock birth, affairs, sexual abuse, alcoholism, workaholism, divorce, abortions, addictions, unstable marriages, enmeshment (overly close relationships), emotional abuse, financial instability, teenage pregnancy, untreated mental illness, domestic violence, incarceration, drug abuse

Earthquake events: Premature death, abuse, suicide, war, cancer, business collapse, infidelity, natural disasters, or immigration from another country.

Considering these lists of family themes and earthquake events. Which of these apply to your family of origin? What are some insights regarding how your family has been impacted, and how this has affected who you are today? What reflections and resolutions do you have from the lists above?

_____

_____

_____

Examples of Reflections and Resolutions on themes and earthquakes:

- I saw that the men in my family did not stay faithful to their wives so I will stay faithful to mine.

- My father and grandfather were alcoholics, so I know what I need to stay away from.

- My family has generations of out-of-wedlock births. It hasn't turned out well for us.

- My parent's addiction decided life for all of us. I'm going to be a better father to my daughter, so she doesn't go through what I went through.

- I don't want my son to have a father who is still broken in some areas because of childhood sexual abuse. I'm going to start going to counseling.

- I am my father's son, but not my father's choices. The cycle of incarceration ends with me.

- I'm not doing myself or my future family any favors by keeping secrets.

Some of us have become stuck in our family's value system and way of relating. You often have to re-organize your life to break cycles, rooting out deeply ingrained family patterns. The process might prove far more difficult than you expect.

In many ways, this process is a continual one. Life will always throw new challenges at us that expose the values and ways of relating from our family background that need to change. An important part of this exercise is determining what newfound realizations you have made. Here's a statement that you might use in your group or even in your own personal time of reflection.

Reflection Questions:
1. What are you beginning to realize?

2. In light of this exercise, what is one step that you can take to change harmful or negative generational patterns that have affected my life?

Examples of Responses

1. I am beginning to realize that changing these family pat-terns is like getting off crack cocaine. Breaking deeply rooted family patterns might prove to be one of the most difficult tasks of my life.

2. I am beginning to realize that real peace is not living in stable misery.

3. I am beginning to realize that the baggage of our families continues to shape us, even after we've left the house.

4. I am beginning to realize that it's not only about changing who you are in front of people, but changing the depth of who you are.

5. I am beginning to realize that some demons are inherited. Others are invited.

6. I am beginning to realize that when you hear the voices that say "You are going to be just like your mom or dad," you have to talk back.

7. I am beginning to realize that if you don't deal with your stuff, your stuff will deal with you.

8. I am beginning to realize that truth and freedom go hand in hand; if you're not living in truth, then you're not free.

9. I am beginning to realize that if I do my work, I can help others do theirs.

10. I am beginning to realize that I was too indoctrinated with my family's script to receive contrary paradigms that might have been better for me.

11. I am beginning to realize that I didn't create the problem, but it's mine to heal.

12. I am beginning to realize that my biological family of origin does not determine my future; God does.

13. I am beginning to realize that to see your drama clearly is to begin to free yourself from it.

14. I am beginning to realize that I can build on the positive legacies and heal the negative ones.

Practical Next Steps

- Pick up information on family backgrounds and how they affect us. I suggest *Unlocking Your Family Patterns: Finding Freedom from a Hurtful Past* by Dr. Henry Cloud, Dave Carder, Dr. John Townsend, Dr. Earl Henslin and *The Genogram Journey: Reconnecting with Your Family* by Monica McGoldrick

- Start a small group based around Part 1 (Self-Awareness) and Chapters 31 to 35 of *Bridge the Gaps (www.thebridge330.com)*.

- Find a therapist. To be sure, much of the territory is beyond my level of expertise, but there are experts who can help you sort through what you inherited and what you want to use going forward.

Exercise 4: Differentiation: Become Your Own Person[1]
Some people lose touch with who they truly are in order to play a certain role in their family. It has been said that the real measure of our sense of self is when we are with our family for an extended period of time. One of the ways we can recognize our need for change is through our relationships and our choices. Here's a scale to reflect on where you are on road to becoming true to yourself or "self-differentiated."

0 – 25
- Can't distinguish between fact and feeling
- Emotionally needy and highly reactive to others
- Much of life energy spent in winning the approval of others
- Little energy for goal-directed activities
- Can't say, "I think…" or "I believe…"
- Little emotional separation from families
- Dependent marital relationships
- Do very poorly in transitions, crises, and life adjustments
- Unable to see where they end and others begin

25– 50
- Some ability to distinguish fact and feeling
- Most of self is a "false self" and reflected from others
- When anxiety is low, they function relatively well
- Quick to imitate others and change themselves to gain acceptance from others
- Often talk one set of principles/beliefs, yet do another

- Self-esteem soars with compliments or is crushed by criticism
- Become anxious (i.e., highly reactive and "freaking out") when a relationship system falls apart or becomes unbalanced
- Often make poor decisions due to their inability to think clearly under stress
- Seek power, honor, knowledge, and love from others to clothe their false selves.

50-75
- Aware of thinking and feeling functions that work as a team
- Reasonable level of "true self"
- Can follow life goals that are determined from within
- Can state beliefs calmly without putting others down
- Marriage is a functioning partnership where intimacy can be enjoyed without losing the self
- Can allow children to progress through developmental phases into adult autonomy
- Functions well – alone or with others
- Able to cope with crises without falling apart
- Stays in relational connection with others without insisting they see the world the same way

75-100 (few people function at this level)
- Are principle-oriented and goal-directed – secure in who they are, unaffected by criticism or praise
- Are able to leave family of origin and become an inner-directed, separate adult
- Sure of their beliefs but not dogmatic or closed in their thinking
- Can hear and evaluate beliefs, discarding old beliefs in favor of new ones

- Can listen without reacting and communicate without antagonizing others
- Can respect others without having to change them
- Aware of dependence on others and responsibility for others
- Free to enjoy life and play
- Able to maintain a non-anxious presence in the midst of stress and pressure
- Able to take responsibility for their own destiny

Emotionally Safe Communities
One thing that love requires is that people know they are not alone.

IN 1965, A REPORT WAS issued by the Department of Labor under the administration of US President Lyndon B. Johnson entitled *The Negro Family – The Case for National Action*. In the report, Thomas Pettigrew's research demonstrated that a stable home is a crucial factor in neutralizing the effects of racial dehumanization.

American politician and sociologist Daniel Patrick Moynihan has acknowledged that there's no adequate way to measure the health or sickness of an ethnic or geographical community, but the considerable body of evidence has demonstrated that the black American social structure has been assaulted and stressed by uprooting, discrimination, and injustice.

One of the conclusions from the board of directors of Harlem Youth Opportunities Unlimited Inc. was that the fabric of the black society has undergone great deterioration. Due to family breakdown, a large number of black youth have not had their emotional needs met. Over the last few decades, black communities have experienced tremendous disruption of family life due to issues of poverty, constant relocation, and a lack of institutional resources and understanding.

According to Dr. Joy DeGruy, author of *Post Traumatic Slave Syndrome*, the trauma of slavery and the legacy of racial dehumanization after slavery such as the Black Codes, lynchings, race riots, and mass incarceration have affected how black Americans relate to the world and how we relate to each other.

As I study this history, one of my main thoughts is that the deterioration and breakdown all have to do with relational bonds being strained. That's a significant part of what has to be healed: the rebuilding of relational bonds.

The story of what happened to black people over the course of American history includes concepts like transgenerational epigenetic inheritance, hypothalamic pituitary adrenal gland and childhood adversity, intergenerational transmission of trauma, etc. These are SAT words that can make these problems sound super-complicated, which they can certainly be.

But on a much simpler level, these concepts describe the ways that we've been wounded and how we can love each other to a healthier sense of self and community. Even more specific than love, the word that keeps coming to mind is safety.

Some people grow up in safe environments. Others grow up in environments focused on survival. When it comes to family, one of the most important questions that I believe should be asked is: Did you feel *safe* in the families you were raised in?

Many people have no idea what life in a safe home would look like. Chances are, if you've never been trained in the practical ways of showing love, you never learned, and you might end up succumbing to the environment you were reared in.

An important factor in sustainable change is creating safety, where people can learn emotionally healthy skills to foster a greater sense of community. These are skills that seem very basic, but when practiced on a consistent basis, they can yield significant benefits in the life of a community.

The following exercises are called Community Temperature Reading. Often, it's not what happens to us that forms us—it's what should have happened but did not. If we want to bring about relational change, we have to give time and attention to the aspects and impacts of emotional safety.

Community Temperature Reading[2]

In relationships, distance is measured in terms of affection more than miles. Relationships grow through the investment of trust, positive exchanges, and a subsequent accumulation of positive experiences.

Unfortunately, many people were raised in homes where appreciation was never expressed, conflicts were not resolved in heathy ways, and important personal information about hopes and dreams was never shared in a safe way. The more negative memories we have with each other, the harder this will be to reconcile.

Emotional health is especially important in our relationships, so that we can manufacture quality memories with one another. Even if the time we have is limited, we can manufacture quality moments, so we have great things to reflect on. Good memories have a positive effect on health and well-being.

Some of the ways you relate to your mentee will be similar to the ways you are relating with your peers. You want to make what's important to them important to you, because this is where they will reveal their hearts and souls.

Every close relationship will have its share of fear, anger, and sadness, but those who are true friends and family stay by your side throughout all these trials. True family members respect and acknowledge God's call on each individual life.

I am the man that I am because someone chose to love me. We all need to feel that we matter to someone and that we belong somewhere. We also need positive input, not just negative. In fact, for every negative comment you hear, you need to hear five positive ones.

Community temperature reading is a way to assess where most of the conversations in your community are on a scale of negative to positive. I think the temperature of the community can be assessed best through the tone and type of the conversations that are had.

Conversations are used to express appreciation, resolve conflicts, share new information, make requests, and share hopes and dreams. In a positive relationship, both sides contribute ideas and both are receptive to listening to the other person. A relationship can only handle a certain number of failed efforts at empathy.

It can be hard to be emotionally open when you've been emotionally closed all your life. If you've endured extreme forms of mental stress, you might have grown up feeling lonely and misunderstood. Many people have never been listened to, by anyone.

We don't need love and belonging from everyone in our lives, but we need to feel that from at least one person. Technology advances, but human nature stays the same. So many people live in a place of emotional exile because the people around them have not learned how to love, and human beings will always need love.

Each of us is harder to understand than we actually realize. Relationships where people lack communication skills will have a very difficult time healing the breakdown. In fact, sometimes people develop a toxic reaction to intimacy. We learn to shutdown genuine expressions of truth and react with defensive anger.

At the root of so much conflict is that what is important to one person is not important to the other person. This tool was designed to honor each person's God-given and unique personality and temperament. The best thing we can do for anyone is to help them find their God-given voice.

1. Appreciations

   This exercise is used to share heartfelt expressions of gratitude. We think of how grateful we feel, but we don't regularly make it a point to share this. It usually is only shared when someone has gone far above and beyond the call of duty. Some families and cultures rarely express appreciations, if ever—but appreciation is vital to the life of any relationship or community.

Think of ways you can express your appreciation for the little things people do every day. Examples to try: "I appreciate you waiting for me the other day when I was running late." "I appreciate you arriving early and getting everything ready before the meeting."

2. Puzzles, not Assumptions

   This exercise is used to get you to be curious instead of making assumptions. People can be baffling. We might say, "I can't think of a reason why she would do that!" in a rhetorical way, but we don't have a genuine desire to learn the cause behind someone's actions. We might say, "They should know." These words come from the pit of hell, emphasizing judgment instead of curiosity. You cannot be angry and curious at the same time. What standards are you imposing on others that they may not be aware of? One of the biggest challenges in relationships is that as people grow into their unique selves, their ideologies on life begin to shift. It's inevitable that beliefs about customs and traditions collide. Are you giving others room to learn or make new choices?

   Assumptions can poison relationships. Instead of assuming, use a word puzzle to keep from making negative assumptions about people, especially when you don't have all the information. Puzzles keep us from jumping to conclusions and wrongly interpreting what is going on around us. Puzzles give us an opportunity to slow down and ask questions instead of making judgments.

Shift your emphasis from expressing anger based on an assumption to finding out more information. Instead of angrily saying, "You didn't call me back" you can say, "I'm puzzled as to why you didn't call me back."

Instead of thinking, *No one cleaned up after the party. I live with slobs!* You can say, "I wonder why they didn't clean up after the party."

3. Complaints with Possible Solutions

   This exercise allows you to validate your grievances about annoyances and small irritations without attacking the other person's character.

   Nothing is wrong with wanting things resolved, but the manner in which we go about finding resolution matters immensely as it relates to building safe communities.

   Just because something is accurate or factual doesn't mean it can't be used in a destructive manner. You can be right about what you said and wrong about how you handle a matter. We've lost civility because we hide behind technology. We need to learn how to talk.

   At one point or another, we all will probably be in situations where disputes with our loved ones could be taken to a worse level. If you don't learn how to heal a breakdown in communication, you risk permanently fracturing the relationship.

All relationships include situations you might not prefer. This is perfectly normal. But do you respond with silence—figuring "If you don't have anything nice to say, don't say anything at all"—or do you just complain about your feelings but fail to offer any constructive suggestions?

Instead of complaining, try to use the phrases "I notice… and I prefer…"

"I notice you often leave the lights on downstairs when you go to bed, and I prefer that before you go to bed, you turn them off."

"I notice that you come to our meetings late, and I prefer that you arrive at the agreed-upon time."

The person making the complaint takes responsibility for a recommendation. Always keep your complaints respectful and light during this exercise.

4. New Information

    This exercise is used to share personal, intimate information about oneself. One of the biggest challenges in relationships is that as people grow into their unique selves, their ideologies, desires, and plans for life begin to shift—but none of us has a real blueprint to share these changes with those we love.

    We need to learn a way to share when we have *news*—which can mean opportunities, events, new decisions, appointments, achievements, or activities. Relationships grow when people know what is occurring in each other's lives. We need to share both the trivial as well as the important things.

When you have news, wait for an appropriate moment and then share it as a statement of fact. "I've decided to go back to school. I've already applied to a few schools." "We're moving out next week. We just closed on our first house." "I just tried that tuna recipe, and it's delicious!"

5. Hopes and Wishes

This exercise is used to share desires for our future in relationships and in life in general. Our hopes and wishes reveal to others the uniqueness of our souls and the most important parts of who we are.

Our relationships become richer as we support and listen to each other's hopes and dreams.

Have the courage to let those you love know what things are most important in the big picture of your life. "I hope we can take time to relax more this year." "I hope to get my PhD in psychology someday." "I want to make enough money to retire early and travel."

To get started with these tools, complete these sentences:

I appreciate……

I'm puzzled by …

I notice … and I prefer……

My new information is….

I hope …

Activity with a Partner
Pair up with a partner and read through the guidelines for the Community Temperature Reading. Think about what kind of conversations you hear the most in your community and how these conversations happen in your life and the lives of those close to you. Facing each other as you speak, take turns sharing, back and forth, as you use the sentence stems. Keep sharing brief and light. Don't respond or interrupt. Only respond to complaints or puzzles with a few words, and work on one category at a time.

Small Group Sharing[3]
In building emotionally safe communities, we have to risk intimate emotional contact. Healthy ways of relating usually conflict with people's cultures and families. This tool can be used with children/families, at the workplace, with friends, or in classrooms. Because communication is also about what's being heard, pay attention to the reactions and interpretations you see.

In groups of three or four, answer the following questions:

1. How did your family express appreciation? Hopes and wishes? Complaints?

2. What was it like for you to express yourself in these different categories?

3. Which was easiest for you? Which was most difficult for you?

Final Question: Of everything you just said, what's the most important thing you would like me to remember?

Part 4: Community issues

You can't change what you don't face, and you can't face what you don't know.

I BELIEVE THE AVERAGE PERSON is a decent person whose social practices and values were shaped by the current social systems. Many of these systems in our nation are designed to make us feel comfortable, entertained, complacent, self-centered, and ignorant of what's happening on the other side of town.

People invested in the status quo and a kind of American patriotism, sometimes chauvinism, have a strong incentive to refuse to acknowledge patterns of injustice against American citizens. American patriotism has transformed into a kind of idolatry, where the country itself becomes the main object of concern or affection, instead of the citizens.

As a black man in America, when I look at the disproportionate statistics of black and white people that depict the wealth gap, achievement gap, incarceration gap, and innocence gap, it's hard to adopt the wholesale endorsement of America's greatness.

When we dissent, it must be for a well-founded reason. Racial inequity in America was put into place intentionally, and was on America's books for the majority of the time the nation has existed. The gaps we see now are appalling, but not surprising. Race was, is, and more than likely will always be, a meaningful difference in America.

White supremacy's stepchild – black self-hatred—is responsible for much of the pathology that occurs in black life today. Like any pathology, it doesn't go away on its own. If it remains unaddressed, it will adapt or get worse.

We can walk and chew gum at the same time. We must not mince words about the reality of life for black people in our world and its causes. In good faith, we must tell the undiluted truth, so that we can be reconciled as people.

Nothing right in the world happens without some discomfort. When we remain ignorant of aspects of our community life, we are complicit in injustice.

I believe each person should take personal responsibility for their choices in life, but also take corporate responsibility to address issues that hurt their fellow man. Change is necessary. We see a growing sense that the current institutions will be unable to comprehensively meet the needs and solve the problems of vulnerable communities, which have a lengthy history of dehumanization.

Some people say that a crisis is a necessary prerequisite to create the urgency of new ideas on how to better live in this world. That is true, to an extent. Groups of people have suffered unnecessarily because they learned to face their issues quietly. If you are silent about issues, the people in power who are invested in the status quo will allow the issues to go unacknowledged—or even worse, they will continue to profit from them.

The less the issues are discussed, the more they will be normalized, which can lead to empathic collapse. The culture will change when it's heard enough that it has to, studied enough that it wants to, and obtained enough that it's able to.

In a *Letter from a Birmingham Jail* written in 1963, Martin Luther King, Jr. expressed his frustration with the white moderate Christians and Jews who praised his goals but cautioned patience and moderation. From Dr. King's perspective, time alone will not heal or bring change. Time is amoral and neutral. Change only happens where there is a resolute, unavoidable, and legitimate impatience that leads to fighting injustice and improving life for black people.

In 1965, a report by the Department of Labor under the administration of US President Lyndon B. Johnson called *The Negro Family – The Case for National Action* acknowledged that this injustice existed. In the report, American politician and sociologist Daniel Patrick Moynihan noted that the black family has been affected by injustice, discrimination, and displacement. While many black people had already reached unprecedented levels of accomplishment, many were falling further behind. That was in 1965. In 2020, this remains true.

I, along with many of my peers, was not taught to be civically engaged. I was taught to focus on my individual success, without consideration of how the systems of world affect people that look like me. We often don't concern ourselves with issues unless or until they affect us personally.

This needs to change. Our young people must begin to develop a consciousness of these issues, so they can wield their future power in a wise way to heal a legacy of racial injustice. The goal of the information I'm presenting here is not to just be intellectually stimulated—it is to raise awareness of the issues that we as a community need to wrestle with.

You can't change what you don't know. To improve the quality of life for people in your community, you need this information, and the information must create productive thought and action.

The role of a mentor is to provide guidance to those they serve and also to promote the awareness of issues that affect people's lives. Awareness creates empathy, which is necessary for action, social change, and justice. Even well-intentioned people lose their motivation to bring change if they have only a vague understanding of the issues affecting people. Their distance from oppressed people robs them of their humanity.

Because the world has grown more socially complicated, we need a more nuanced understanding of these issues. Disparity doesn't always equal discrimination. We can't just point to the pollution. We must go upstream to identify the source of the pollution.

Black people can no longer point to visible villains like police dogs and segregated water fountains, diners, buses, and schools. Black life and life for Americans in general is complicated by several issues, and the solution doesn't always have a clear target. We have to learn how systems interact in people's lives.

As you read this section, I'd like you to approach the topics with an understanding that these issues are complex and deeply rooted in systems and structures designed to bring about certain outcomes in society. Prejudice in America was long in the making, and it may not be fast in the unraveling.

In the spirit of Dr. King's words, we must exercise an unavoidable impatience and commitment in facing and understanding these issues. Let's get started.

10: Collateral Consequences of a Felony

"Doom to you who legislate evil, who make laws that make victims— laws that make misery for the poor, that rob my destitute people of dignity, exploiting defenseless widows, taking advantage of homeless children." Isaiah 10:1-4, MSG

EACH YEAR, 620,000 PEOPLE ARE released from federal and state prisons across the country. That's more than 10,000 people each week returning to one of this nation's communities.

Unfortunately, 60 to 70 percent of them will return to prison within three to five years. Sadly, the journey back into society presents itself with many pitfalls. For those returning after having served time in prison, it's vital to re-establish community or even form a new community, better than the one that was left behind.

As mentors, you might take on the role of helping someone returning from prison to find a new sense of self and a new community. You might help them build a new life after prison.

In order to remove the stigma associated with prison, it's important to understand that most people convicted of felonies got there because of plea bargains.

Jonathan Frejuste

Understanding of Plea Bargains and Racial Implications

The plea bargain might be considered the defining feature of the American criminal justice system. In plea bargaining, a defendant (someone charged with a crime) is offered a chance to skip the trial and either return home or serve a lesser sentence—if they plead guilty.

Of course, the best outcome for the defendant is to be found innocent or be acquitted of all charges. This will allow the defendant to avoid both incarceration and the collateral sanctions of being a felon. But many people accused of crimes know this is probably not going to be an option.

Going to trial can be risky, especially if the defendant lacks the resources necessary to hire private attorney services. The offer of a shorter sentence becomes an especially attractive option if the defendant knows that a guilty verdict at trial will automatically earn him a long prison term.

The trade-off is that the defendant becomes a confessed felon, for life.

When we talk about second chances for ex-convicts, we are assuming that they got a first chance. But as civil rights attorney Michelle Alexander, author of *The New Jim Crow* discusses, thousands of people are in prison, simply because they were too poor to access the resources needed to give them a fighting chance in court.

According to Bryan Stevenson, founder of the Equal Justice Initiative, a human rights organization in Montgomery, Alabama, our criminal justice system treats you better if you're guilty and rich than if you're innocent and poor. According to the Bureau of Justice, between 90 and 95 percent of people in prison today confessed to crimes to accept a plea bargain.

As a society, instead of painting the incarcerated with a broad brush, we need to understand what factors may have led to their incarceration. One of the main factors is prosecutorial discretion.

Prosecutorial Discretion

Research into the difference between the plea bargains and trial outcomes showed the plea bargain produced vastly different outcomes for people of color. The primary factor was prosecutorial discretion.

Prosecutors have been found to use threats to pressure defendants into accepting plea bargains. They want to secure a conviction, even when the evidence of a crime is flimsy.

What other factors determine the outcomes? According to the Bureau of Justice, gender and age showed limited and inconclusive correlation to outcomes. However, not surprisingly, race played a huge role.

Black defendants are less likely to received reduced sentences from the plea bargaining process, largely because of prosecutorial discretion. Considering that 95 percent of elected prosecutors are white, and that inequality often tracks across racial lines, black people have good reason to mistrust the American justice system.

For more information, read these insightful Equal Justice Initiative articles discussing this issue:

a. Article Title: "Study Finds 95 Percent of Prosecutors Are White" Website: https://eji.org/news/study-finds-95-percent-of-prosecutors-are-white/

b. Article Title: "Research Finds Evidence of Racial Bias in Plea Deals" Website: https://eji.org/news/research-finds-racial-disparities-in-plea-deals/

Types of Collateral Consequences

People leaving prison expect their re-entry into life outside to be hard. They have to re-earn the public trust. They are told that if they knock on enough doors and work hard, they can pull themselves up by their own bootstraps.

It seems obvious that successful reintegration includes having the rights of citizenship. But the full implications of legal decisions are often unfamiliar, not only to the general public, but also to attorneys and courts. The very rights won in the civil rights movement are stripped away with a felony conviction. People who serve their time are still kept shackled.

It's as if the law is designed to look at ex-felons as having a shattered character. That's not coming from me. That's coming from the United States Commission on Civil Rights in the June 13, 2019 report *Collateral Consequences: The Crossroads of Punishment, Redemption, and the Effects on Communities*.[4] In this report, the commission majority approved several key findings:

1. Collateral consequences of a felony (conviction) intensify the punishment beyond the court-imposed sentence and unduly hinder a returning citizen's ability to reintegrate into society.

2. Many collateral consequences have no connection to the crime or to public safety.

3. The public, the lawyers, and the courts often are unaware of the entirety of the collateral consequences, the length, their connection to public safety, and whether they are discretionary or mandatory. The convicted person generally lacks notice of the collateral consequences, yet he or she might be restricted from adopting a child, getting a real estate license, or becoming a lawyer.

Some examples of lifetime bans for people convicted of felonies in certain states include:

   a. Adoption – See adoption laws by state: https://adoptionnetwork.com/criminal-background-checks-for-adoption-by-state

b. To become a lawyer. See the laws by state: http://www.ncbex.org/assets/BarAdmissionGuide/NCBE-CompGuide-2019.pdf

c. To sell real estate – See the laws by state: https://helpforfelons.org/can-a-felon-become-a-real-estate-agent/

d. There are new editions uploaded annually. Google the following: "Comprehensive Guide to Bar Admission Requirements 2019"

4. There is barely sufficient evidence that collateral consequences keep additional crimes from happening. In fact, studies show that collateral consequences that are irrelevant to public safety *increase* recidivism, mainly because they keep a returning citizen from receiving personal and family support.

Has our justice system's perspective been helpful in achieving justice, or is it more a matter of revenge? As you review these findings, you'll see that it seems like it's been the latter. Fortunately, our society is beginning to wake up to the fact that the system is not working and is, in fact, inhumane.

My intent is to make the general public aware of the unreasonably harsh consequences of felony convictions in order to provoke thought on the underlying intent and motivation of the laws and regulations. Right anger can help us protect and serve something good. Discontent with an unfair system can create a commitment to human integrity and the social fabric.

Society uses punishments to deter those who would violate conventions—but the punishments must be just. Through a politics of fear and anger, our society has become irrational. We are keeping millions of people from growing beyond what they did and achieving what they can become.

About 70 million Americans have a felony conviction. A felony conviction impacts an ex-felon's ability to successfully reintegrate into society by making it harder to vote, work, find housing, or get government assistance. We might ask, "Are the people coming out of prison who have been disproportionately sentenced going to have the same experience as those who were freed from slavery?" The first aspect to consider is whether we will make an intentional effort to help returning citizens participate in the political process.

1. **Voting**

About 6 million returning citizens cannot vote because of a felony conviction. See the voting rights by state at this site: https://felonvoting.procon.org/view.resource.php?resourceID=000286

2. **Housing**

Housing insecurity and homelessness are a huge problem for returning citizens and can lead to higher rates of recidivism. The most immediate and pressing need upon release from incarceration is often finding a place to live; eight out of ten formerly incarcerated individuals say they have faced denial of housing or ineligibility because of their or a loved one's conviction history. Men who have been in prison are twice as likely to become homeless as men without a history of incarceration. According to the US Commission on Civil Rights, homeless people of color are more likely to have an incarceration history than white homeless people. This can be explained by the disproportionate rate of the incarceration of people of color, particularly black men.

See the information below on housing issues for the formerly incarcerated and the resources available.

Article Title: "Formerly Incarcerated People Are Nearly 10 Times More Likely to be Homeless"

Website: https://nlihc.org/resource/formerly-incarcerated-people-are-nearly-10-times-more-likely-be-homeless

Article Title: "Nowhere to Go: Homelessness among formerly incarcerated people"

Website: https://www.prisonpolicy.org/reports/housing.html

Resource: Connecting People Returning from Incarceration with Housing and Homelessness Assistance

Locate information on local homelessness resources at the website:

https://www.usich.gov/resources/uploads/asset_library/Reentry_Housing_Resource_Tipsheet_Final.pdf

3. **Employment**

   a. Having a job is vital to someone successfully re-entering society. Employment allows one to regain a sense of purpose and to become self-sufficient. Research also shows that employing ex-convicts contributes to a strong economy, stable communities, and helps to reduce recidivism. Of more than 44,000 federal and state collateral consequences for felony convictions, about 70 percent relate to employment. Barriers to employment affect the well-being of not only ex-felons but also their families and communities, which can have public safety implications. According to the Department of Justice, a past criminal conviction reduces the chances of getting a job by 50 percent. One in four Americans are kept out of the workforce due to a felony conviction, resulting in billions of dollars in lost output.

b. Racial Implications: According to the US Commission on Civil Rights, 60 percent of black applicants with a felony record received no job offers or callbacks, compared to 30 percent of white applicants with felony records.

c. Public Safety Concerns: Reasonable employment restrictions cover certain types of felonies. For example, a convicted sex offender should not be allowed to run a day care center. But irrational restrictions undermine the in-tent of promoting public safety and cost-effective criminal justice practices.

d. Disadvantages of incarceration: Some with felony records experience disadvantages that challenge their employability. These disadvantages include substance abuse, limited work experience, physical or mental health conditions, and inadequate education. They may lose their social networks and/or be connected with harmful social networks while behind bars. About 18 percent of non-incarcerated people have a high school diploma. Over 40 percent of those incarcerated do not have a high school diploma. Almost 50 percent of non-incarcerated people have college experience. Only 13 percent of those incarcerated have college experience.

e. Occupational Licensing / Ban the Box

   i. About 30 percent of US employees must have a license to perform their jobs. Occupational licenses serve the purpose of ensuring that the consumer is given quality goods and services. According to the National Inventory of the Collateral Consequences of

Conviction, more than 13,000 licensing restrictions apply to people with a criminal conviction. Research shows that occupational licensing burdens have a correlation with recidivism.

ii. Due to the risk of continued rejection, some people are more willing to suffer through financial insecurity. It's understandable for employers to want dependable and trustworthy workers, but with 70 million people with a criminal conviction, it's safe to say that there's a great probability that valuable potential employees are overlooked. As a result, ban-the-box initiatives have passed in several states. Ban the box is a civil rights campaign aimed at the box on job applications inquiring about an applicant's criminal record. The purpose is to give returning citizens a fair chance.

iii. To learn more about regulation of occupational licenses and ban-the-box laws for felons by state: https://ccresourcecenter.org/state-restoration-profiles/50-state-comparisoncomparison-of-criminal-records-in-licensing-and-employment/

4. **Public Benefits / Food Stamps**

   a. People coming home from prison often lack support to find self-sufficiency. Government benefits such as food stamps and welfare payments created to bridge the gaps for low-income families include TANF (Temporary Assistance for Needy Families) and SNAP (Supplemental Nutrition Assistance Program). In 1996, the federal government passed the Personal Responsibility and Work

Opportunity Reconciliation Act (PRWORA). This welfare-reform law blocked only those with felony drug convictions—and no other kinds of felonies—from receiving assistance. Some states have lifted this ban completely or partially. Other states are reluctant to lift the ban at all.

See which states have or have not lifted the ban at the following site: https://www.themarshallproject.org/2016/02/04/six-states-where-felons-can-t-get-food-stamps

5. **Psychological Distress**

   a. People on probation or parole are more likely to experience psychological distress than those with no criminal justice involvement. Without government support systems, they are often unable to seek mental health care. See Chapter 41 – Mass Incarceration and Reentry of *Bridge the Gaps*.

What Can be Done

NYU Professor of Clinical law Anthony Thompson encourages his students to question why things are done. I echo the sentiment. We have to rethink punishment as a moral concept.

Is the goal of criminal justice to take revenge by keeping a returning citizen from experiencing the law's protection, or should we be allowing people to reintegrate into a more redemptive society with the tools they need to thrive? Because of the nature of the collateral sanctions for convicted felons, this is a "roll-up your sleeves" type of issue. To resolve this issue will take work.

1. Know what resources are available and find ways you can support ex-convicts.

a. **Help for Felons** is an organization dedicated to providing direction and support to returning citizens, inmates, and felons. This website will point you in the direction of resources such as housing, employment, reentry programs, and financial assistance in each state.
Website: https://helpforfelons.org/

b. **Reform Alliance**—The mission of the REFORM Alliance is to dramatically reduce the number of people who are unjustly under the control of the criminal justice system, starting with probation and parole. To win, we will leverage our considerable resources to change laws, policies, hearts, and minds.
Website: https://reformalliance.com/

c. **Collateral Consequences Resource Center** is a non-profit organization established in 2014 to promote public engagement on the many issues raised by the collateral consequences of arrest or conviction.
Website: https://ccresourcecenter.org/

d. **The National Inventory of Collateral Consequences** catalogs the collateral consequences imposed by the statutes and regulations of all fifty states, the federal system, and the District of Columbia, Puerto Rico, and the Virgin Islands. Each consequence is given a brief description and categorized by a number of features.
Website: https://niccc.csgjusticecenter.org/

e. **The Marshall Project** is a non-partisan, non-profit news organization that seeks to create and sustain a sense of national urgency about the U.S. criminal justice system through award-winning journalism and partnerships between news outlets and public forums. The Marshall Project strives to educate and enlarge the audience of people who care about the state of criminal justice. Website: https://www.themarshallproject.org/

2. Play a part of the finding opportunities for felons.

   a. **Second Chance Pell Grants**

      i. In 1994, Congress banned Pell grants to felons. Pell grants are need-based financial aid designed to help undergraduate students from low-income families afford college. In 2015, the Obama administration launched a Second Chance program to provide Pell grants to incarcerated individuals again. Efforts are underway by criminal justice reformers to repeal the ban on Pell grants.

         1. The Restoring Education and Learning Act of 2019, introduced on 4/9/2019 (H.R. 2168) is a bill focused on the reinstatement of Pell grant eligibility for incarcerated individuals. This is a bipartisan effort that would improve public safety, save taxpayer money, and curb recidivism. Website: https://www.congress.gov/bill/116th-congress/house-bill/2168/text

      ii. **Federal Ban-the-Box Legislation**

1. S. 387 is a bill introduced on February 7, 2019. If signed into law, it would amend federal law to prevent federal employers and contractors from inquiring about a job applicant's criminal history until after the applicant has received a conditional job offer.
   Website: https://www.congress.gov/bill/116th-congress/senate-bill/387/text

3. Know your legislators and pending state bills.

   a. Here's the website for the New Jersey Legislature: https://www.njleg.state.nj.us/

      i. Find Your Legislator: https://www.njleg.state.nj.us/members/legsearch.asp

      ii. Find the bills that are being put forth in the legislature: https://www.njleg.state.nj.us/bills/bills0001.asp

Some highlights of 2019 Legislation:

1. **Bill S4154** revises expungement eligibility and procedures, making it easier for convicted felons to clear their records. It includes a new "clean slate" automated process to render convictions and related records inaccessible; creates an e-filing system for expungements; eliminates expungement filing fees; and appropriates $15 million to DLPS for implementation. This was signed into law in December of 2019.

2. **Bill A5823**, signed into law in December of 2019, removes the prohibition on voting by persons who are on parole or

probation due to a conviction for an indictable offense under any federal or State laws.

Article Title: "Governor Murphy Signs Major Criminal Justice Reform" https://www.nj.gov/governor/news/news/562019/approved/20191218a.shtml

    a. **Bill A5089**, introduced in February 2019, eliminates past conviction of indictable offense as disqualifier for jury service.

3. Support in-prison programs with post-release value. Research shows that the most successful programs begin while a person is incarcerated. These include pre-release vocational training, halfway houses, work-release programs, and mental health/substance abuse programs.

    a. **Prison Fellowship** has a mission to restore those affected by crime and incarceration. They offer in-prison mentoring, service to children through Angel Trees (facilitating the delivery of Christmas gifts from incarcerated parents to their children), and justice reform work.
Website: www.prisonfellowship.org

    b. **Federal Bureau of Prisons**: The BOP contracts with residential reentry centers (RRCs), also known as halfway houses, to provide assistance to inmates who are nearing release. RRCs provide a safe, structured, and supervised environment, as well as employment counseling, job placement, financial management assistance, and other programs and services. RRCs help inmates gradually rebuild their ties to the community and facilitate supervising returning citizens' activities during this readjustment phase.

i. Website: https://www.bop.gov/inmates/custody_and_care/reentry.jsp

More Resources

Breaking the cycles that keep released convicted felons from reintegrating into their communities requires that we grow in our knowledge of the issues. Here are some additional resources:

- *The New Civil Death: Rethinking Punishment in the Era of Mass Conviction,* by Gabriel J. Chin, University of Pennsylvania Law Review (April 1, 2013)

- "Ex-offenders face tens of thousands of legal restrictions, bias and limits on their rights," *ABA Journal* (June 1, 2013)

- *Collateral Consequences of Criminal Convictions: Law, Policy and Practice*, 2012-2013 ed., Thomson West Publishers (2013)

11: Children of Incarcerated Parents

ONE OF THE BEST ASPECTS of prison ministry for me is having the ability to create countercultural environments where men can share honestly about their hopes, dreams, pains, and fears. Most, if not all, or these men were raised in environments where they didn't have the opportunity to feel heard, valued, and affirmed. The majority of these men feel the deep pain of not being able to see their children. The toughest guys I've ever met become emotionally fragile at the thought of what they are unable to prevent from happening to their children because they are in prison. Sadly, their fears are real.

Nearly three million children in America have a parent in prison. These young people are often the invisible victims of incarceration. Of the 2.3 million people in prison, more than half are parents of children under the age of eighteen. Most of those parents are serving time for a non-violent crime.

Children of offenders are six times more likely than their peers to end up in jail. Black children and Hispanic children are more than seven times more likely than their white peers to have an incarcerated parent. Fathers make up 90 percent of incarcerated parents; 40 percent of them are black.

These children face:
- Trauma from a parent's incarceration

- Potential placement in the foster care system and possible termination of their parent's custody rights
- Psychological problems including depression, withdrawal, anxiety, shame and guilt, and Stress
- Social problems including hostility toward siblings and caregivers, aggression, and anger

They are also more likely to:
- Witness violence in their communities
- Be exposed to drug and alcohol abuse
- Experience economic/monetary hardship
- Be suspended or expelled from school.
- Experience Internalizing problems: depression, withdrawal, anxiety, shame and guilt, stress
- Experience externalizing problems: Hostility toward siblings and caregivers, aggression, anger

When, as a mentor, you come across a situation with a mentee who has an incarcerated parent, you can rely on a framework or set of best practices to navigate the situation.

1. If/when explaining what is happening, here are the scenarios that can possibly come-up and dialogue that you can use to guide any conversations.
- If the parent has been convicted:

"Mommy/Daddy is in a place called prison. It's not your fault that he/she is not with you.

Sometimes people go to prison when they break a grown-up rule called a law."
- If the parent has not been convicted:

"Mommy/Daddy may have broken a grown-up rule called a law. He/she is in a place called jail.

People are trying to figure out what happened. I will let you know once I have more information."

- If a jail/prison visit is allowed:

"I'll let you know when you can visit Mommy/Daddy. You can write letters and draw pictures for them if you want to."

1. Help the child share his or her feelings. Review the list in Chapter 10's Tool—No More Shame. Be patient when he/she answers. Let the mentee know that it's okay to share feelings, even if they want to say things that feel hard to say or scary. Encourage your mentee to use art sup-plies if they prefer to draw their feelings.

2. Help the mentee feel secure by reassuring him/her of what will happen going forward. Children need to know where they will live and with whom; who will drop them off and pick them up from school; what kinds of activities they can expect to be available (sports programs, music lessons, etc.)

Resources

See the following list of resources for clinical professionals, child welfare/social work, children parents, caregivers, law enforcement, corrections personnel, school administration, and teachers for more information on helping your mentee who has an incarcerated parent:

1. Children of Incarcerated Parents - https://youth.gov/youth-topics/children-of-incarcerated-parents

2. Coping With Incarceration - https://sesamestreetincommunities.org/topics/incarceration/

3. On Sesame Street's YouTube channel you can find several short clips that give advice and sample scenarios. Search for Sesame Street in Communities – Little Children, Big Challenges: Incarceration. Several short clips that give advice and example scenarios.

Mentoring

If you are interested in mentoring the child of an inmate, you can learn more at Angel Tree Mentoring. Studies show that the single most effective strategy for limiting destructive behavior and building character in children at risk is having a mentor. As a mentor, you can help a young person:

- Stay motivated and focus on education.

- Help them face challenges.

- Improve their attitude.

- Develop skills that will help them in different dimensions of life.

To get started, you can visit - https://www.prisonfellowship.org/about/angel-tree/mentoring/ or call 1-800-55-ANGEL to find out more.

Recommended Resources

These can be found on www.amazon.com, www.audible.com, your local Barnes & Noble, hulu.com, or Netflix.com.

Documentaries:

13th by Director Ava Duvernay *When They See Us* by Ava Duvernay

Books:

Incarceration Nations: A Journey to Justice in Prisons Around the World by Baz Dreisinger

Just Mercy by Bryan Stevenson

Writing My Wrongs: Life, Death, and One Man's Story of Redemption in an American Prison by Shaka Senghor

Post-traumatic Slave Syndrome by Joy DeGruy

The Miseducation of the Negro by Carter G. Woodson

Letter to a Young Brother by Hill Harper

12: Innocence

The struggle for justice doesn't end with the ones we know about. The struggle is for all those who came before the ones we know about and the ones who will come after.

According to Barbara O'Brien, Michigan State law professor, there is no longer any doubt that innocent people are sent to prison on a regular basis. Unfortunately, the vast majority of wrongful convictions are never discovered.

Fortunately, our society is shifting in its perception of the criminal justice system, largely through literature and cinema that is awakening the American psyche to see the patterns of injustice. Books like *The New Jim Crow* by civil rights attorney and Stanford Law School professor Michelle Alexander and *Just Mercy* by NYU Law Professor Brian Stevenson are illuminating the ways in which injustice has been designed and perpetuated in the criminal justice system.

Documentaries like *13th* and the TV miniseries *When They See Us* by Golden Globe-winning and Academy Award-nominated director Ava Duvernay give us information, but also help us see the emotional landscape of the experience of injustice by placing us in the shoes of the person or people experiencing injustice.

Serving the cause of helping wrongfully convicted people get out of prison is similar to helping people escape from slavery. It's a commitment to abolishing systems of injustice, and it is no small task.

What people often don't realize is that the situation that mobilized Rosa Parks and Dr. Martin Luther King, Jr. was a sixteen-year-old drummer and grocery delivery boy named Jeremiah Reeves. In 1952, Reeves was having a consensual relationship with a white woman customer. When their relationship was discovered, she screamed rape. Jeremiah was brought to the Kilby prison. Law enforcement officials strapped him to an electric chair and threatened to electrocute him unless he admitted to the rapes of white women that summer. He confessed under duress and was later convicted. He was executed on March 28, 1958 at twenty-two years of age. Sadly, this is not the only case of its kind involving false ac-cusations against black defendants and unjust treatment by the criminal justice system.

Here are some statistics as of 2017:

1. Of the 367 DNA exonerations to date, 61 percent are black, according to the Innocence Project. A DNA exoneration happens when evidence of a crime is submitted for DNA analysis, which wasn't available at the time a crime was committed, and conclusively proves that a convicted person was not guilty of the crime.

2. Black exonerees spend an average of 10.7 years in prison before release, compared to 7.4 years for white exonerees, according to the National Registry of Exonerations.

3. Of the 164 convicts who survived Death Row—which meant they were in the long process of being executed—84 are black, according to the Death Penalty Information Center.

4. Innocent black people are seven times more likely than innocent white people to be convicted of murder, according to the National Registry of exonerations.

5. Innocent black people are more likely to be convicted and receive harsher sentences for sexual assault than innocent white people, according to the National Registry of Exonerations.

6. Black people are twelve times more likely to be wrongfully convicted for drug felonies than white people, according to the National Registry of Exonerations.

7. According to the National Registry of Exonerations, of the 2,364 exonerations, almost 50 percent of the convicted individuals were black. That's nearly four times the percentage of the population of black people in America.

Bryan Stevenson, the founder of the Equal Justice Initiative, describes a continuum stretching from slavery to lynching to mass incarceration and the death penalty. In the 1930s and 1940s, in reaction to a strong anti-lynching movement, white racists switched their strategies: They decided to stop lynching black people from trees and to lynch them in the courtroom instead.

The statistics bear out this history. Being wrongfully convicted is a nightmare you can't wake up from. One normal reaction is to get angry, which can prompt an innocent convict to take action. That's a good thing. But it becomes bad when the anger turns into bitterness, rage, and psychological dysfunction.

And what about *our* reaction to discovering that this injustice exists? We should be furious about the situation, but not derailed by it. Let's focus on actionable items.

What Can Be Done:

Decide to donate your time and/or financial resources to one of the organizations that work to free innocent convicts. See the list under resources.

Resources

1. **The Innocence Project (www.innocenceproject.org)**

Exonerations to Date: 367
Founded in 1992 by Barry Scheck and Peter Neufeld at Cardozo School of Law. Their work is to exonerate wrongly convicted people through DNA testing and to ultimately reform the criminal justice system to prevent future injustice.

2. **The University of Chicago Law School Exoneration Project (https://www.law.uchicago.edu/clinics/exoneration and https://www.exonerationproject.org/)**

Exonerations to Date: 15.
Focuses on cases involving convicted men and women who claim to be, and we believe to be, innocent of the crimes for which they stand convicted. In this course, students work on actual post-conviction litigation representing individuals who are asserting their innocence as well as advancing related claims associated with their wrongful convictions.

3. **The Center on Wrongful Convictions (law.northwestern.edu/legalclinic/wrongfulconvictions/)**

Exonerations to Date: 40+
Dedicated to identifying and rectifying wrongful convictions and other serious miscarriages of justice. To date, the Center has exonerated more than forty innocent men, women, and children from states around the country, and it receives thousands of inquiries a year. The CWC also houses some of the nation's leading legal experts on false confessions and police interrogations and has helped exonerate more than twenty false confessors.

4. **The NYU School of Law Center on Race, Inequality, and the Law (https://www.law.nyu.edu/centers/race-inequality-law)**

Works to highlight and dismantle structures and institutions that have been infected by racial bias and plagued by inequality. Coordinates curricular development and serves as a resource for faculty whose teaching or scholarship addresses subjects related to race, ethnicity, and inequality. The Center also encourages public conversations with stakeholders, affected communities, thought leaders, advocates, and students; shapes policy, engages in multifaceted advocacy, and provides training on issues of race and inequality; and leverages the collective power of partnerships with a diverse array of allies committed to progressive social change. With a foundation in New York City, deep connectivity to the world of practice, and a global perspective, NYU School of Law is ideally suited to developing a center to examine and address issues of race, inequality, and the law using a multi-disciplinary approach.

13: Healing: No Longer Used to Dysfunction

"When the country is in chaos, everybody has a plan to fix it— But it takes a leader of real understanding to straighten things out." (Proverbs 28:2)

BAD THINGS GROW NATURALLY. GOOD things have to be planted. I've never seen anyone plant weeds. Weeds grow on their own. Conversely, I've never seen beautiful gardens that were not intentionally planted, watered, and cultivated.

If change is to take place in our communities, we have to see it as important enough to be proactive and intentional. Just because you have learned to live with injustice doesn't mean you have to. A part of our healing comes when we are no longer accustomed to dysfunction.

At the end of the 1965 report *The Negro Family – The Case for National Action,* American politician and sociologist Daniel Patrick Moynihan says that the objective of the study was not to provide solutions, but to define the problems in the black community in 1965.

That objective was the focus for three main reasons:
First, many people, within and outside of the government, believed black people's problems were not very serious. Once black people got the right to vote (Voting Rights Act of 1965) and segregation ended (Civil Rights Act of 1964), they felt, the problems would solve themselves. It turns out that was incorrect.

Second, Moynihan's view was that the problem is so large and interrelated, there is no way to list a few programs and solutions and think that would solve the problem. Such minimal efforts would be incomplete. Employment affects educational aspirations and achievement affects family stability, and family stability affects employment. It's a cycle. Before we list any solutions, we have to understand the interrelated nature of the problems.

Third, several prominent leaders believed that black people's problems were beyond the control of the government. Moynihan's research concerning black educational achievement and the inverse correlation between welfare and employment indicated otherwise.

Moynihan concluded that 300 years of injustice had brought about structural distortion (loss of normal functioning) in the life of black people in America. From his perspective, the cycle of problems affecting black people would continue without the white world's interference. In other words, black people's problems would feed on themselves. White racism lit a match, walked away, and now the forest would burn itself down.

In light of his conclusions, Moynihan believed that the best way to address the problems of black Americans was to focus on healing the black family structure. This varied greatly from the government's view.

In 1965, the policy of the United States was to bring black people into an equal sharing of the rewards and responsibilities of citizenship through government programs designed to improve the resources and strength of black people. But these programs have proven ineffective.

The current state of affairs shows that more work must be done. Waiting for the government to solve all problems in America is foolish. Like any sickness, if you don't treat it soon enough, it gets worse. Are we willing to re-evaluate our philosophies and paradigms, or are we going to stay loyal to the dysfunction that results in wasted lives and regrets?

We have to re-establish norms that cater to the healing of the disadvantaged, underserved, under-resourced, and vulnerable—not the comfort of privileged people. As Toni Morrison expressed, we must insist on being *shocked* by dysfunction instead of dying inside because we see so much of it.

We must never normalize dysfunction, because then we won't do anything to prevent it. We cannot change what we have learned to tolerate.

Considering the legacy of white supremacy, its brutality against black bodies, the gross miscarriages of justice resulting in black deaths and false imprisonments, and the devastating effects on the black psyche can leave us shell-shocked and feeling helpless. But radical civil rights leaders—from W.E.B. Dubois to Carter G. Woodson to Malcolm X to Martin Luther King, Jr.—had a solution.

They modeled and preached that the most revolutionary thing you can do is love black people enough to reorder your priorities, challenge long-held beliefs, change relationship dynamics, and shift the way you understand and interact with the world.

Some things are believed because they are factual; some things are believed because they are repeated continuously. As a mentor, you must be prudent in your beliefs, because "the simple believe anything, but the prudent give thought to their steps." (Proverbs 14:15, NIV.)

I've provided tools here that can help black people recapture a sense of culture, accelerate vocationally, and stabilize emotionally. I hope to see black people heal the self-hatred, restore safety in the family, detach from the dehumanizing messages spread in the media and our society, and gain consciousness of the injustices that resemble historical patterns.

We live in a polarizing time. Whenever there is an accusation of racism, you will find people on both sides of the conversation without either party having heard the details of the case. All of this comes from the ugly, racist history that we haven't faced.

This bears repeating: Our racist history was not done accidentally. It cannot be undone accidentally. It will take intention and resolve to undo our flawed past.

Sustainable social change rarely comes without discomfort, particularly when implementing tough lessons. If any section of this guide made you angry or uncomfortable or both, then I did my job right. Sustainable change doesn't happen when people are comfortable. It happens when people are unsettled by the things they discover.

Ironically, it's not always the new lessons that give us a challenge. The old lessons need to be heard again, because the older we get, the more we realize our need for reminders. Just because you've heard it once doesn't mean you have it. Some truths are learned over time and in different seasons. We revisit things based on where we are, socially and emotionally.

Your level of commitment to change will be reflected in your effort to apply these tools.

This guide is an invitation for mentors, as leaders on the ground, to review the tools sequentially or at your discretion and then to use them to bring about a change in the area that you deem to be most pressing: personal development, emotional health, racial healing, or social justice.

Some of the tools within the guide are complex and will require a constant pursuit of knowledge, critical thinking, and emotional maturity. Maturity is having a sense of self that's both courageous and considerate. I say this because we need to be cautious about boisterously claiming what needs to be done. We all "see through a glass darkly" (1 Corinthians 13:12, KJV.) With these tools, we're trying to sort out which issues come from culture, history, family, and you.

I believe that each person is responsible for the choices they make and for their actions. Ultimately, your destiny is for you and you alone to manifest. I also believe that a person's environment significantly impacts their ambitions. People often become what the environment tells them to become.

As mentors, we are called to create, shape, and maintain a culture that supports healing, productivity, and a strong sense of self. I don't have an *either/or* perspective but a *both/and* perspective. No one person has all the answers, and our wisdom evolves over time. When I look at what I believed ten years ago, I shudder—mostly at my tone.

As our perspectives expand, we may or may not change our positions, but we will most certainly change our tone. This type of thinking goes against a prevailing practice associated with "cancel culture," which assumes that one group or person has a social and ethical awareness exclusive to them and no one else.

Some people believe that they are wiser and more anointed than others. There's no room for that if we are to change society. These are hard issues that we bathe in prayer, investigate and plan to heal with diligence, shape with counsel, and alter by necessity.

Malcolm X said you need to be careful with condemning those who don't know what you know or think as fast as you think, because there was a time when we all were ignorant of such matters. We need to continually inform our opinions, because no one is safe from ignorance.

We should make it a goal to contribute more than criticize. There may be evidence that proves you right and evidence that proves you wrong. Once you know the truth, you are responsible for addressing the issues you uncover with full integrity. However, you will need wisdom, humility, emotional maturity, and most importantly, courage to speak inconvenient truth to power and to do so respectfully, honestly, and clearly. That is my prayer for us all.

I want to encourage you not to allow confusion, tough topics, conflict, and discouragement to rob you of initiative. We can't change the world with ideas in our minds alone. We need conviction in our hearts.

Dr. King told us the men are measured by where they stand during moments of controversy and conflict. I'll take it a step further. I come from a faith tradition grounded in the life of Jesus. I am called to be a peacemaker, not a peacekeeper. "Blessed are the peacemakers"—not peacekeepers. (Matthew 5:9, NIV).

You can never have true peace by pretending that what is wrong is right. This path is not for the faint of heart. Fortunately, we have someone we follow who is the perfect example of perseverance. Jesus wanted to quit. "Father, if you are willing, please take this cup of suffering away from me. Yet I want your will to be done, not mine." (Luke 22:42, NLT).

Jesus stayed committed because he remembered who he was and who gave him his assignment. Jesus was willing to disrupt the status quo for the sake of a principled belief in God. He wasn't a thermometer, but a thermostat. He was countercultural for a noble reason.

I have an unflinching and undying belief in the ability of our community to be better, but I'm not blind to the reality of the situation. It can be difficult and confusing. The way to keep going when things get hard is to follow the example of those who broke cycles. Then do something bigger than yourself for someone other than yourself.

The first person to work for is God. Always leave God in the equation when you are trying to bring about change. Historically, progress for black people came when they were in touch with the power of their agency and the need for urgency.

As a mentor, your ability to affect change in the world is not contingent on the level of schooling you have, your grades in school, or the professional status you hold. Your ability to affect change is contingent on your dissatisfaction with the status quo and your willingness to, with integrity, flesh out the tools you have received and the ones you have learned from your journey of change. The first person you have to change is yourself.

The faith I have is in God, not in America. While we can pray for America and work to make it better, we must recognize that it's foolish to put faith in governments made of human leaders. "Don't put your trust in human leaders. Don't trust in people who can't save you." (Psalm 146:3, NIRV).

America was defective from the start, and the work to make America a place where everyone can freely live has mainly been done by the conscientious among us who recognized that America won't work until we do.

I pray this book is a blessing and a catalyst for change in your life, the lives of those you serve, and this nation. I am who I am because someone loved me. Blessings.

Recommended Resources / Reading List

These can be found on www.amazon.com, www.audible.com, or your local Barnes & Noble.

Books:

Incidents in the Life of a Slave Girl by Harriet Jacobs
Lessons from History by Jawanza Kunjufu
The Autobiography of Malcolm X by Alex Haley
Race Matters by Cornel West
The Miseducation of the Negro by Carter G. Woodson
Between the World and Me by Ta-Nehisi Coates
Black Theology of Liberation by James Cone
Daily Motivations for African-American Success by Dennis Kimbro
The New Jim Crow by Michelle Alexander
Medical Apartheid by Harriet Washington
Strength to Love by Dr. Martin Luther King, Jr.
Post-traumatic slave syndrome by Dr. Joy DeGruy
100 Years of Lynching by Ralph Ginzburg
Long Walk to Freedom by Nelson Mandela
Where Do We Go From Here? By Dr. Martin Luther King, Jr.
Black Bourgeoisie: The Book That Brought the Shock of Self-Revelation to Middle-Class Blacks in America by E. Franklin Frazier
The Short and Tragic Life of Robert Peace by Jeff Hobbs

Why It's So Hard to Talk to White People About Race by Robin DiAngelo
Just Mercy by Bryan Stevenson
Democracy in Black by Dr. Eddie Glaude
Lies My Teacher Told Me: Everything Your American History Textbook Got Wrong by James W. Loewen

Endnotes

1   Scazzero, Pete and Geri. *Emotionally Healthy Skills 2.0: Discipleship that Deeply Changes Your Relationship with Others.* Zondervan, 2017

2   Scazzero, Pete and Geri. *Emotionally Healthy Skills 2.0: Discipleship that Deeply Changes Your Relationship with Others.* Zondervan, 2017

3   Ibid

4   https://www.usccr.gov/pubs/2019/06-13-Collateral-Consequences.pdf

www.ingramcontent.com/pod-product-compliance
Lightning Source LLC
LaVergne TN
LVHW051726080426
835511LV00018B/2906